FUNCTIONAL SKILLS IN LANGUAGE AND LITERATURE

FUNCTIONAL SKILLS IN LANGUAGE AND LITERATURE

Sonu Marwah

ANMOL PUBLICATIONS PVT. LTD.
NEW DELHI-110 002 (INDIA)

ANMOL PUBLICATIONS PVT. LTD.

Regd. Office: 4360/4, Ansari Road, Daryaganj,
New Delhi-110002 (India)
Tel.: 23278000, 23261597, 23286875, 23255577
Fax: 91-11-23280289
Email: anmolpub@gmail.com
Visit us at: www.anmolpublications.com

Branch Office: No. 1015, Ist Main Road, BSK IIIrd Stage
IIIrd Phase, IIIrd Block, Bangalore-560 085 (India)
Tel.: 080-41723429 • Fax: 080-26723604
Email: anmolpublicationsbangalore@gmail.com

Functional Skills in Language and Literature

First Edition, 2010

ISBN 978-81-261-4514-0

PRINTED IN INDIA

Printed at Mehra Offset Press, Delhi.

Contents

Preface

The textbook provides a didactic, up to the minute approach to the common and uncommon situations experienced in practice, giving advice about a huge range of conditions and problems that present in an emergency department. The information provided is easily accessed and presented in a way that both new and experienced individuals can obtain authoritative advice.

Among the essential items in this collection are Linguistics and Phonetic which include fundamental theoretical statements, structural analyses of individual skills in language, explorations of the connections between language and words. This will become a basic book for contemplating the function of language in literature--a project that will continue to engross the keenest readers.

Author

Chapter 1

History of English

ENGLISH LINGUISTIC

This is not a conventional history of English. Rather, it tries to show how the discipline of linguistic history may be pursued — a rather different matter. It does this by using selected phenomena in the history of English to exemplify the dynamic processes of change involved. In so doing it tries to address the question of linguistic change: why does change happen, and why does it happen at the time and in the way that it does? In answering these questions, this book, rather obviously, holds it as axiomatic that human language is both a cultural and a systematic phenomenon, and that both these characteristics need to be borne in mind when addressing the question of linguistic change.

English, a West Germanic language originating in England, is the first language for most people in Australia, Canada, Ireland, New Zealand, the United Kingdom, and the United States. It is used extensively as a second language and as an official language throughout the world, especially in the Commonwealth of Nations, in countries such as in India or South Africa, as well as in many international organizations. Modern English is sometimes described as the world lingua franca. English is the dominant international language in communications, science, business, aviation, entertainment, and diplomacy and also on the Internet.

It has been one of the official languages of the United Nations since its founding in 1945 and is considered by many to be on its way to becoming the world's first universal language. The influence of the British Empire is the primary reason for the language's initial spread far beyond the British Isles. Following World War II, the increased economic and cultural influence of the United States led to English permeating many other cultures, chiefly through development of telecommunications technology.

Because a working knowledge of English is required in many fields, professions, and occupations, education ministries throughout the world mandate the teaching of English to at least a basic level in an effort to increase the competitiveness of their economies. On the one hand, it is held here that the various changes at an intralinguistic level which are held to be the prime concern of writers of linguistic history-changes in writing systems, pronunciation, grammar or lexicon-cannot be meaningfully accounted for without reference to the extralinguistic contexts (historical, geographical, sociological) in which these phenomena are situated.

Language is plainly a social phenomenon-if societies did not exist, there would be no language-and it follows from this that an asocial approach to its study has a comparatively limited (because formal) interest. This conclusion applies most uncontroversially to diachronic linguistics (i.e. time-situated linguistics).

If we attempt to explain language change entirely intralinguistically, without ultimate reference to extralinguistic factors, then, it is argued here, the explanation will ultimately fail. But it is also held here that linguistic change can operate intralinguistically, that is, without immediate reference to external, non-linguistic factors. The key argument in support of this axiom is that linguistic changes, once they have themselves been implemented, interact with each other to produce further change.

To clarify these points, it may be useful to model the structure of natural language diagrammatically. The deepest level of language, in this diagram, is semantics, that is, the level of meaning. Meaning is expressed linguistically through the grammar and lexis of a language; in turn, the grammar and lexis of a language are transmitted to other language-users through speech or (a comparatively recent development in human history) through writing. The model of language has its uses, but it is important to be aware of its limitations. It is essentially a static model, a snapshot; it depicts what happens when a single linguistic 'event' (a word, a grammatical construction, a sound or a spelling) takes place.

It is hierarchical in orientation, placing semantics at the top of a tree in which transmission occupies a lowly position. Above all for the purposes of this book, it is limited because it does not indicate any point where change might take place. There are methodological advantages to treating each level of language (written and spoken transmission, grammar, semantics and lexicon) separately, for it is obvious that to attempt to cover every level at once brings with it a threat of incoherence. Nevertheless the approach has dangers.

What evidence we have indicates that the human brain uses each level of language in an integrated way, handling them all simultaneously and interactively, and in diachronic study it will frequently, if not generally, be found that change in one level of language relates intimately to change in others. If language is systematic-and it must be, for otherwise it would be impossible to use it to express meaning, however broadly we define that concept-then movement in one part of the system must have an effect or effects on other parts.

Languages, in short, are systems in which everything is connected to everything else. This structural notion is the major insight of linguistics since the modern discipline was founded in the nineteenth century, and it is at the heart of the subject's claim for non-trivial status. In sum, we must expect that any given linguistic event is the result of complex interaction between levels of language, and between language itself and the sociohistorical setting in which it is situated.

It is therefore necessary, in our modelling of language, to supplement the simple communicative model with a non-hierarchical one. This latter model allows for the process of change; disruption and subsequent reaction can happen at any point in the system, and thus any model of language reflecting these processes must be of necessity non-hierarchical. The interactive nature of the phenomenon, of course, makes the investigation of linguistic change a matter of engaging with complexity; and this complexity might lead students of the history of English to despair of finding any generally acceptable truths on which to base their discipline. There is, in fact, a respected and respectable tradition in the linguistic sciences which holds that the only valid goal of diachronic linguistic enquiry is description, and that the discussion of causation is not a proper question for researchers to address.

The outcome of this distinction can be seen in the practice of diachronic linguistic enquiry. Some books are essentially lists of observations, and these may be termed chronicles-not necessarily a hostile criticism, for such collections of observations are the bedrock of deeper understanding. In a sense, the notion of 'chronicle' correlates with the synchronic (i.e. time-independent) approach to linguistic study, in which the purpose of the discipline is to formalise the rules of a given state of language without relating these rules to their antecedents or successors; the true chronicle, with its annalistic approach, may be seen as a series of synchronic snapshots which happen to have been arrayed in chronological order, an ordering which makes no connective reference or causative link to what happens before or after.

Most of the readers of this book will have already encountered such annalistic approaches, and may have even formed the impression that such chronicles are what the historical study of English is about. But this conclusion, it is held here, is wrong; the practice of linguistic historiography is to do with the interpretation of these observations, and it is historiography, not chronicle-making. Since this book sets out to be an historical account, it is orientated in accordance with the practice of historiography as established by tradition: it seeks answers to the question 'why?' through the observation of correspondences.

When historians seek to account for a particular event in the past-say, the French Revolution-then they will look for its causes in the state of society within which the event took place: the financial and political bankruptcy of the monarchy, the oppression of the Third Estate, the coexistence of advanced Enlightenment ideas in France with revolution in the United States, and so on. It is by seeking to answer such questions that the discipline of history progresses, although few historians nowadays would claim to have final solutions to the questions which history poses.

Similarly, the explanations put forward in this book for changes in the history of English have the validity of historiography; they are attempts to show why certain things happen when they do, argued (it is hoped) rationally from the observation of correspondences, and they are of course falsifiable, that is, open to being superseded by other explanations. Of course, it is widely accepted by scholars in many disciplines that neutral observation, the goal of the chronicle-maker, is something of a myth, for our position of observation (our point of view) conditions what is observed. Nevertheless, the disabling nature of this so-called 'observer's paradox' can be overstated.

Observers of language can strive for neutrality on the basis of shared terms of reference, even if they necessarily fail to achieve absolute objectivity because conditioned by their own intellectual horizons. The answer to the problem is not, it is held here, to cease making observations and hypotheses, but rather to continue to make observations and hypotheses from various points of view.

The question has been addressed by philosophers since at least the eighteenth century. English is an Anglo-Frisian language brought to southeastern Great Britain in the 5th century AD by Germanic settlers from various parts of northwest Germany (Saxons, Angles) as well as Jutland (Jutes). Prior to the invasion of Britain by these Germanic tribes, the native Britons spoke an early form of Brythonic (the ancestor of Modern Welsh).

Unlike in Gaul and Hispania, the indigenous population did not adopt Latin as a native language during the Roman occupation, where it was mainly confined to the Roman cities and garrisons. The degree to which the original Celtic-speaking inhabitants remained or were displaced by the Germanic invaders is a matter of some debate. Recent genetic studies together with a re-evaluation of archaeological evidence suggest that the native Celtic population were not substantially displaced in any part of Britain. If correct, this interpretation of events would imply that the native Celts in the south and east of Britain, gradually adopted the language and culture of a politically and socially dominant ruling class.

Celtic languages survived in parts of the island not colonised by the invaders: Scotland, Wales, Cornwall, and, to some extent, Cumbria. The dialects spoken by the invaders eventually coalesced to a degree and formed what is today called the Old English language, which resembled some coastal dialects in what are now northwest Germany and the Netherlands. Throughout the history of written Old English, it remained a highly synthetic language based on a single standard, while spoken Old English became increasingly analytic in nature, losing the more complex noun case system, with a heavier reliance on prepositions and fixed word-order.

This is evident in the Middle English period, when literature is first recorded in the various spoken dialects of English of the time, after written Old English lost its status as the literary language of the nobility. It has been postulated that the early development of the language may have also been influenced by a Celtic substratum.

Later, it was influenced by the related North Germanic language Old Norse, spoken by the Vikings who settled mainly in the north and the east coast down to London, the area known as the Danelaw. Then came the Norman Conquest of England in 1066. For about 300 years following, the Norman kings and the high nobility spoke only Anglo-Norman, which was very close to Old French.

A large number of Norman words found their way into Old English. Later, a large number of words were borrowed directly from Latin and Greek, especially for scientific and technical terms, leaving a parallel vocabulary that persists into modern times. The Norman influence strongly affected the evolution of the language over the following centuries, resulting in what is now referred to as Middle English.

During the 15th century, Middle English was transformed by the Great Vowel Shift, the spread of a standardised London-based dialect in government and administration, and the standardising effect of printing. Early Modern English can be traced back to around the time of William Shakespeare.

LANGUAGE DEVELOPMENT

For the majority of children, starting school means confronting new ways of using language. These include using language to accomplish new types of tasks and new expectations for how they will structure what they say. Schooling brings new kinds of interaction, where students are often required to state information that in an everyday context could be taken for granted, and to specify relationships between concepts in some detail.

Language is a beautiful gift. With it we can share our wants, our needs, our thoughts, our feelings, and everything that makes us human. If you spend time with a child, you have the power to give and nurture this gift of communication. Many factors affect the rate at which a child develops language. Sometimes language development slows down while a child is learning other skills, such as standing or walking. In other words, the bulk of the child's concentration and energy may be going to gross motor development at this point with little reserve for the development of language.

The amount and kind of language the child hears may also affect the rate of language development. For example, if the child is hearing two languages at home, his or her brain is trying to learn two sets of vocabulary, process two sets of speech sounds, and understand two sets of grammatical rules. That is a lot of work! It may take longer to begin talking, and still the child may at first feel comfortable speaking in only one of the languages.

Some children who are immersed in a new language at school may be silent for a long period of time. In addition, students are expected to begin using language in a new mode, writing, which brings with it new ways of grammatical organization. These new ways of meaning-making enable participation in a wider range of tasks and contexts, so it is important that all students have opportunities to develop their language potential as they progress in schooling. Some children's ways of making meaning with language enable them to readily respond to the school's expectations, but the ways of using language of other students do not. The language students bring from their communities to school is the means through which they engage new "schooled" knowledge.

For this reason, it is important to value a wide range of ways of using language at school, giving different languages, dialects, and ways of meaning more social value by having them shared in the schooling context. But it is also important to provide all students with access to academic ways of using English so they can participate in new kinds of learning at school. All children enter school with language resources that have served them well in learning at home and that have enabled them to be interactive and successful members of their families and local communities.

But many children lack experience in making the kinds of meanings that are expected at school, or with the kinds of written texts and spoken interaction that prepare some children for school-based language tasks. This lack of experience makes it difficult for these students to learn and to demonstrate their learning. Schooling is a context in which the kinds of meanings that are made are quite different from the meanings made in more informal contexts of everyday life.

Language is used in school contexts in ways that are integral to construing the academic and social knowledge that schools aim to develop. As students move into middle school and secondary school, the tasks they are asked to do become more and more dependent on control of a wide range of linguistic resources.

While these ways of making meaning may appear to set up barriers for children from backgrounds that have not prepared them for participation in this context, the ways of meaning are integral to accomplishing the goals of schooling. Learning and language are closely related, and for success at school, students need to come to understand the context of schooling and the linguistic choices that realise that context. Under the influence of the work of Vygotsky, among others, there has been increased recognition of the role that language plays in the development of social and cognitive processes. Vygotsky argues that language and thinking develop simultaneously in social interaction.

The development of particular ways of thinking occurs through the linguistic tools that the society uses and that become part of the socio cultural experiences of the child. This means that the kinds of conceptual knowledge that children develop depend on their social experiences and ways of interacting with others, with language the primary semiotic system through which this interaction takes place.

Much of the knowledge that schooling aims to develop in the child is not available just through everyday experience in the world; it needs to be articulated in ways that abstract from everyday life as children engage in structured experiences that provide new perspectives on the world and enable them to generalize their experience. Vygotsky describes such knowledge as "scientific" concepts, different from the "everyday" concepts that emerge through the less structured experiences of everyday life.

Vygotsky believes that both scientific and everyday concepts develop through scaffolded interaction with more experts others who work with learners to help them perform at levels that they would be unable to achieve independently; what Vygotsky calls the "zone of proximal development." Through social interaction of this kind, children are challenged to do more than they can on their own.

This suggests that a clear understanding of the role language plays in this socialization would require analysis of the structure and uses of language itself. But in fact, language is the element of learning that is most unanalyzed and least often explicitly addressed. A Vygotskyan perspective illuminates how differences in socialization practices mean that students from different backgrounds come to school with divergent preparation for using language in the ways expected at school, but does not offer concrete solutions that are specifically bound to the nature of language. A linguistic approach, on the other hand, can show how the structuring of new kinds of knowledge depends on new ways of using language and can identify the features of the language that enable schooled ways of learning.

Describing learning from a linguistic perspective, Halliday focuses on developments in the grammar that are needed to accommodate the construal of more complex kinds of meanings as children learn. Using a complementarily similar to that of Vygotsky's "everyday" and "scientific" concepts, Halliday describes how children learn to reconstrue "common sense" knowledge in a more abstract mode as they reproduce it as "educational" knowledge, and finally to construe knowledge in specialized and technical language.

This perspective offers a framework for understanding how language evolves over time in the child in ways that enable learning, as learning and learning new language occur simultaneously. Adopting this view of the relationship between language and social context and language and thinking has major implications for how the challenges of schooling are understood.

The activities that students are asked to engage in result in the development of knowledge and language related to the goals of those activities. Language is the primary means through which school activities are conducted and students' development is realized and evaluated. Both Halliday and Vygotsky view language learning as integral to, not separate from or prior to, cognitive development.

In learning language in interaction with others, children "appropriate the knowledge and practices of their culture" as they develop scientific, non-everyday concepts that draw on ways of using language that are not part of everyday experience.

A better understanding of the ways language construes academic knowledge is important for students and teachers, linguists and language researchers, textbook writers and administrators. This research that demonstrates the ways language socialization practices prepare some children for the contexts of schooling. It also reviews descriptions of school language use that highlight the linguistic choices that are highly valued in school tasks. It is these choices that can be characterized as the language of schooling. The functional linguistic analysis that follows in later chapters links the language features with the social contexts they realise to show the close relationship between language and context, and to illustrate the challenges for students whose socialization has not prepared them to participate fully in the school context.

CHANGE IN LANGUAGE

So far, language change has been discussed without further definition or explanation. Yet the question 'what is language change?' has to be confronted at an early stage, for, as we shall see, its definition sets the goals for our enquiry. The distinction may be made between potential for change, implementation (itself including triggering or actuation) and diffusion.

The potential for change exists when a particular speaker or group of speakers makes a particular linguistic choice at a particular time; implementation takes place when that choice becomes selected as part of a linguistic system; and diffusion takes place when the change is imitated beyond its site of origin, whether in terms of geographical or of social distribution. Strictly speaking, the first of these phenomena is not to be included as part of the typology of change. The continual flux of living languages means that new variant forms are constantly being created in a given linguistic state. However, these variants are not themselves linguistic changes; rather, they constitute the raw material which is a prerequisite for linguistic change.

A linguistic change happens only when a particular variable is selected and a systemic development follows. In that sense, language change begins with implementation; when implementation of potential for change is for some reason triggered in a linguistic system, then we can speak of a linguistic change. The diffusion of the phenomenon within a particular speech-community is, it is held here, a further process which can be counted as part of the particular change involved; it may, of course, itself have further effects.

It will be observed there that the potential for change, the set of 'variational spaces' within a given linguistic system, is always present. However, a particular interaction of processes-extralinguistic with intralinguistic, or intralinguistic with intralinguistic-at a particular time and in a particular place triggers the implementation of change, with subsequent diffusion of that change within and beyond a particular speech-community. Subsequently, other changes can be triggered in turn.

FORM AND FUNCTION

In pursuing the aims described, two key terms will be used on a number of occasions; it is therefore appropriate to offer some definitions at this initial stage. These are the terms *form* and *function*. These terms are used technically in many disciplines (e.g. in architecture), so it is perhaps worth taking time to define the special ways in which they are used here.

By *function* is meant intralinguistically the role individual linguistic items play within an overall linguistic system, and-and this is an extension of traditional usage, although quite commonplace in sociolinguistic literature-also extra linguistically the role linguistic systems play in society. By *form* is meant the various linguistic items themselves.

Thus a pronoun (form) may act (function) as the subject or object of a clause; and a particular usage (form) may signal the role (function) of its user in relation to other users; or, to put matters less abstractly, a particular formal usage such as double negation *(I don't know nothing),* acting functionally in intralinguistic terms as an intensifying marker of negativity, typically functions extralinguistically in contemporary British society as a stigmatising item, signalling membership of a particular (and non-prestigious) social group.

SOCIOLINGUISTICS AND PRAGMATICS

The linguistic discipline which deals with the function of language in society may be subdivided into two related subdisciplines: sociolinguistics and pragmatics. Sociolinguistics is perhaps the better established of these two, in the sense that it has been practised for several decades by a number of major scholars of whom perhaps the most important are William Labov, Peter Trudgill, and James and Lesley Milroy. It deals with the ways in which membership of social groups is signalled through linguistic choices, and it will be observed that insights from sociolinguistics inform many aspects of this book.

The work of researchers like Labov, Trudgill and the Milroys has broken new ground in showing how linguistic usages of very delicate differentiation demonstrate membership of distinct social groups, and they have gone on from this insight to develop important perspectives on such matters as the linguistic difficulties suffered by underprivileged groups in society, and the causes and mechanisms of linguistic change.

The sociolinguistic approach is not, however, the only valid one in considering language in use. In recent years, another discipline has emerged which also deals with social interaction: pragmatics.

Pragmatics, which has been defined as 'the study of how utterances have meanings in situations', emphasises how language functions as a means of communication, and various regulative principles have been identified which describe the pragmatic strategies of interpersonal communication which human language-users adopt. One of the most important of these is the philosopher H.P. Grice's Co-operative Principle, which sets out in maxim fashion the constraints which govern conversation.

The Principle may be summarised briefly as follows:

1. Quantity: Give the right amount of information, i.e. (a) make your contribution as informative as required, (b) do not make your contribution more informative than is required.
2. *Quality:* Try to make your contribution one that is true, i.e. (a) do not say what you believe to be false, (b) do not say that for which you lack adequate evidence.
3. *Relation:* Be relevant.

4. *Manner:* Be perspicuous, i.e. (a) avoid obscurity of expression, (b) avoid ambiguity, (c) be brief (avoid unnecessary prolixity), (d) be orderly.

The Co-operative Principle, Grice held, governs all speaker-hearer/writer-reader communications. To communicate with someone else, it is necessary to co-operate with them linguistically; and, to co-operate with someone linguistically, it is necessary to use language they can understand. Thus extralinguistic pressures affect the linguistic usages of those subjected to those pressures.

It would perhaps be more correct to write of the re-emergence of pragmatics as a discipline. Students of the history of linguistic thought have shown that many modern notions of sociolinguistics and pragmatics have their origins in the work of nineteenth-century (and earlier) philologists and philosophers.

More recent work in the pragmatic and sociolinguistic analysis of speaker-interaction has distinguished between accommodation theory and identification theory, and these notions have significance for a more general theory of language change. Accommodation theory seeks to relate any given linguistic act to the relationship between particular interlocutors, and is a development of the co-operative notions set forth above.

Identification is a broader notion which might be taken to comprehend accommodation theory. It tries to span the divide between pragmatics and sociolinguistics; it holds that any particular usage at any particular point in time is the result of an 'act of identity', in which speakers are seen as modifying their behaviour to accommodate to group norms.

Thus, 'the individual creates for himself the patterns of his linguistic behaviour so as to resemble those of the group or groups with which from time to time he wishes to be identified, or so as to be unlike those from whom he wishes to be distinguished'.

It is an observed fact that speakers use language not just to communicate needs and to transmit information, but also to signal their and others' social standing. Identification theory is functional, in the broad sense used in this book, in that it situates any individual linguistic act in relation to its social setting.

CLASSIFICATION OF LANGUAGE

The English language belongs to the western sub-branch of the Germanic branch, which is itself a branch of the Indo-European family of languages. The question as to which is the nearest living relative of English is a matter of some discussion. Apart from such English-lexified creole languages such as Tok Pisin, Scots (spoken primarily in Scotland and parts of Northern Ireland) is the Germanic variety most closely associated with English.

Like English, Scots ultimately descends from Old English, also known as Anglo-Saxon. The closest relative to English after Scots is Frisian, which is spoken in the Northern Netherlands and Northwest Germany. Other less closely related living West Germanic languages include German itself, Low German, Dutch, and Afrikaans.

The North Germanic languages of Scandinavia are less closely related to English than the West Germanic languages. Many French words are also intelligible to an English speaker (though pronunciations are often quite different) because English absorbed a large vocabulary from Norman and French, via Anglo-Norman after the Norman Conquest and directly from French in further centuries.

As a result, a substantial share of English vocabulary is quite close to French, with some minor spelling differences (word endings, use of old French spellings, etc.), as well as occasional divergences in meaning, in so called "faux amis", or false-friends. Over 380 million people speak English as their first language. English today is variously estimated as the second, third, or fourth largest language by number of native speakers.

All estimates have it trailing Mandarin Chinese, and other estimates are mixed as to whether it outranks Hindi, Spanish, and a combination of the various Arabic dialects. However, when combining native and non-native speakers it is probably the most commonly spoken language in the world, though possibly second behind a combination of the Chinese languages. Estimates that include second language speakers vary greatly from 470 million to over a billion depending on how literacy or mastery is defined.

There are some who claim that non-native speakers now outnumber native speakers by a ratio of 3 to 1. The countries with the highest populations of native English speakers are, in descending order: United States (215 million), United Kingdom (58 million), Canada (17.6 million), Australia (17.5 million), Ireland (3.8 million), and New Zealand (3.4 million).

Of those nations where English is spoken as a second language, India has the most such speakers ('Indian English') and it has been claimed that, combining native and non-native speakers, India now has more people who speak or understand English than any other country in the world. Following India are the People's Republic of China, the Philippines, Nigeria, and Germany.

English is the primary language in Anguilla, Antigua and Barbuda, Australia (Australian English), the Bahamas, Barbados, Bermuda, Belize, the British Indian Ocean Territory, the British Virgin Islands, Canada (Canadian English), the Cayman Islands, Dominica, the Falkland Islands, Gibraltar, Grenada, Guernsey, Guyana, Isle of Man, Jamaica (Jamaican English), Jersey, Montserrat, Nauru, New Zealand (New Zealand English), Ireland (Hiberno-English), Pitcairn Islands, Saint Helena, Saint Lucia, Saint Kitts and Nevis, Saint Vincent and the Grenadines, Singapore, South Georgia and the South Sandwich Islands, Trinidad and Tobago, the Turks and Caicos Islands, the United Kingdom (various forms of British English), the U.S. Virgin Islands, the United States (various forms of American English), and Zimbabwe.

In many other countries, where English is not a first language, it is an official language; these countries include Cameroon, Fiji, the Federated States of Micronesia, Ghana, Gambia, India, Kiribati, Lesotho, Liberia, Kenya, Namibia, Nigeria, Malta, the Marshall Islands, Pakistan, Papua New Guinea, the Philippines, Puerto Rico, Rwanda, the Solomon

Islands, Samoa, Sierra Leone, Singapore, Sri Lanka, Swaziland, Tanzania, Zambia, and Zimbabwe. It is also one of the 11 official languages that are given equal status in South Africa ("South African English"). English is also an important language in several former colonies or current dependent territories of the United Kingdom and the United States, such as in Hong Kong and Mauritius. English is the language most often studied as a foreign language in the European Union (by 89% of schoolchildren), followed by French (32%), German (18%), and Spanish (8%).

It is also the most studied in the People's Republic of China, Japan, South Korea, and Taiwan. It is worth noting that English is not an official language in either the United States or the United Kingdom. Although the U.S. federal government has no official languages, English has been given official status by 25 of the 50 state governments.

REGIONAL VARIETIES

The expansion of the British Empire and—especially since WWII—the primacy of the United States have spread English throughout the globe. Because of that global spread, English has developed a host of English dialects and English-based creole languages and pidgins.

The major varieties of English each include, in most cases, several sub varieties, such as Cockney slang within British English; Newfoundland English, and the English spoken by Anglo-Québecers within Canadian English; and African American Vernacular English ("Ebonics") and Southern American English within American English.

English is a pluricentric language, without a central language authority like France's Academic française; and although no variety is clearly considered the only standard, there are a number of accents considered as more formal, such as Received Pronunciation in Britain or, formerly, the upper-class Bostonian dialect in the U.S.

Scots developed — largely independently — from the same origins, but following the Acts of Union 1707 a process of language attrition began, whereby successive generations adopted more and more features from English causing dialectalisation. Whether it is now a separate language or a dialect of English better described as Scottish English is in dispute. The pronunciation, grammar and lexis of the traditional forms differ, sometimes substantially, from other varieties of English.

Because of English's wide use as a second language, English speakers have many different accents, which often signal the speaker's native dialect or language. For the more distinctive characteristics of regional accents, see Regional accents of English speakers, and for the more distinctive characteristics of regional dialects, see List of dialects of the English language.

Just as English itself has borrowed words from many different languages over its history, English loanwords now appear in a great many languages around the world, indicative of the technological and cultural influence of its speakers. Several pidgins and creole languages have formed using an English base, for example Tok Pisin began as one.

There are many words in English coined to describe forms of particular non-English languages that contain a very high proportion of English words. Franglais, for example, is used to describe French with a very high English word content; it is found on the Channel Islands. Another variant, spoken in the border bilingual regions of Quebec in Canada, is called Frenglish. Norwenglish is a form of English containing many words or expressions directly copied from Norwegian.

Chapter 2

Function and Role of English

LANGUAGE DEVELOPMENT

It is held in this book that the functions of language, both intralinguistic and extralinguistic, are crucial in accounting for linguistic change. To dismiss functional pressure as being at all influential in the direction of linguistic development would be extreme. To take a simple example: the history of the English pronouns shows a steady replacement of many less distinctive native h-types by markedly distinctive forms borrowed from or influenced by Scandinavian (e.g. they, their, them and, probably, she).

The shift from native to Scandinavian forms seems to coincide with the rise in importance of pronouns as grammatical 'tracking-devices' as the older inflectional mechanisms fell into decay; and there are therefore both intralinguistic (system-based) and extralinguistic (contact-based) issues involved in explaining the change.

Although functional explanations of such developments, as we shall see, are not in themselves enough-and are certainly not comparable with the predictive explanations considered satisfactory in the physical sciences-it is surely perverse to see them as inherently implausible and philosophically untenable.

A parallel can be drawn here with the investigation by palaeontologists of biological evolution: the prehistoric ichthyosaur (a reptile) and the modern dolphin (a mammal), although of quite distinct genetic ancestries, bear a strong resemblance to each other, and biologists accept that both evolved to perform much the same function in the ecosystems within which they lived. A similar ecology has constrained evolution at two periods widely separated in time: function has constrained form.

As has been frequently pointed out, however, linguistic function cannot alone be the determining factor for linguistic choice. The strongly functional argument that linguistic change can be avoided because of systemic communicative pressures is untenable, since in that case change would never occur; change, it could be argued, is inherently dysfunctional in communicative terms since it impedes social interaction. For instance, when older generations call for a definition of new terms like nerd or geek they are demonstrating communicative breakdown with their children, whose choice of these terms is a way of distancing themselves socially from those same older generations.

It is therefore necessary to take account of formal as well as functional factors in discussing linguistic change; and the formal input to linguistic change lies in the field of variation. Usage varies not only from user to user, but also within an individual user's own variety of language (her or his 'idiolect'). Individual items are reflected variously in utterance depending on such extralinguistic factors as the age, sex and social origins of speaker and addressee, and on the degree of formality adopted or on the field of human activity within which the utterance occurs.

Thus we address an elderly aunt in one way, but a political rally or a husband/wife in others; and the circumstances of delivery of language can vary from an idle conversation over the cornflakes to a formal lecture. Because of the characteristics of language just described, it is argued in this book that both formal and functional aspects of language need to be taken into account when discussing and explaining linguistic change.

Although it is important to distinguish between the two in order to make clear the processes and mechanisms involved, it is nevertheless the case that an approach to the historical study of language which is purely formal or purely functional has severe limitations in explanatory power. The relationship between user and system seems to be a dynamic one, in which

In addition, an explicit focus on the linguistic features of the language of schooling can raise students' awareness of the choices available to them for writing the texts of schooling and can help reveal the layers of meaning in the texts they read. This chapter also outlines new directions in research on the language of schooling that can bring a theoretically motivated analysis of language to educational issues.

LANGUAGE TESTING

In language assessment, particular language tests are designed for particular purposes (i.e., proficiency, diagnosis, placement, and progress), and if applied to other purposes, may result in inappropriate evaluations of students' language ability. Tests have specific uses, and classroom tests can be used to evaluate specific curricula. Gronlund says that validity is "the extent to which inferences made from assessment results are appropriate, meaningful, and useful in terms of the purpose of the assessment".

Language proficiency tests and diagnostic tests are not specific to any one curriculum, but on the other hand, progress assessments should evaluate students' ability to implement the language knowledge and skills that they have learned through their studies in a particular course, and placement assessment seeks to determine the level of students' knowledge/skill with reference to placement within a particular curriculum.

With respect to assessment to place students into a specific curriculum, test content needs to be based on the material presented in the curriculum, which in turn should be based upon real-world tasks of English language use. Bailey says, "Since the purpose of a placement test is to assign students to particular levels of a programme, then it makes sense that the content of the test should be related to the curricula of those levels".

Thus, the purposes of programme level placement tests in non-Western developing countries differ from those of high-stakes international tests (such as the Test of English for International Communication - TOEIC or International English Language Testing System — IELTS), which evaluate general

English language proficiency. But often such general proficiency tests are used for placement purposes in developing countries simply because they are readily available and have high face validity. This practice can be a problem because these standardized tests are not meant to evaluate specific curricular content.

In fact, they are designed to lessen cultural bias by removing explicit cultural references - references that are the regional uses of English that the language learners in particular regions do in fact need to know. Educational Testing Service and University of Cambridge ESOL Examinations, the developers of two widely used, high stakes tests (the TOEIC and IELTS), have taken considerable measures to exclude content that could be offensive or highly inappropriate for test takers world-wide who are from extremely diverse cultural backgrounds.

Green and Jay (2005), in discussing quality control for IELTS content, explain efforts "to ensure that all material is culturally appropriate and accessible world-wide".

The *TOEIC Technical Manual* states "every effort is made to ensure that the test is unbiased and culturally relevant to our many candidates worldwide". Also, the Association of Language Testers in Europe (2005) recommends avoiding cultural bias in choosing texts for assessment, citing problematic materials such as local newspapers, or texts referring to war, death, politics, or religion.

Despite increased awareness of issues of culturally inappropriate content in English materials, culturally inappropriate content is still a problem. While it can be argued that inappropriate use of tests is the responsibility of the users, that is, ministries of education and/or school administrators, test users in developing countries may have few options when the only tests available are designed for other contexts.

Yet by eliminating problematic culturally explicit content (a practice appropriate for large-scale international tests), the ability to evaluate accurately real-world English language use in specific regions is lessened. Invalid testing due to cultural differences between test maker and test taker is a form of test bias, known as cultural bias. In language assessment, Bachman and Palmer consider the effect of cultural bias in second/foreign language testing, including assessing cultural bias as part of evaluation of the test's usefulness.

They note the possibility of decreased reliability in the sense that test takers would not be able to perform to the best of their ability as would be possible for them in their own cultural setting, and the consequently different test results would be a manifestation of the testing procedure instead of the students' ability. Palomba and Banta point out that test "data are unreliable to the extent that score variance is due to measurement error". If measurement error were to result from cultural bias, it would decrease test reliability.

In addition to affecting reliability in assessment, cultural bias impacts construct validity. In other words, a test does not actually measure the construct that it was designed to evaluate if it is distorted by cultural bias. Culturally biased test content is a threat to validity through construct under-representation or construct-irrelevant variance, meaning that the attribute in question is not being fully evaluated and that factors unrelated to that attribute may affect the outcome of the evaluation.

If a developing nation's department of education desires its citizens to learn English as a lingua franca within the national sociocultural context, yet language assessment is based on Western sociocultural norms, then questions of construct under representation and construct-irrelevant variance in the assessment may legitimately be raised.

ISSUES IN LANGUAGE

The theory that informs current educational practice is often constructed as a debate between proponents of mutually exclusive views that are often set up in terms of "meaning" versus "form." Such narrowly articulated controversies, however, fail to provide teachers with guidance about effective ways to focus on language as students read and write in various school subjects.

Discussions of writing pedagogy, for example, are often polarized around a distinction between "writing as product" and "writing as process" approaches. Supposedly the "product" oriented pedagogy is concerned only with the text the student produces and pays no attention to the process and stages that the writer and text are engaged in. On the other hand, "process" writing approaches are said to be concerned only with assisting students in brainstorming, drafting, revising, and editing without teaching form or grammar. But this distinction presents a false dichotomy.

Both process and product are important in writing instruction. Without a focus on form and attention to different register expectations, process-oriented approaches can easily become trivialized. Students may not be pushed to attempt unfamiliar genres if they are only encouraged to be expressive and write on whatever topics they wish.

This deprives students of opportunities to learn more than they already know and means that students are not prepared for writing in all subject areas. On the other hand, focus on product alone, without consideration of the contexts of writing and the process through which a text is developed, can result in formulaic responses that do not make the full range of meanings that the student is capable of. Products and processes need to be considered together, with the product of the process in focus throughout as students are challenged and assisted in writing new genres with more advanced register features.

In teaching reading, educators are similarly presented with a polarized controversy regarding the appropriate approach, with debates about whether to teach phonics or "whole language". The phonics movement assumes that learning the sound—letter correspondences will make good readers, and the tasks that are typically required of students in learning to read through phonics approaches include an abundance of worksheets, short answers, and activities that require little production of extended discourse.

Whole language approaches, on the other hand, stress the importance of a meaning based approach to reading and argue against a focus on form. But neither of these approaches prepares students for reading the difficult texts they encounter in the later years of schooling. Phonics approaches can trivialize the reading process by reducing reading to decoding. Whole language approaches, without a focus on the language in the text, can deprive students of valuable tools for understanding. In either case, teachers who have been prepared to use these approaches may not be equipped to raise students' awareness about the linguistic features that construe different kinds of meanings in different types of texts.

The emphasis in schools is too often on mechanical writing tasks such as spelling tests and grammar drills, while academic discourse forms that truly lead to success at higher levels of schooling, such as well-developed explanations, discussions, and arguments, are not explicitly presented and analyzed for their language features. In fact, much is left implicit in issues related to language. Outside of English classes and writing programmes, the typical writing assignment is a first and final draft, written in class.

Students often receive instruction about writing only after the writing tasks are completed, meaning that writing is more often assessed than taught. Teachers' feedback on student writing tends to focus on correction of errors at the sentence level or generalized comments on content, and writing is often corrected by teachers in ambiguous and inconsistent ways. This is highly problematic in terms of language development, because even when "errors" are corrected, students' writing may still not realise the academic registers that are expected in the genres they write.

Writing courses that take process approaches often focus only on personal genres, especially in courses for developing writers. Teachers are encouraged to draw on students' personal experience and allow them to use the registers they are comfortable with, on the grounds that pushing students to write in an academic style forces them to conform to models that are not of their cultures and that do not bring out their own personalities, and on the grounds that through frequent opportunities to write about what they are interested in, their writing will develop and mature.

But studies of students' writing do not support this. For example, when Aboriginal children in Australia were encouraged to choose their own topics for writing tasks, they chose a narrow range of familiar topics, such as visiting friends, hunting, sporting events, movies, and TV. They invariably produced recounts—simple sequential retelling of events. So instead of encouraging writing development, this approach actually limited their development.

Students typically work with a very narrow range of genres in the early grades, getting little experience and practice with the more complex genres that will be demanded of them in middle and secondary school and beyond. The most dominant form of writing in the lower grades is personal writing, as students are most commonly asked to write narratives, including recounts. Factual or analytical writing is rare. Articulation from the early grades into the late grades is inconsistent and does not systematically prepare students for what they will be expected to do at high school and beyond, building from the more narrative genres to the more analytical.

In a study of writing in secondary schools, Applebee found that weak writers and second language writers typically got few opportunities to write analytically. Poorer writers were asked to write in personal and imaginative modes and were expected to do only about half as much factual writing as better students. Better writers were assigned a higher proportion of information-based writing. This means that the writers who needed the most help were not engaged in tasks that gave them experience with academic registers.

In critiquing ESL writing instruction that is modeled after process approaches designed for native speakers, Hinkel argues that such approaches ignore issues related to the development of grammar and lexis. She demonstrates that the kinds of writing assignments students are given influence the types of texts they write. The assignments that ask for personal experiences lead to personal narratives or essays about students' beliefs or opinions. When given such tasks, students use examples rather than argumentation, relying on conversational rather than academic registers. Hinkel argues the need for a focus on the textual functions of grammatical structures in writing instruction.

Teachers need to create opportunities for students to write different types of texts and help them focus on how those texts are most effectively constructed so that students can extend their repertoires and make register choices that realise new and more challenging genres. As Shaughnessy notes, students do not choose a style of discourse, but rather are confined to particular styles because of their unfamiliarity with academic writing.

All students need to be able to address questions directly, defend those parts of their writing that are open to argument, and engage in other such academic language moves. These are not abilities that students will develop without assistance, as performing these functions requires use of academic register features that are not part of oral language competence and that are not developed through personal and narrative writing. For the past generation, pedagogical approaches for both second language learners and native speakers have de-emphasized any focus on form.

This philosophy against focus on form is most evident in approaches to second language acquisition that base themselves on Krashen's Input Hypothesis and Comprehensible Input constructs. This popular theory suggests that all that students need for language learning is plenty of comprehensible input, and that any focus on grammar is counterproductive. This theory was initially a reaction to an ineffective pedagogy focused on learning grammar rules. But in devaluing any focus on form, this approach ignores the differences between interactional registers and academic registers and the role of language in construing meanings in school subjects.

Students with fluent oral English, but little experience outside of school that leads to development of academic language, may need explicit focus on form in the context of purposeful learning of the registers and genres which enable them to participate in today's complex society. Students may be fluent in spoken English and still lack basic resources for reading and writing academic registers. When such students' reading and writing performance is weak, they are at risk of being placed in inappropriate instructional programmes. If it appears that their English is fluent, their problems may be viewed as cognitive; that they lack the intellectual skills they need for success at school.

Students are often tracked from the earliest years into programmes that provide differential access to advanced literacy. Rose illustrates, for example, how university students classified as "developmental" are placed in courses where they work through grammar exercise books and are given no experience with the critical writing tasks that their regular courses will demand.

These low-level courses focus on discrete skills that the students seem to lack, even while the students often have well-developed reasoning abilities which the courses never allow them to demonstrate.

At the same time, students who display their abilities in more expected ways go into programmes that allow them to further develop their linguistic resources and demonstrate their abilities through creative and challenging assignments. "Process" vs. "product" in writing instruction and "phonics" vs. "whole language" in reading instruction are debates that distract educators from the key issues in developing students' advanced literacy.

Christie argues that these dichotomous ways of thinking about language development fail to provide adequate guidance for teaching because both lack a sufficient understanding about differences between written and spoken language.

Without an understanding of the differences between ordinary interactional language and the language of schooling, teachers are inadequately prepared to address the challenges of the registers of advanced literacy.

Literacy learning goes on throughout one's lifetime and is never finished. Approaches that reduce literacy development to the learning of discrete elements like phonics, or expect students to be able to get meaning from text without attention to the forms that construe the meanings, lack the crucial component that functional approaches provide; a way of introducing students to the lexical, grammatical, and discourse features of academic registers that make the technical and specialized meanings that enable students' participation in advanced literacy contexts.

LANGUAGE INSTRUCTION AND ASSESSMENT

Recognizing the importance of correspondence between target language use, instruction, and assessment is an important step in finding a solution to the problem of inappropriate language instruction and testing, particularly when it stems from sociocultural bias from the use of Western tests in non-Western regions.

Bachman and Palmer state that testers want to "make inferences about test takers' ability to use language in a target language use domain a set of specific use tasks that the test taker is likely to encounter outside of the test itself". Brown and Bailey, among other assessment experts, suggest that placement test content be based upon the instructional content of the curriculum into which students are to be placed.

Thus we see in task-based assessment a three-fold relationship between tasks of real-world English language use, tasks for English instruction, and tasks for English language placement. The Connecting Point between Teachers, Testers, and Learners, illustrates the centrality of real-world English language use tasks to language instruction and assessment. In developing countries, there is a need for culturally appropriate tests of real world non-Western English language use to place students into language programmes which are seeking to instruct them in the English that they need in their specific region.

If the purpose of language assessment is to measure the practical language ability of students in real-life settings, then language assessment must correspond to tasks of target language use in authentic contexts. Assessment based on such real-world use of English language use has the advantage of being culturally specific, thus removing culturally in appropriate content. Brown, Hudson, Norris and Bonk suggest that, although there are challenges yet to be overcome, task-based language performance assessment offers a considerable advantage in evaluating test takers' ability to use the target language (i.e., English) in real-world communication. Such task-based language performance assessment would be based on needs analysis of daily tasks in real-world settings that require the use of English in actual communication.

Once tasks of real-world English language use are identified, test items can be developed for placement testing. But first it is necessary to identify how the target language is used in daily life. Various writers have defined task differently, and in this report, "task" focuses on authentic language use tasks accomplishing a real-world goal.

In developing placement tests, language teachers and school administrators ultimately want to know if their students are able to use the target language in real-life communication (which ideally are addressed by the curriculum). Referring to tasks to be used in language assessment, Bachman says, "Task specifications constitute the definition of the content domain to which our assessment-based inferences about ability extrapolate or the domain of real-life tasks which we want to predict".

Such tasks can be identified through sociolinguistic research investigating how language is used in social interaction. Specifically, this research investigates task descriptions of non-Western English language use, utilizing Bachman and Palmer's (1996) definition: "an activity that involves individuals in using language for the purpose of achieving a particular goal or objective in a particular situation".

In particular, this project identifies three tasks of non-Western English language use that are culturally appropriate in some regions but inappropriate in others. The resulting task descriptions are the informants' accounts of regionally specific uses of English explained in their own words.

LEARNING THE LANGUAGE

The notion of cultural incongruence or mismatch has been used to explain students' failure at school, but it is not enough to identify mismatches between the home and school and allow students to work in the genres of their home cultures. It is important to draw on the language students bring to school, but it is also necessary to help them develop new ways of making meanings that call for new forms of expression. Middle-class families apprentice children into ways of using language which will later be highly valued, but it also argued that it is not reasonable to expect that this kind of experience can be provided by teaching parents to adopt the strategies that researchers see middle-class parents using. Ways of making meaning vary across social groups in ways that are functional for those social groups.

The contexts and power relationships are different for people of different social and cultural backgrounds, and forms of interaction that do not correspond to deeper meanings and roles of participants are unlikely to be successful. So attempts to replicate middle-class parents' approaches are unlikely to work. Instead, schools need language development approaches that provide meaningful experiences with new subject matter and enable a focus on the linguistic features of the texts students read and write about that new experience.

Development of academic registers is a different task for students from different backgrounds. For some, the language expectations of schooling fit seamlessly into their home and community language styles, providing further reinforcement for abilities that they are developing in a wide range of social contexts. Their out of-school experiences socialize them into the ways of using language that are valued at school, so they can rely on their intuitions about language to achieve success. But other students have not had the kinds of social experiences that lead to this kind of understanding.

For these students, learning academic registers is like learning a second language in a context where little reinforcement is available outside of the classroom. The learning of new registers, like learning a second language, requires appropriate input, opportunities for interaction and negotiation of meaning, and relevant focus on the form that language takes in different settings and as it is used for different tasks. But classroom contexts, as currently constituted, are seldom sites where such language development can flourish. The ability to use the grammatical and lexical strategies of academic registers in writing and to recognize the meanings they make in the texts they read does not just come naturally in students' ordinary language development.

Socialization into new registers depends on having interaction that is meaningful in the new contexts where those registers are functional. This is similar to what is needed in early first language development, where what is most important is a consistent attempt by adults to understand the meaning intentions of the child and a willingness to make those intentions the basis for further conversation.

Second language acquisition research also shows that language development requires meaningful and purposeful interaction with an interlocutor who is willing to pursue the meaning-making moves of the learner. Our schools currently serve many second language learners, speakers of nonstandard dialects of English, and other students with little experience outside of school with academic ways of making meaning.

These students need meaningful input and opportunities to engage with texts and tasks in purposeful ways if they are to develop new language resources. They need interaction with knowledgeable interlocutors in ways that enable them to explore and negotiate meaning. And finally, they need a pedagogy that scaffolds language learning and learning through language.

None of these conditions is typically available to the learners in our schools. Classroom interactional patterns have been the focus of much research, and a common pattern of whole-class teacher—student interaction, the initiation-response-evaluation (IRE) sequence, also called the initiation-response-follow up (IRF) sequence, has been criticized as a barrier to providing students with the negotiation of meaning that promotes language development.

During these events, the teacher asks questions and evaluates students' responses as together they construct a particular interpretation or understanding of classroom content. Such interaction is criticized on several grounds: that most responses by students during this activity are single words or short phrases, that typically only a limited number of students volunteer to participate, that instruction and practice in formulating linguistically elaborated responses is typically not provided, and that the teachers' interpretations are always dominant, as they control clarification questions and which topics introduced by students will be followed up in subsequent discussion, limiting students' opportunities to negotiate meaning or pursue their own questions or ideas.

Other researchers have looked at this activity differently, showing that the IRF sequence can function in different ways in the classroom. Whether or not this participation structure is effective in helping students learn depends on how the teacher uses it, and at what point in the lesson.

Wells and Christie both point out that this discourse form can contribute to the development of students' understanding of language and content when teachers are clear about its purposes and goals. In the middle-school science classroom that Christie reports on, the IRF sequence actually enables the development of scientific discourse as it provides a context in which teacher and students together reconstrue the knowledge they have developed in technical and grammatically metaphorical language.

Christie traces the development of the "text" in this unit from the initial topic, "why the parts of a machine work" to its reconstrual as "mechanical advantage." The curriculum unit builds students' linguistic and scientific knowledge through hands-on experimentation and teacher explanation.

The IRF sequence occurs at the point where the students need to construct a taxonomy that will inform the collaborative science activities they are about to engage in. The IRF interaction scaffolds the development of new scientific knowledge using new linguistic forms, and small group work then provides opportunities for students to experience and discuss together the new concepts they are learning.

The unit culminates in oral and written reports in which students draw on academic register features to display the new knowledge they have developed. So the IRF sequence can play a crucial role in joint construction of patterns of use of the technical language that is necessary for student learning when it is structured to help students reconceptualize knowledge they have developed through experience as formal knowledge construed through new linguistic resources.

The kind of language students hear and read at school is also an important element in promoting academic language development. Often students whose reading skills are weak are given simplified texts that do not present the same content their grade-level peers are learning. Reading a simple narrative about the experience of a Civil War soldier, for example, when the grade-level standards call for students to understand the war's causes, deprives the weaker readers of access to learning opportunities.

From this perspective, texts used in instruction need to be good examples of real genres, "not just something enjoyable to engage children or a way to practice decoding". This suggests that teachers need to be conscious about the features of the texts they teach and engage in activities that make those texts meaningful.

Teachers also need to use academic registers and help students understand new ways of using language. Students cannot learn academic registers and academic content when the spoken explanations they hear lack the technicality they need to develop language resources for disciplinary work in different subject areas. Khisty, for example, in an ethnographic study of middle-school mathematics instruction, demonstrates that little real "math" language was actually used in the classrooms she studied.

Teachers mainly demonstrated procedures for performing calculations, and expected students to memorize these without discussion of conceptual factors in learning math or interaction about math concepts. The language that teachers used lacked technicality, as they attempted to express difficult mathematical concepts in words and phrases that carry little math meaning and can, in fact, be ambiguous.

For example, in asking a student to simplify the fraction 16/10 to get the answer 8/5, the teacher asks "Can you go down any lower?" Students need critical discussion of concepts through academic registers that construe the meanings they are expected to learn. Content knowledge and skills cannot be separated from the linguistic means through which that knowledge and skill is manifested. This is recognized to some extent by research in English as second language pedagogical contexts, where a focus on content-based language has been promoted.

Approaches to content-based language instruction can be enriched through an understanding that language and content are never separate; that "content" in school contexts is always presented and assessed through language; and that as the difficulty of the concepts we want students to learn increases, the language that construes those concepts also becomes more complex and distanced from ordinary uses of language. Such an understanding implies that focus on language itself is important for helping students learn the concepts of school subjects.

Christie points out that all teachers are teachers of language in this sense, "for language is the behavioral resource of central significance in the forms of learning for which schools are particularly responsible". She suggests that "where curriculum activities are designed so that children ... explore new experiences and acquire new information, they are encouraged to employ their linguistic resources, thus mastering an expanding range of new registers".

Classrooms can provide contexts for language development when students are engaged in exploring new ideas and content through meaningful experiences and activities and then assisted in developing spoken and written texts that draw on features of academic registers that are functional for presenting and discussing the new ideas and content.

Teachers need to be aware of and explicitly teach the strategies they expect students to use in classroom interaction, helping students develop skills of questioning and discussion that enable them to develop linguistic capacities that display their knowledge. If students are unable to draw on the meaning-making resources of academic registers, they are unable to demonstrate what they know.

KNOWLEDGE OF LANGUAGE

The ability to draw on the meaning potential of the registers expected in schoolbased tasks does more than just help students expand their knowledge of language. It enables them to learn the subject matter of advanced schooling and to think in new ways. Learning is in many ways a linguistic process, and the construal of non-everyday meanings in non-congruent grammar involves thinking in ways that *are* the content of school subjects and academic disciplines.

Painter suggests that "strategies or processes of learning—classifying, comparing, generalising, making cause—effect links, hypothesising, inferring and so on—all are most usefully seen ... as ways of mobilising the linguistic resource into text, rather than ways of doing some essentially non-linguistic, non-visible mental process". New ways of using linguistic resources enable students to develop the meaning potential that allows them to participate in the powerful forms of discourse in our society.

A pedagogy that focuses on language as a meaning-making resource puts the priority on helping students use language in new ways, rather than on teaching them "thinking skills" in isolation from content and language. In teaching writing, the focus can be on enabling students to marshal new linguistic resources for organizing and presenting the points they want to make.

Shaughnessy suggests that weak writers often do not lack ideas; instead, they lack knowledge of the discourse organizing strategies and grammatical choices that are needed to produce effective writing. She points out that "not only do [basic writing] students produce essays that are full of points but the points they make are often the same ones that more advanced writers make when writing on the same subject.

The differences lie in the style and extent of elaboration". She suggests that the notion that students need to be taught to "think" is based on the belief that the student's writing problems reflect an inability to conceptualize and that this condition may respond to direct instruction that concentrates on the thinking process rather than on writing.

She criticizes this view as a confusion of the analysis of thought with the generation of thought, pointing out that it underestimates the intellectual sophistication of the students and does not address their need to learn the ways of writing that are highly valued.

Veel suggests that academic registers construe "distinctive and favoured ways of thinking about the world; ways which we recognize as 'scientific,' 'logical' and 'rational'. Similarly, Lemke argues that "what we call 'thinking logically' is for the most part simply using language according to genre patterns ... to teach 'logical thinking' is simply to teach the uses of these genres".

Instruction can help learners gain access to educational discourses of the kind they might not otherwise become familiar with in their daily lives, at the same time providing them with conceptual tools for reflection on language as they engage in activities that help them develop new knowledge.

This reflection on language can also help students see how the linguistic choices of writers embed different ideological positions and make certain ways of thinking appear natural. Christie suggests that the teaching of a functional grammar "develops a critical capacity to interpret and challenge the ways language makes meanings".

This calls for an active role by educators in raising students' awareness of the power of the language. In order for students to engage in critical dialogue with institutions and social forms, they need to understand how the ideas, beliefs, and attitudes that make up a world view or a political position are embedded in texts and literacy practices. It is only through such understanding that students can examine the underlying assumptions and messages that promote certain perspectives and hide others.

As Veel notes, "language is constitutive of meaning and social context, not simply a conduit or tool to transmit thought or reality. The language ... makes possible some ways of thinking about the world and simultaneously prevents, or at least marginalizes, other ways of thinking". Understanding this power of the academic registers enables the meanings they make to be questioned and challenged, and the ideologies that these discourses embed to be understood and critiqued.

Knowledge about academic language gives students access to participation in the social contexts in which new knowledge is shared in the various disciplines. Learning to use academic registers is necessary if students are to make the kinds of meanings that are expected and functional in schooling. Having gained control of the registers, students can then manipulate them and use them to construct the diversity of meanings that reflect their own cultural contexts and goals. Getting control of the academic registers can enable students who are now marginalized to participate in constructing new kinds of meanings.

Functional linguistic analysis provides a framework and tools to enable students to develop strategies to analyse the ways language is used in school to serve dominant interests and silence others, and to examine how institutions and social organizations are maintained and reproduced through the use of language. New kinds of meanings will emerge as students make academic registers their own. All language is constantly in a process of variation and change due to the ways it is used by speakers for social purposes.

Different uses of academic registers inevitably contribute to maintaining or challenging the way things are. Knowledge of grammar, when seen from this perspective, is a form of social knowledge that can help students gain control over the valued genres in our society and, by participating in those genres, contribute to the social changes that are necessary for true equity of opportunity in schools and beyond.

Developing the ability to participate in the texts and contexts of schooling gives students the choice to challenge or support current institutions and social forms as they come to understand how language functions to establish and maintain social practices and to articulate different ideological positions. In school contexts, students come to new knowledge through language. The dense and abstract language characteristic of the texts of advanced literacy construes the specialized and abstract knowledge that students are expected to develop as they move into secondary school and higher education.

The linguistic challenges of schooling come from the specialized ways that language construes experience and social roles simultaneously in the densely structured texts of various subject areas. As demonstrated in this book, the register features of schoolbased tasks such as expository essays, and of science, history, and other disciplines, are functional for their purposes.

These features enable the language of schooling to make the disciplinary meanings through which knowledge is shared and developed. A greater awareness of the linguistic basis of this meaning making can broaden participation in the many contexts of learning that are realized in the language of schooling.

This has presented tools that can make visible the means by which language construes meanings in the texts of schooling. Recognizing the meanings in the grammatical choices reveals the basis for valuing certain ways of using language. In addition, the tools of systemic functional linguistics provide a means by which teachers and students can focus on language in functional ways that make explicit the different kinds of meanings that texts construe, providing a theoretical link between language and context that can help teachers and students recognize the functional value of linguistic choices.

Helping students understand how different forms construe different meanings gives them more choices about how they represent themselves as writers and gives them tools for getting meaning from the texts they read. This has drawn on research from a range of theoretical and methodological perspectives to show that there are common findings that emerge from the study of language use at school.

The value of the functional linguistics perspective on these findings is to situate the difficulty of learning academic content in the language through which content is taught and learned, and to see the learning of language and content as inextricably linked, rather than as separate processes. Characterizing the complexity of the language in terms of the clause structures that condense information in the nominal group and call for conjunctive strategies of integration allows us to reflect on the meanings construed in the language in ways that are open to analysis and discussion.

The systemic functional linguistics framework provides a metalanguage for talking about language that can bring a unified perspective to findings across a range of studies. The analyses presented here provide a general description of the language of schooling that is of course only partial and incomplete. More research from the functional linguistics perspective is needed to provide a deeper understanding of the challenges of the language of schooling; both the challenges of the genres and the challenges of developing facility with the register features.

More analysis of the functional uses of language in the context of particular genres can contribute to better understanding of the ways that grammatical elements are employed in the construction of spoken and written texts. In particular, we need a better understanding of the linguistic demands that new educational standards and examinations present at different levels and in different subject areas.

This research also needs a pedagogical dimension, examining when different genres can be introduced, how best to introduce them, and studies of the development of students' linguistic awareness about them. Students who are still developing academic registers make grammatical choices that are different from those made by more proficient writers, producing a different structure of information from what is expected. Understanding the challenges of the later years of schooling is important for enabling students to go beyond initial literacy to work with the dense, abstract, and technical texts of advanced literacy.

In addition, research is needed on how teachers develop an understanding of the functionality of language. Teacher education programmes are not grounded in the linguistic basis of learning, nor do they typically prepare teachers to help students understand the linguistic challenges of their subject areas. More research is needed on ways of preparing teachers to focus on how language construes meanings in the disciplines they teach. All teachers need strategies for talking about language features; research is needed to develop programmes that begin to reach teachers for whom language has not been a focus of attention.

And to accomplish these goals and to engage resources for research, it is also important to expand the awareness of educational administrators, teachers, and researchers about the role of language in education. Greater awareness about the linguistic expectations of schooling has the potential to bring about new ways of thinking about what is valued at school. Making the expectations of schooling explicit is a way for educators to examine those expectations.

Analyzing texts and tasks and evaluating their effectiveness for the purposes of schooling can help make educators more conscious of the real expectations that underlie learning activities and may lead to a reassessment of what is valued and encouraged. Research on standards and other assessment issues from a functional linguistics perspective can lead to new pedagogies that integrate language development into disciplinary learning in ways that acknowledge the linguistic challenges.

The linguistic framework provided by Halliday's theory offers tools for expanding the awareness about language of all those engaged in education and other social processes. As a theory of language that demonstrates the close link between the contexts of language use and the kinds of spoken and written texts that emerge from those contexts and in turn shape those contexts in particular ways, it can add a dimension to the explanations that sociolinguistics, applied linguistics, and educational linguistics offer for understanding issues of language and learning.

Adopting this way of talking about and analyzing grammatical forms and discourse structures offers a perspective within which a broad range of researchers can engage in discussion about the role of language in social contexts of various kinds. To make English easier to read, there are some simplified versions of the language. One basic version is named *Basic English,* a constructed language with a small number of words created by Charles Kay Ogden and described in his book *Basic English: A General Introduction with Rules and Grammar*. The language is based on a simplified version of English. Ogden said that it would take seven years to learn English, seven months for Esperanto, and seven weeks for Basic English, comparable with Ido.

Thus Basic English is used by companies who need to make complex books for international use, and by language schools that need to give people some knowledge of English in a short time. Ogden did not put any words into Basic English that could be said with a few other words, and he worked to make the words work for speakers of any other language. He put his set of words through a large number of tests and adjustments. He also made the grammar simpler, but tried to keep the grammar normal for English users.

The concept gained its greatest publicity just after the Second World War as a tool for world peace. Although it was not built into a programme, similar simplifications were devised for various international uses.

Another version, Simplified English, exists, which is a controlled language originally developed for aerospace industry maintenance manuals. It offers a carefully limited and standardized subset of English. Simplified English has a lexicon of approved words and those words can only be used in certain ways. For example, the word *close* can be used in the phrase "Close the door" but not "do not go close to the landing gear".

Chapter 3

Status of Language

EVIDENCE

Texts are never simply illustrative of past states of the language, for every text has a special context which conditions its contents. Thus in an historical study such as this book it is important from the outset to face up to some of the problems with which texts confront us-problems which vary diachronically.

It is necessary, in other words, to examine the nature of the evidence for the history of English from various stages in that history; and this chapter demonstrates some typical evidential problems from the three stages of the language conventionally distinguished: Old, Middle and Modern English.

PHILOLOGY AND LINGUISTICS

Before doing so, however, it must be noted that such a linking of textual analysis to more general linguistic concerns is not a feature of scholarly practice which has been invariably accepted by all linguistic historians.

Since the end of the Second World War, two traditions of enquiry into the history of English can be distinguished: the 'philological' and the 'linguistic'. These traditions have from time to time been seen as mutually antagonistic, although there are signs that a scholarly rapprochement between them is beginning to emerge.

The term 'philology' has a number of meanings; on the continent of Europe, for instance, it is often used to refer to literary rather than to linguistic studies. Perhaps its most common use, however, is to refer to the close study of the language of individual texts from the past, as opposed to 'linguistics', which may be crudely defined as the scientific study of language, whereby observed facts are placed within a larger conceptual framework.

Many scholars have come to see philology as old-fashioned, not concerned with the larger theoretical picture which is considered by some the true domain of historical linguistics, and therefore trivial; traditional philology certainly suffered, at least in British universities, from such atomism, and it is probably for this reason that it has come, at least for the time being, to lose its centrality within the larger domain of English studies.

Philology seemed to be-or perhaps more correctly seemed to have become-not so much 'theory-free' as 'theory-innocent', and thus ultimately intellectually unsatisfying.

Yet it could be argued that a tendency has developed amongst some modern linguists to allow theory to overwhelm data; and the data-centred discipline of philology can be regarded therefore as useful corrective to a tendency to overgeneralise.

The necessity of bringing together these two approaches to the historical study of language is emphasised when we judge the evidence for the history of English. In the Old and Middle English periods, the main sources of information are literary and documentary manuscripts, supplemented to a limited extent by inscriptions on stone, wood, metal or bone, and by place-names, and complex questions of context and transmission surround all these texts.

In the Early Modern English period, things seem at first sight more hopeful; the evidence of the manuscript is supplemented not only by that of the printed book but also by that offered by the first serious writers on the English language: the spelling-reformers, the early phoneticians and grammarians and the early lexicographers.

Many of these scholars were excellent observers of the language of their time; however, their evidence always needs to be judged in the light of contemporary prescriptive attitudes to speech and writing. Only in the nineteenth and twentieth centuries, with the rise of the scientific study of contemporary language, does the evidence become in any sense complete; but, even then, there are problems to do with the sheer quantity and range of the material collected, and with the theoretical assumptions which governed its collection.

Hie direct evidence for past states of the language, therefore, survives in patchy and fragmentary ways; and, although this direct evidence can be supplemented by the indirect evidence to be derived from processes of linguistic reconstruction, these latter methods not only present problems of their own but also themselves depend on the historical record.

Unlike the modern sociolinguist or diaiectologist, historical linguists cannot choose their informants for their social class or geographical setting; we have to make do with what the vagaries of time have left us, and, very frequently, we depend on the merest hints to help us construct our hypotheses about past states of the language.

It is therefore important not to draw linguistic conclusions from textual data without first subjecting the texts to careful examination. 'Every text has its own history' could be taken as the key axiom which underlies-or should underlie-philological practice.

To refer simply to diatopic ('through-space', i.e. geographical) and diachronic ('through-time', i.e. historical) variation in texts is not enough; texts need to be contextualised, so that the true status of the information they contain may be ascertained.

WRITING AND SPEECH

Perhaps the most important point to make about the evidence for past states of the language is that, until the very end of the nineteenth century, direct (as opposed to reconstructed) evidence is to be found solely in the written record. Thus the most important act of evidential contextualisation needed in an historical study of English is a clarification of the relationship between the written and spoken modes of language.

For most of the language's history, the written mode is all that survives; and this fact raises problems of how far writing maps onto speech.

It is, of course, obvious that the writing-systems of the world used today do not have any clear relationship to the sounds which, often at some removes, they represent: the relationship between symbol and sound is arbitrary, not necessary.

Thus, in alphabetic scripts, Cyrillic 'means', whereas Roman 'means' [w] in English and so on. This complexity is compounded by the appearance of conventional uses based upon distributional distinctions (e.g. has two different phonic significances in Present-Day English yacht, many), and by diachronic variation. As an example of the latter, the representation of might be examined, for this sound has been represented very variously in spelling during the history of English.

An examination of the Linguistic Atlas of Late Mediaeval English yields a broad range of forms for Present-Day English sh- in 'shall' as recorded in manuscripts, for instance chal, scal, schal, shal, ssal, sal, xal; with the possible exception of the initial x- in xal, none of these spelling-variants seems to signify any sound other than.

At a more general level, the written mode is traditionally taken to represent a more formal register than the spoken mode: thus the distinction between language appropriate for, say, a conversation and, for example, a learned article. On the other hand, and despite the existence of conventional usages (e.g. 'silent ' or 'silent ' in forms such as life, knight), it is plain that English alphabetic script has evolved so that the symbols generally and typically represent vowels of some kind, whereas etc. are used generally and typically to represent consonants.

And there are obviously areas of discourse where the distinction between formal written language and less formal speech becomes hard to draw, such as in the academic lecture.

There are two important points to make here. One is that the modes of speech and writing should be treated by historians of a language as distinct manifestations of that language, with important implications for the methodology of linguistic historiography.

The second point, however, is equally valid: there is an obvious connection between the written and spoken modes, because both are manifestations of (i.e. transmission-mechanisms for) the 'same' language.

EVIDENCE FOR ENGLISH

The problem of evidence for the history of English is at its most acute for the period up to c. 1250, that is, the Old English and post-Old English periods.

It is usual to classify the extant Old English texts as belonging to four dialect-groupings: Old Northumbrian and Old Mercian, West Saxon and Old Kentish. We will be returning to the meaning of these labels shortly; ut, before we do so, we might note that the evidence for each of these dialect-groupings varies in extent very considerably, both diachronically and diatopically.

It includes the major inscriptions in runes, the ancient Germanic alphabetic system. The virtue of the table given below is that it shows up the massive gaps in the written record, and that the pattern of gaps and entries does seem to correlate with historical events.

Thus the seventh and eighth centuries, the period of Northumbrian hegemony in England, are unsurprisingly also the time when most texts traditionally called 'Old Northumbrian' survive; in the eighth and ninth centuries Mercia held primacy amongst the Anglo-Saxon kingdoms, and 'Old Mercian' texts predominate; and, in the tenth and eleventh centuries, the period of the supremacy of Wessex, by far the largest number of texts are 'West Saxon'.

The table has obvious flaws, however, and these need to be spelt out rather carefully. First of all there is the question of what we mean by the labels 'Northumbrian', 'Mercian', 'Kentish' and 'West Saxon'.

Northumbrian	*Mercian*	*Kentish*	*West Saxon*	*Date (century)*
Ruthwell Cross; early texts of Cædmon's Hymn; Bede's Death Song; Auzon Casket	Corpus glossary	-	-	seventh/eighth
Liber Vitae	Epinal/ Erfurt glossaries; Vespasian Psalter Gloss	*Codex Aureus; Charters*	Early WS texts names (e.g. Parker Chronicle)	ninth
Lindisfarne Gospels Gloss; Ru2	Ru1; Chad; (ancestor of AB-language)	*Psalms; Hymns; Glosses*	Late WS texts (e.g. certain MSS of Ælfric)	tenth/eleventh

It is obvious, from their descendants in the much better attested Middle English period, that these various Old English dialects can be given a roughly geographical ordering, even if the placings can scarcely be as accurate as that achieved in detailed surveys of present-day varieties of English. It is perhaps best to see these terms as typological expressions, useful ways of expressing broad diatopic relationships between bodies of texts.

Just how rough these expressions are, however, is indicated when we move to a second caveat about the table: the way in which it places each text in a clear-cut relationship of descent and difference. The trouble is that many-if not most-of these texts are situated in quite complex linguistic and textual networks. Thus the Erfurt glossary was almost certainly copied by a scribe whose first language was not English, with all the implications that has for the status of the text as linguistic evidence.

The Vespasian Psalter Gloss, although the major ninth-century Mercian text, was copied in Canterbury, possibly by a non-Mercian scribe working from a Mercian original. The ninth-century Kentish Charters differ from the tenth-century Kentish Psalms in that many of the former show (so it is often, if controversially, claimed) the impact of Mercian orthographic tradition while the latter are influenced by West Saxon remarks, 'West Saxon is fighting against the strong tradition of Mercian spelling'.

The whole question of the relationship between the corpora of Early and Late West Saxon texts is a complex one; it has been traditional to refer to the writings of King Alfred's day (the late ninth century) as exemplifying 'Early West Saxon' whereas those of Abbot Ælfric's time (the early eleventh century) are often termed 'Late West Saxon', yet the relationship between Early West Saxon and Late West Saxon is distorted if the material remains which make up the latter are taken as descended straightforwardly from the former.

The relationship between the Lindisfarne Gospels Gloss and the Mercian portion of the Rushworth Glosses ('Ru1') is an intricate one; but this did not stop Farman, the Mercian glossator of this part of the Rushworth Gospels, feeling and reflecting the impact of what must have been an incipient West Saxon standardised written language. This list of special cases could be greatly expanded.

Finally, some broad coverage across the country. Such an impression is quite fallacious. Apart from West Saxon, the dialect materials from Anglo-Saxon England are slight and fragmentary, and major parts of the country are almost entirely unrepresented (e.g. East Anglia).

It seems that what the written evidence of Anglo-Saxon England supplies us with is a set of snapshots of individual usages, of varying evidential value, giving us an idea of the kinds of language found in a few regional centres of the period. This picture corresponds with what we know of Anglo-Saxon writing abilities in the vernacular: something restricted to the monastic scriptorium.

It is in this sense that some distinguished scholars have spoken of the impossibility of Old English dialectology, if our aim is to produce something comparable to the modern Survey of English Dialects; and it seems certain, despite some researchers' gallant attempts, that quantitative surveys comparable to those carried out by modern sociolinguists are not an appropriate methodology for the study of the language of this period-the material remains to allow for statistical analysis of the kind favoured by such investigations are simply not to be had. However, it is possible to make some interesting typological statements, and the investigation of scriptorial practices remains a valid goal of enquiry.

A similar situation may be found when we turn to the manuscript-evidence for the post-Old English/transitional Middle English period, that is, from the Norman Conquest up to c. 1250. Until the middle of the thirteenth century, manuscripts in the vernacular continued to be produced in England; a remarkable fact is that more manuscripts in what is conventionally called 'Old English' survive dating from after the Norman Conquest than from before it.

But these texts were generally produced under a conservative scriptorial system which survived in only a few regional centres, for instance Worcester, and which could enforce a normative spelling-system; in less geographically and politically peripheral scriptoria, such as Canterbury, the vernacular was replaced much earlier by Latin as the language of written record.

Even in the West Midlands, this scriptorial system had broken down by the middle of the thirteenth century as a result of wider vernacular literacy and demand for books; it has usually been argued that, sustained by the close supervision associated with monastic discipline, the system could not survive in the looser institutional structures needed to produce books rapidly. And in some parts of the country, such as the North or the extreme South-West, conditions were such that vernacular literacy to all intents and purposes seems to have disappeared for much of the Middle English period. The evidence for post-Old English remains patchy.

Moreover, the manuscripts which do survive raise textual problems in many ways similar to those raised by the Old English evidence; for instance, the texts associated with and derived from the much-copied early-thirteenth-century handbook for solitary religious women, Ancrene Wisse, make up a very high proportion of the texts located on this map. Without them, a large portion of the evidence for transitional Middle English would disappear.

And yet there is evidence that these texts were in some sense and at some point in their transmission standardised, that is, focused on a conventionalised usage, traditionally localised at the North Herefordshire religious house of Wigmore Abbey. The evidence for the central period of Middle English is much fuller. The most important source of information for much of this period, as for Old English, continues to be the corpus of surviving manuscripts.

But whereas the manuscript-remains from the period up to 1250 are comparatively scanty, the manuscript-evidence for Middle English after that date is very considerable indeed. Moreover, its evidential value is qualitatively distinct. Middle English is 'dialectal' rather than 'standardised'; a debased vernacular for much of the period, English did not achieve the status of availability for all possible registers until well after the end of the Middle Ages-arguably, not until the nineteenth century, when French was replaced by English as the language of acts of parliament.

The reason for this debasement of English is historical. Although there is good evidence that the Norman aristocracy learnt English fairly quickly after the Conquest-a trend encouraged by the events of 1204, when the rulers of England lost control of Normandy and those barons who owned land in both countries (as many did) had to choose between their English and Norman estates-nevertheless French remained the language of prestige and sophistication during the Middle Ages. Since no general norm of written English was taught until at least the fifteenth century, the written mode of Middle English reflects the diatopic variation of the spoken medium more clearly than ever since.

Despite this plethora of evidence for contemporary linguistic variation, however, it was until comparatively recently (and, in some circles, remains) scholarly practice to confine the discussion of the dialectal manifestations of Middle English to a rather small set of texts considered to be of first-class evidential value: thus the primacy in this scholarly tradition of authorial holographs, which are supposed to give precise information about the language of a (comparatively) fully contextualised individual.

During the Middle English period, such texts are unhappily few: Dan Michel's Ayenbite of Inwyt is one such, as are the holograph writings of the poet and scribe Thomas Hoccleve (early fifteenth century), or much of the fascinating late-medieval collection of papers and letters collected by and for the Paston family of Norfolk.

To these might be added-albeit somewhat controversially-the English poetry of John Gower, William Langland and possibly even Geoffrey Chaucer himself, all of whose usages may be reconstructed from the evidence of manuscripts copied around or just after the time of the poets' deaths. Any discussion of the language of these authors, especially in the field of phonological reconstruction, has in the past been usually restricted to the analysis of poetic rhyming or metrical practice. Such an emphasis on authors derives from the traditional primary philological goal of textual criticism: the construction of the 'critical edition', whereby the authorial text could be presented to a modern audience free from an assumed overlay of scribal accretion and corruption.

However, the completion of the Linguistic Atlas of Late Mediaeval English (LALME) in 1986 has meant a massive addition to the body of localised and localisable texts for the period 1350-1450, and hence a liberation from the restricted corpus hitherto studied.

The focus of LALME is on individual scribal usage rather than on that of the author-thus scribes are granted equal importance to authors in terms of their status as linguistic informants-and on the written language as an object of interest in its own right rather than as indirect evidence for the spoken mode. LALME covers the period 1350-1450, and the reasons why it ends at the later date are obvious: it is from that time that standardisation of the written mode obscures the earlier pattern of richly recorded dialectal variation.

By the sixteenth century, in England at least, the public written mode of the vernacular had become standardised-focused-in a way which points forward to the fixed and educationally enforced standard of present-day written English. The use of printing for reproducing English texts from the end of the fifteenth century provided prescriptive norms for contemporary manuscript-usage, a development which correlates with the contemporary growth in vernacular literacy.

Printing was introduced into England, it seems, as the result of popular demand for the rapid production of books. Its invention correlates with the growth of a larger distinct reading public, that is, notably in London and the rest of the prosperous South and East, a literate, upwardly mobile, urban middle class.

It is worth recording that upper-class readers still demanded lavishly decorated manuscripts for presentation to them; printed books were essentially aimed at the emerging middle classes, for whom the traditional workaday manuscripts were a poor second-best. During this period, the origins of Present-Day English society, with its modern class-gradations, may be detected; and these class differences are marked by linguistic standardisation in both written and spoken modes.

For information about the spoken mode during the Early Modern English period we depend not so much, as in the Old and Middle English periods, on the evidence supplied by variant spellings and grammatical forms in written texts (although informal writings from the period do sporadically reflect contemporary speech-habits in ways which are disguised in contemporary printed books, and deserve more attention than they are often given).

Rather, students of Early Modern English speech depend on the interpretation of contemporary statements about the language: the works of the orthoepistical writers and the early English grammarians and lexicographers. Even here, it is important to note that the evidence of these early commentators cannot itself be taken at face value. A number of writers claim usages as authentic which are at obvious variance with the facts, misled by their own conception of what is more or less prestigious practice.

Helpful extra information about pronunciation is given by rhyming practices and, even, puns; and there is also the evidence provided by, for instance, writers of the time attempting to represent, frequently for the purposes of parody, the variousness of contemporary spoken language; good examples of the latter are to be found in Shakespeare's representation of non-standard speech, such as in Edgar's 'countryman's' language in King Lear.

However, these practices, too, can be affected by the growth of prescriptive norms, and a degree of formalisation cannot be ruled out even (perhaps especially) in parodic writing-just as present-day stage Glaswegian is not to be too closely identified with the actor's target for imitation, 'real' Glaswegian. Rhymes and puns, archaistic grammar or vocabulary, can be conventional, and not a true reflection of the spoken mode of the time. It is therefore important, in studying the language of this period, for a third source of evidence to be brought into consideration: the evidence of Present-Day English itself. Present-Day English is made up of many varieties; and many of these varieties themselves contain residualisms which illuminate the earlier history of the language.

RECONSTRUCTION

So far in this chapter, we have been concerned with the analysis of direct, that is extant, evidence for the historical study of English. There is, of course, another, indirect source of evidence for states of the language in the past, which has proved particularly useful when engaging with pre-historic matters (i.e. discussion of linguistic events which take place before the period of written records). This source lies in the well-established methodologies associated with comparison of recorded language-states and subsequent reconstruction of common unrecorded ancestor-forms.

A simple example of comparative reconstruction (as it is called), that is, reconstruction based on the data of more than one related language or variety, is given by Lehmann, who cites the contrast between British, Australian and North American pronunciations of the words atom, bitter and little. In some varieties of American English (AE), the medial -t- is voiced, so that atom and Adam, bitter and bidder are pronounced alike (i.e. they are homophones); this usage contrasts with that of British English, where atom, bitter have medial/t/beside medial/d/in Adam, bidder.

Pronunciations like those of British English (BE) are also found in other varieties of English, for example in Australia (AusE). Such comparisons enable the linguist to reconstruct a *proto-form* or *etymon*. The implication of this diagram is that American English had undergone an innovation not experienced by the other varieties in question.

This simple reconstruction is supported by an examination of words made from the same base in American English, such as hitter American English/'h d r/beside hit American English/

h t/. The voiceless/t/in the verb suggests that the American English pronunciation of hitter with/d/, the derived noun, not shared by British English and Australian English, is an innovation.

Beside comparative reconstruction, historical linguists also have had recourse to *internal reconstruction.* Internal reconstruction, as its name suggests, uses data from within one variety-which itself might be reconstructed-for reconstructing its ancestor. Again, Lehmann gives a simple example of this procedure. He notes that an earlier American English/t/ became/d/in certain environments.

Both methods are well established in scholarship, and have proved themselves to be a valuable resource of indirect evidence for historical study. However, there are problems about these methods which, when the disciplines of reconstruction were first established during the nineteenth century, were perhaps not addressed as fully as they might have been.

Table. Internal Reconstruction

tick	sin	bid	hit
ticker	sinner	bidder	hitter
ticking	sinning	bidding	hitting
ticks	sins	bids	hits
red	black	fast	fat
redder	blacker	faster	fatter

In essence, these problems centre on the question of uniformity that the proto-language represents a uniform state from which subsequent varieties have diverged. The evidence of present-day and historically recorded languages is that such uniformity is a fiction; any single language is a congeries of varieties which have emerged through processes of complex interaction with each other.

Furthermore, the techniques of reconstruction can be taken only so far back. It has been a presumption of most linguists that all human languages have an ultimate common ancestor, but the reconstruction of this ultimate proto-language has not proved possible. Languages borrow material from other languages as well as inherit it from their ancestors, and the further back the reconstruction is taken, and the more languages there are for comparison, the smaller the amount of inherited material there is.

In such circumstances, it is worth reminding ourselves that any set of reconstructed proto-forms is an abstract representation of an underlying system, not reflecting the surface variation of which natural languages consist; a useful formalisation, but limited if our aim is to use such formalisations as evidence for the processes involved in linguistic change.

It is for this reason that this book, although it deals with a few problems where reconstruction of some kind is necessary, has avoided dealing with language-states such as Proto-Germanic, where only reconstructed forms can be adduced as evidence. It is worth noting, moreover, that reconstructions of proto-languages depend on the earliest historical data available; and the earliest data for English from the Anglo-Saxon period themselves need textual analysis before they in turn can be used for reconstruction.

PROBLEMS OF TEXTUAL ANALYSIS

At the beginning of this chapter, reference was made to the necessity for textual analysis before linguistic deductions can be legitimately made. In what remains, some textual problems characteristic of the various periods of English conventionally distinguished will be discussed, exemplifying the kinds of difficulty which the diachronic linguist needs to confront.

An Old English Problem

The first example will be taken from the Old English period that is the period roughly from the arrival of the Anglo-Saxons in England up to the Norman Conquest of 1066. A typical linguistic innovation, observable in Present-Day English and referred to from time to time elsewhere in this book, is that which scholars refer to as 'misadaptation' or 'hyperadaptation' or, sometimes, 'hypercorrection'. Hyperadaptation is characteristic of socially mobile, upwardly aspiring people; such folk are weakly tied to the social network they are attempting to leave, and similarly weakly tied to the target-class at which they are aiming.

A good example in Present-Day English is the spread of initial by habitual 'h-droppers' to environments where it is not used in 'standard' speech and where it has no etymological justification, for instance for 'I'. Such innovations can become objects of mirth and parody. But they are of interest to linguists because they display the classic features of an innovation, being produced by a group of upwardly aspiring people with weak ties in the community both to their social origins and to their social target.

Such hyperadaptations can be found early in the history of English. An eighth/ninth-century copy of the Gospels in Latin, was given an Old English interlinear gloss in the tenth century by two scribes whose names are recorded in the manuscript: Farman and Owun. The book belonged in 1650 to John Rushworth, deputy clerk to the House of Commons, and he donated it to the Bodleian; it is therefore known as the Rushworth Gospels. Farman's portion consisted of the gloss to Matthew, Mark 1-2, and a small portion of John; Owun wrote the rest.

The colophon indicates that Farman wrote 'æt harawuda', usually identified as Harewood near Leeds in Yorkshire. Owun seems to have been a Northumbrian. The two scribal contributions are traditionally known as Ru1 and Ru2 respectively. It has long been recognised that Farman's glossing differs linguistically from the Old Northumbrian of Owun, but accounting for the difference was controversial before R. Menner's study of 1934.

Until that date, it was a persistent belief that Ru1 was 'a kind of mixture of Mercian and West Saxon'; and some scholars had concluded that this mixed variety existed because Farman was copying a West Saxon gloss and interlarding it with his own (Old Mercian) forms. Menner showed convincingly that Farman was a translator of the exemplar before him. The basis of his proof was that, in his glossing of Mark, Farman used as his exemplar the Old Northumbrian gloss to the Lindisfarne Gospels, which still survives: 'this is obvious...from his frequently copying the variant glosses and even a marginal expansion from Lindisfarne'; the gloss to Matthew, however, was derived independently. Careful comparison of the two sets of glosses in Ru1 shows few linguistic differences between them. What differences there are can be explained in terms of what has been called 'constrained usage':

One may...risk the deduction that in copying another gloss Farman would avoid a word that did not belong to his own dialect, but might on the contrary follow his original in the use of words that would not be his choice in an independent translation.

Although Menner vindicated Farman's usage as his own, his work left a number of questions unanswered. In terms of the traditional Old English dialect typology, Farman's language remained mixed in appearance, and his writing included a number of forms which seemed not to be etymologically justified.

The key work on Farman's usage remains Kuhn's study of e and œ in Ru1. Kuhn demonstrated that Farman's peculiarities could be accounted for in terms of hyperadaptation (although Kuhn did not use the term) in the direction of West Saxon, a dialect which, in the generations after Farman, became prestigious and was therefore imitated in the written mode outside its area of origin.

Probably the clearest instance of this behaviour, fully documented by Kuhn, is Farman's use of œ for the isolative development of both West Germanic a and West Germanic e. As a Mercian, Farman might have been expected to share the development of these sounds found in the chief Old English 'Mercian' text, the ninth-century gloss to the Vespasian Psalter; but there are some interesting differences.

Because of a prehistoric Old English sound-change known as 'second fronting', the gloss to the Vespasian Psalter has e for West Germanic a where West Saxon has œ. Farman, however, generally has œ; beside dœg, other common forms are œfter, fæder, hrœgl etc. He uses e only rarely, for instance hweþre. Kuhn shows that Farman uses œ to e as the reflex of West Germanic a in the proportion 25:2.

Farman's usage here may seem unexceptionable; we know little enough about the true geographical extent of second fronting in the Old English period, and it could be argued that the sound-change simply did not reach 'æt harawuda'. However, this position cannot be sustained when we examine the reflexes of West Germanic e in Farman's glosses.

Unless affected by neighbouring sounds, the reflex of West Germanic e has been astonishingly stable in the history of English, and e is the usual form in all Old English dialects. Yet Farman uses œ for e in West Germanic e-words in the proportion of 5 *œ* to 9 *e*-a remarkable statistic. Thus forms such as *œfne, cwœþende, stœfn, þœc, þægn, wœr* appear. A. Campbell objected to a 'general identification of œ and e' in Farman's idiolect, and drew attention to the restricted set of words in which œ for e occurred.

Campbell did not, however, make as clear a distinction as he might have done between writing and speech; and this held him back from accepting Kuhn's explanation of these forms, even though he felt that the 'cause of these abnormal spellings requires investigation'. Kuhn, having found similar behaviour in the eleventh-century *Worcester Chronicle,* explained Farman's usage as follows: Farman was a Mercian whose native speech must have been essentially the same as that of the scribe who glossed the Vespasian Psalter, but whereas the latter was writing with a minimum of outside influence, Farman was trying to imitate the language of his temporal and ecclesiastical superiors.

As a consequence of this imitation, he introduced numerous Saxonisms into his glosses, among them œ instead of e for [West Germanic] a. He, like the Worcester scribe, carried the imitation too far, and wrote œ frequently for [West Germanic].

In other words, Farman hyperadapted in the written mode. His hypercorrection, moreover, can be accounted for in terms of what may be termed weak cultural ties; Farman was not a West Saxon, but aspired to West Saxonism. This makes him a typical innovator; but it also makes his evidence for Old Mercian problematic.

A Middle English Problem

Until quite recently, Middle English scholars generally held to the dictum, perhaps most clearly enunciated by J.R.R. Tolkien, that the language of a Middle English text was a reflection of its textual transmission.

Since Middle English was the age when dialectal variation was reflected in the written mode, and therefore scribal idiolects varied very considerably, and since most Middle English texts other than authorial holographs were the result of scribes copying the work of other scribes whose idiolects almost necessarily differed to a greater or lesser extent from their own, it was assumed that any given scribal copy was written in what became called a Mischsprache, a 'mixed language', to which each scribe involved in transmitting the text had contributed some element.

It was therefore assumed that texts other than holographs-which were felt to be in some sense 'pure'-were of very limited linguistic value. The publication of LALME has, however, revised scholarly opinion on this matter. It is now held that the problems of interpretation raised by scribe-author interaction in the copying of Middle English texts can be overcome.

The means by which this has been done have been set out in a series of ground-breaking articles, which established a typology of scribal practice. This typology, which is clinal, divides the habits of copyists of Middle English manuscripts into three categories:

1. *Literatim*-copying, whereby a scribe reproduced, letter-by-letter, the forms of an exemplar;
2. Translation, whereby scribes converted the language of their exemplars into their own language;
3. Something between these two poles.

Examples of all three kinds of behaviour are not hard to find in Middle English texts:

- The Cotton text of The Owl and the Nightingale,

although copied by one hand throughout, is written in two distinct spelling-systems which fall into two distinct sets of stints.

- A comparison of William Caxton's text of Malory with Caxton's own prose shows that, in this instance, the printer had imposed his own spellings on whatever exemplar was being presented to him. This was not Caxton's usual practice, as is demonstrated by his retention of particular spelling-usages characteristic of especially prestigious text-descent, e.g. his prints (in verse) of John Gower's Confessio Amantis or (in prose) of Nicholas Love's translation of the Mirror of the Blessed Life of Jesus Christ .
- The Titus manuscript of Ancrene Riwle seems to be written in a mixture of 'AB-language' and North-West Midland Middle English; even if the manuscript were still written by a literatim-copyist, it suggests very strongly that a mixed language lies somewhere in the ancestry of the text.

M. Benskin and M. Laing, as well as engaging with the mechanisms involved here, distinguish subcategories, for example progressive translators, who begin as literatim-scribes but become translators as copying proceeds, or constrained scribes, whose repertoire of forms is partially but not wholly activated by their exemplars.

They conclude that, during the period covered by LALME, 2-type scribes, or scribes who tended towards 2-type behaviour, were by far the most common kind. This insight makes scribes as well as authors legitimate objects of investigation. The processes involved in scribal translation may be illustrated by an examination of four texts of a major Middle English poem, the Cursor Mundi.

This lengthy (about 30,000 lines) spiritual history of humanity from the Creation to the Day of Judgement survives in nine fourteenth-century manuscripts or manuscript-fragments in a number of Middle English dialects. Short parallel passages derived from four manuscripts. All contractions have been silently expanded, but the texts are otherwise as they appear in the manuscripts. MS C has a number of features which characterise it as Northern. Late Old English a is reflected as in strang 'strong' 5, bald 'bold' 7; the weak adjective ending -e, which was lost early in Northern England, has disappeared in the strang strijf 'the furious strife' 5, even though the stress-pattern of the verse indicates that it probably appeared in the authorial original, and the present plural ending is -is in lesis 'lose' 6; Norse-derived pronominal forms, þer, þam 'their', 'them' appear in 6, 26, and sere 'various' 12, 23 is also of Scandinavian derivation.

MS F is similarly marked by Northern forms. Late Old English â appears as in nane 'none' 10; *-e* seems no longer to reflect any phonetic fact, and thus appears unhistorically, for example þousande 'thousand'; the present plural ending in -s appears in dos 'do' (rubricated heading); a Norse-derived form, þaire 'their' 6 appears beside native ham 'them' 26; sere 'various' is replaced by native mony 12, but retained as sere 23. Probable Norse-derived forms in MS F but not in MS C include til 'to' 14.

MS G is something of a mixture. Late Old English â appears as in strong 5, bolde 7, non 'none' 10. The weak adjective is no longer inflectionally marked: þe strong strijf 5, but this practice is more widespread in late-fourteenth-century Middle English than it was earlier in the century. However, men cals 'men call' in the rubric at the head of the passage shows the characteristic Northern present plural ending, þaim 'them' 26 appears, and sere 'various' 23 is retained.

MS T is in a markedly distinct dialect from the other three manuscripts. Old English â appears as, in longe 5, bolde 7, noon 'none' 10 etc. There is some evidence for the retention of the weak adjective as a living feature of the language: þe longe strif 5; and the present plural is the Midland -en in callen (rubric), ernen 'desire' 1, duden 'did' 12. hem 'them' 26 appears for MS C's þam, and mony appears instead of sere.

It is from the evidence of such texts, both localised by internal reference and localisable by subsequent deduction, that LALME was created. The coverage it achieved is illustrated in the map already referred to, which indicates the locations of every localised and localisable text used in the published atlas.

The distinction between 'localised' and 'localisable' is methodologically important; localised texts form a group of materials, largely documentary and thus usually brief, which are firmly identified with a particular locality. They supply the anchors to which other longer texts, generally literary, may be 'tied' or 'fitted' typologically (both terms frequently used in the literature).

The following hypothetical and simplified example may illustrate the process. A short document, which we shall call Text Z, contains a for 'he', meche for 'much', scholle(n) for 'shall'. Another, much larger literary text, Text Y, contains the same features, and thus may be associated with Text Z; but the larger text by its very nature yields a good deal more information about other items and their forms as well as a, meche, scholle(n). Thus the information gained from the exercise is greatly increased.

The fit-technique, as it is known, is typologically governed; thus a further text, Text X, may have a, meche but not scholle(n), and is therefore to be placed at some remove from Texts Y and Z in the direction of other texts which do not have scholle(n). Once fitted, the literary texts localised in this way may themselves be used for further localisations; a typological matrix has been established within which other texts as yet unstudied may be placed.

As with the Old English example of Farman, however, it is sometimes dangerous to take Middle English texts at face value. MS Manchester, Chetham's Library, A.6.11 (6696) is an early-sixteenth-century copy of John Gower's late-fourteenth-century poem, the Confessio Amantis. At the end of the manuscript appears the name 'Notehurste'.

This word also appears in another manuscript, MS Glasgow, University Library, Hunterian V.2.8, a copy of the alliterative Gest Hystoriale of the Destruction of Troy, and it refers to Nuthurst in South Lancashire, where the Chetham family lived. Both manuscripts were copied by the same scribe, Thomas Chetham (c. 1490-1546), probably for his own use. The

Glasgow Gest Hystoriale is localised entirely plausibly by LALME to the South-East Lancashire/Cheshire border; but the linguistic evidence presented by the manuscript needs to be judged with some care.

It seems probable that Chetham's behaviour here is of the kind called 'constrained'. In such an interpretation, mony etc. would represent Chetham's core repertoire of forms-forms which he will always use, because others are outside his linguistic 'horizon'-while his variation between, for example, she when copying Gower and ho in the Glasgow Gest shows the activation of one of two possible variables in his repertoire when one of them appears in his exemplar.

If this hypothesis is correct, it reminds us of the vagaries of textual survival; if the Chetham Gower had not survived, then we would not be aware that Chetham's repertoire of possible variation covered such a comparatively wide spectrum of forms.

ENGLISH EXAMPLE

In Middle English phonological studies, the evidence of rhymes has long been used as a primary source of information. Comparison of rhyming forms with distinct etymologies enables the investigator to reconstruct authorial pronunciation as well as localise the place of origin for the text. Of course, this procedure depends on an assumption: that Middle English authors attempted exact rhyme.

Although this assumption has sometimes been challenged, it is nevertheless plausible in medieval conditions. Middle English poets were closer to oral traditions of verse than those of the present day; verse was, we know, commonly rather than rarely read aloud; and thus a forced rhyme would be stylistically foregrounded more obviously than would now be the case.

In the postmedieval centuries, however, a practice of 'conventional' rhymes developed, whereby poets rhymed forms which had once been entirely acceptable acoustically but which sound-change had made no longer current. Thus, for instance, William Blake rhymes mine: join in a poem of 1783, even though these words (as in most varieties of Present-Day English) almost certainly no longer contained the same vowel in his variety.

Similarly, the practice of 'eye'-rhyme, whereby written similarity outweighs spoken distinction, seems to have become common from approximately the same date; thus Robert Burns, in his Augustan (as opposed to Scots) verse, can make play with the similar visual appearance of rough and plough/bough, even though the rhyming elements of the three words were differently pronounced in the incipient standardised forms of spoken English (both English and Scottish) at the time.

The simple Bard, rough at the rustic plough, Learning his tuneful trade from ev'ry bough. In these lines there is an ironic contrast between the Augustan register of language (in which the three words are eye-rhymes but not ear-rhymes) which 'linguistic acceptability...is...increasingly vested in the visual rather than the aural', reflecting a shift from the world of orality to that of the literary poet with a literate reading public. Burns, of course, a man keenly conscious of the interaction of social settings, is playing on this historical development in The Brigs of Ayr, contrasting the oral and quasi-mythical Scots world of the 'simple Bard' with the literate, Augustan English of the opening of the poem.

The problem of conventionality in rhyming practice, and what that means for the phonological interpretation of poetic usage, is acutely presented by the rhyming practice of John Keats. Keats suffered at the hands of his first reviewers, and one of the grounds of their criticism was his habit of rhyming such pairs as higher: Thalia, thorns: fawns, thoughts: sorts, indicating that his accent was non-rhotic (i.e. 'non r-pronouncing'; cf. Southern English beside Scottish and some US pronunciations of bar).

In Present-Day English, of course, non-rhotic accents are (in the United Kingdom, if not invariably in the United States) prestigious, being associated with Received Pronunciation, but at the beginning of the nineteenth century such rhymes were regarded by many people as 'Cockney', and therefore inappropriate for serious literary discourse. Thus John

Lockhart in Blackwood's Edinburgh Review criticised Keats as without 'learning enough to distinguish between the written language of Englishmen and the spoken jargon of Cockneys'.

It is significant that Lockhart criticises Keats for deviance from a norm derived from written usage. And as late as 1877, Thomas Hood the younger considered that 'such atrocities as "morn" and "dawn", ..."fought" and "sort", are fatal to the success of verse'.

It has been shown, however, that Keats's lack of rhoticity was not wholly stigmatised by contemporaries. B.H. Smart, for instance, in his prescriptivist A Grammar of English Sounds, comments that 'the smooth R, is often pronounced with so little force, as to be, in fact, nothing more than the vowel sound AH'.

Although in his earlier A Practical Grammar of English Pronunciation (1810) Smart seems to have regarded non-rhoticity as something Londoners were 'too liable' to exhibit-since the written mode was seen by him as offering a guide to correct pronunciation-nevertheless he seems to accept it as characteristic of quite large numbers of persons whose social status is not in doubt.

And an analysis of the rhymes of, for example, P.B. Shelley shows that poets of impeccably upper-class descent were fully capable of using non-rhotic rhymes without receiving any comparable attack from contemporaries. L. Mugglestone has pointed out that part of Lockhart's venom may be due to his Scottish origins; the accents of Present-Day Scots and Scottish English are still rhotic, and Lockhart's attack on Keats's usage may have been an assertion of the value of a Scottish accent as well as of the primacy of writing over speech.

Vocalisation of r may have been sporadically stigmatised, as a failure to pronounce a letter sanctioned in writing; but, in general, the disappearance of postvocalic r in upper-class nineteenth-century speech, and not just in that of Cockneys, is clearly attested.

Thus the attack on Keats by Lockhart and others is not a simple attack on some linguistic deficit; it is rather the use of any tool to hand to aid a knocking review. The three examples discussed above-Farman, the Chetham Gower, Keats-all demonstrate how textual analysis and an understanding of context help our understanding of linguistic output. A theme of this study is that an understanding of texts in relation to their contexts is essential to an adequate theory of diachronic linguistics; thus philology and linguistics are ideally complementary disciplines for students of the history of a language, and not competitive paradig m, a theoretical paradigm for the historical study of English will be sketched in, based upon a linking of philological and linguistic traditions.

Chapter 4

General Linguistic

MODEL

The Origin of Species, linguists such as Auguste Schleicher and Max Muller (Lectures on the Science of Language, 1861-1864) had used Darwinian ideas for their own purposes; and by the end of the century evolutionary notions had become central to linguistic enquiry. Thus Hermann Paul, in the 'Neogrammarian bible' of late-nineteenth-century philological study Prinzipien der Sprachgeschichte, held that linguistic change was to do with 'the greater or lesser fitness of the forms which arise'; in other words, the Darwinian-or perhaps, more correctly, sub-Darwinian-notion of 'the survival of the fittest' could be adapted for the use of historical linguists.

'The survival of the fittest', of course, is a phrase which has been widely reinterpreted by thinkers subsequent to Darwin. For Paul, the phrase meant survival of variant forms of highest frequency in a particular speech-community. Thus, he would hold that, when the p of Proto-Indo-European 'became' the f of Proto-Germanic, the former sound survived in some languages such as Italian (e.g. padre, pesce) but evolved in others (e.g. Present-Day English father, fish) because the Germanic community had determined (unconsciously, over many millions of usage-occurrences) that an f-type realisation of an earlier p was appropriate, and that other realisations were eccentric and thus insufficient for the clear expression of meaning. That this notion was itself insufficient was demonstrated by Ferdinand de Saussure; the Neogrammarians, in the opinion of de Saussure and his followers, did not emphasise sufficiently the role of system in the operation of language. De Saussure pointed out that views such as Paul's did not distinguish clearly between what he called langue and parole. Parole is linguistic substance, the forms which survive over time, but forms perform different functions at different times in their history depending on the langue, or system, within which they work.

Thus Proto-Indo-European p/Proto-Germanic f, although the latter developed historically from the former, are distinct because the two sounds had different functions within the two langues, Proto-Indo-European and Proto-Germanic; the p> f shift took place because of system-change during the divergence of Proto-Germanic from the other Indo-European dialects. In Saussurean terms, simple variation is not change; linguistic change occurs when a systemic development takes place.

However, this insight did not entail a dismissal by de Saussure of the Darwinian model; rather, de Saussure's ideas on variant forms acquiring useful functions (and discarding unneeded ones) as langue changed were closer to true Darwinian theory than Paul's, and placed linguistic Darwinism on a firmer theoretical footing.

The Saussurean model has remained a dominant one for historical linguists ever since. However, Darwinian theory has not remained static, and developments of evolutionary theory over the last hundred years or so have implications for linguistic modelling.

MUTATION AND SELECTION

Darwinian theory, as developed by the late twentieth century, rests upon an understanding of two basic mechanisms: (1) biological mutation and (2) natural selection. Mutations are spontaneous, random errors in genes transmitted from one generation to another; their effect is to produce a pool of variation within a given biological 'community'-a beak becoming a little longer here, a claw becoming a little shorter there. These mutations are non-teleological, in the sense that they are not directed preferentially towards any particular improvement from generation to generation. What appears to be direction is what Dawkins has referred to as 'the blind watchmaker': natural selection, operating on a pool of available genetic material.

Natural selection is a relentless slight bias in death rates, or a slight bias in reproductive rates, among the individuals within a species. Given enough time, small changes in lineages accumulate into large differences between species. Given even more time, lineages diverge yet further until we have descendants as different as elephants from moles, or squid from warthogs.

Recent study of this process in evolutionary biology is exemplified by the recent work of P. and R. Grant on the Darwin's Finches of the Galapagos Islands of the Eastern Pacific. These birds all appear to descend from a single lineage which arrived in the Galapagos a few million years ago-perhaps blown off course by an unusual storm. Since that time they have diverged into thirteen separate species, each one specialised for a particular way of life on the islands. One incident in the evolution of the finches is of particular relevance:

1977 was a drought year in the Galapagos, and 1983 a year of unprecedented floods. After the drought, a higher proportion of large-beaked finches were found to have survived. After the floods, small-beaked finches predominated, presumably because they were better equipped to pick up the smaller seeds that wet weather favours. Reversals of this kind are common.

Long-term evolution will result only if there is a sufficiently drawn-out trend in a particular direction-as there often is, especially when evolving enemies such as predators or parasites are involved rather than just the caprices of the weather.... The drought of 1977 did not induce beak-enlarging mutations, nor did the floods of 1983 provoke opposite mutations.

The mutations had already happened, regardless of the weather. Droughts and floods enter the story only afterwards. In other words, certain tiny mutations in form, easily within the range of natural variation, are favoured for functional reasons by the environment in which they are situated; and these mutational choices, which Dawkins has elsewhere referred to as the 'small-change' of evolution, steadily accumulate to produce such a shift in form that it is possible to speak of the emergence of some new species of creature. The process described here is slow, since Darwin's Finches reproduce only annually; but biologists have found empirical support for Darwinian theory in studying the evolution of such creatures as fruit-flies, where many generations can emerge within a few days, and through the use of computer-based modelling.

PROGRESS IN LANGUAGE AND LITERATURE

It is held here that the model of evolution established in biology is also at least partially applicable to linguistic evolution. To describe linguistic change as evolutionary is, of course, in one way a metaphor, since the notion of evolution was first established in biology and has simply been transferred to linguistic study by analogy. The 'language instinct' certainly appeared in humans as a result of evolution, and bears all the hallmarks of having emerged through straightforward evolutionary processes.

As proof of this, we might notice, for instance, how-typically in biological evolution-the articulators used for human speech, such as tongue, teeth, nasal cavity and so on, had physical functions to do with eating and breathing before they developed secondary, speech-forming functions (cf. animals with tongues, teeth etc. but without speech); in biology, this process has been termed exaptation, and the term has recently been applied to linguistic evolution as well.

It may be permissible, however, to argue that historical linguistics is literally an evolutionary discipline, since the mechanisms of change with which the subject engages seem to work in evolutionary ways. Most notably, linguistic evolution seems to work through a 'blind watchmaker', or (using another frequent metaphor) through a 'hidden hand'. There remain, however, two important differences between biological and linguistic evolution. The first difference is one which is more apparent than real. Some early evolutionary biologists interpreted Darwin's theory to mean that there was an overall direction in evolution, in which more 'advanced' creatures succeeded more 'primitive' ones.

This view is no longer held in quite the same terms by modern evolutionists, although it remains part of the popular understanding of the theory; it is now felt by evolutionists that an amoeba (for instance) does a perfect job for the environment in which it exists, and in such an environment a human being (for instance) would not be nearly as efficient.

Dinosaurs were magnificent and complex creatures, comparable with many twentieth-century organisms, but the environment in which they lived changed and they became extinct. Much of the appeal of the modern ecology or 'green' movement lies in the way in which it has engaged with this notion of the 'equality of species'.

The older view of evolutionary progress had a certain vogue in the nineteenth century, correlating with contemporary ideas about the perfectibility of humankind, and it is therefore not surprising to find some nineteenth-and early-twentieth-century linguists extrapolating from this misunderstanding of Darwin's theories and introducing notions such as 'progress' or 'decay' into their linguistic speculations.

Thus O. Jespersen wrote in 1922 that in 'the evolution of languages the discarding of old flexions goes hand in hand with the development of simpler and more regular expedients that are rather less liable than the old ones to produce misunderstanding'. It is now generally held that linguistic evolution does not work in this way, however.

It is no longer believed by serious linguists that any language, at any point in its history, is any more or less 'primitive' or 'advanced' than any other; the language of the 'primitive' Bushmen is just as complex (or simple) in grammatical, phonological or lexical terms as the language of an 'advanced' European, and thus the adjectives complex and simple, difficult and easy are really inappropriate as neutral descriptors of natural languages. After all, many readers of this book may find Old English difficult-but the Anglo-Saxons, eleven hundred years ago, evidently did not. The second difference is a more significant one. In biological evolution, species diverge from each other so that it is possible to classify them as separate; they do not genetically come together again.

For example, the three orders of nature known as birds, insects and mammals undoubtedly share a common ancestor, a proto-form, which lived many thousands of millions of years ago; but it is possible to classify birds as a group separate from mammals and insects because all birds share a common ancestor which differs from the distinct common ancestors of mammals and insects. Languages do not behave precisely in this way. Present-Day English is a Germanic language, descended, like Present-Day German, Swedish, Dutch etc., from a common ancestor.

But English has also, during its history, taken on characteristics from non-Germanic languages with which it has come into contact, such as French. It is an important principle of biological classification ('cladistics') that separate orders, species etc. cannot overlap in evolutionary terms, and this distinction might be expressed notationally thus: (birds) (mammals) (insects).

However, languages cannot be separated in this way; were we to express the relationship between German, English and French using a similar notation we would arrive at a formula something as follows: (German (English) French). It follows from this formula that, unlike in biology, acquired characteristics in language can be inherited, for-for instance-English speakers can take on French vocabulary and integrate it into a system which can be then passed on to their successor language-users.

LINGUISTIC VARIATION AND CONSTRAINT

Corresponding in language to the minute mutations of biological evolution are linguistic variants. All living languages vary-the only ones which do not are dead ones, such as Latin, or formal ones, such as mathematical or logical notations. For instance, a single speaker can vary quite radically in the way he or she realises an individual linguistic item on different occasions-at its simplest, exemplified by the way in which many speakers of English have in their repertoire of usage two pronunciations of the stressed vowel in the item either, or different stress patterns for the word adult.

Most obviously, languages vary diatopically, that is, through geographical space, and we therefore distinguish between, for instance, Scottish and English accents or grammatical and lexical usage. However, variation can also arise within dialects or even individual linguistic repertoires because of such factors as age, social class and the level of formality adopted.

Such variation is a property of all natural languages, and it lies at the heart of linguistic change, for change depends on the availability of different choices. When a particular variant-innovation becomes adopted systematically by other speakers and used 'conventionally to communicate particular forms and meanings', it is possible to speak of linguistic change having taken place.

Since Weinreich et al. (1968), three stages in the operation of linguistic change have been generally distinguished by linguists: actuation, implementation and diffusion. A slightly modified version of this categorisation is adopted here: the potential for change, the triggering and implementation of change, the diffusion of change.

The potential for change exists in the particular linguistic choices made by particular language-users at a particular time; such choices may be compared with the constant process of biological mutation; it is constantly taking place, for it exists in the perpetual ebb and flow of linguistic variation. When linguists refer to linguistic change, they tend to refer to implementation and diffusion, that is, the systemic development.

Corresponding to natural selection in language are the constraints which govern communication within a given speech-community and therefore regulate the processes of implementation of change. These are the constraints of pragmatic interaction and of social setting; thus usage can only vary in so far as it remains broadly meaningful to the interlocutor, and there are powerful forces to do with social stigmatisation which constrain expression in other ways.

In pragmatic terms, it makes sense to use as little effort as possible to express meaning. However, this effort cannot be too little; the production of differentiated meaning is clearly a matter of speaker-hearer interaction, and the demands of communicative efficiency are such that a whole series of cues, not just one, must be offered to the hearer by the speaker. Languages need such redundancy, for no two speakers have the same usage, and to attempt to distinguish meaning on the basis of single cues would risk unintelligibility.

But if too much redundancy is maintained, or if the cues which are chosen are contradictory (e.g. an intended statement is expressed with intonation appropriate to a question), the system undergoes pressure. Such an opposition correlates with functionalist views of language, in which a 'principle of least effort' is balanced against a 'principle of maintaining intelligibility'. Notions such as these are well established in the literature.

A key notion in this context is that of variational space. Variation is possible because individual linguistic items occupy fairly broad slots in the langue within which they are situated, and their realisations in parole can therefore vary quite widely. Variational space is relevant to all levels of language. Thus, for example, the realisations of the vowel-phoneme produced by seventy-six different speakers in terms of recorded sound-frequencies.

These speakers all considered that they were producing the 'same' sound; but the records show that, although there are clearly defined limits for these realisations, there was nevertheless considerable phonological space within which they could take place.

This variation is not inefficiency, but communicatively necessary. Any two speakers will have, to a greater or lesser extent and as the result of slight physiological and social differences, a differing set of realisations for a particular phoneme, and it is therefore important for communicative purposes for each speaker to have a fairly wide tolerance of others' usages.

Similarly, in grammar, formal and informal usages can exist side by side within the same variational space, for instance isn't and is not occupy the same slots in the sentences That isn't right and That is not right, and, although one usage is more formal than the other, there are situations when either is suitable. Other sources of variation in grammar are to do with stress, and with analogy. The most obvious examples of analogous usage are produced by children acquiring linguistic skills.

When children say mouses for mice, or singed for sang, or mines (cf. yours, hers, his) for mine they have observed certain regularities in language and have extrapolated by analogy to regularise historically inherited forms which seem to them irregular.

A similar process is found in 'non-standard' English spoken by adults; thus foots for 'feet', a common usage in children's speech, has been recorded in adult language by dialectologists in (for instance) Present-Day East Suffolk, buyed for 'bought' in Present-Day Devon, and *badder* for 'worse' in Present-Day Cumberland.

All such examples, of course, are commonplace in those varieties of speech which are comparatively unconstrained by the pressures of formal and normative education. It is the custom of modern parents and teachers to correct such analogical creations and for adult users of such forms to suffer social stigmatisation; but, with reference to earlier times, before prescriptive norms of language became established; it is easy to conceive of a situation where analogical reorganisations would have been widely imitated.

Thus, Present-Day English those, a form entirely acceptable in the modern prestigious language, arose in the late Middle Ages through analogy: a prototypically plural inflection was added to earlier tho (from Old English þa), and the resulting form has been accepted into Present-Day English prescribed usage. The new, analogically produced form those seems to have been favoured in the standard language because it corresponds to an ancient contrastive usage ('ablaut'), whereby front vowels correlated with nearness (thus *these*) and back vowels with distance (thus *those*).

On the other hand Present-Day English yous ('you' pl.), a more recent analogical creation found in many varieties of the language, providing speakers with a potentially useful singular/plural distinction in the paradigm for the second-person pronoun and correlating with other grammatical markers such as the form of the verb *to be,* has not been so accepted; it appeared after the emergence of prescriptive norms, and has thus been stigmatised.

As for the lexicon, it is a proven fact that words mean different things in different contexts, and therefore have a fairly broad variational space. For instance, the expression to let the cat out of the bag has both a literal and a metaphorical significance: literally, a feline is liberated, but metaphorically, a truth (usually unwelcome) has been revealed, and this metaphorical usage would seem-in my own variety, at any rate-to be now more commonplace.

Another source of variation is to do with linguistic register: thus, two words may denote the same referent-for example, begin and commence-but have very different connotations (in this example, to do with levels of formality).

This second example shows what happens when two words from different language-families-here, Germanic (begin) and Romance (commence)-are brought together within the same language: the two words, because first heard in different (and socially charged) circumstances, develop different connotations. A similar example is the contrast between destroy and break up.

Yet another kind of variation is demonstrated by the difference in connotation of the words ordure and shit; the usage of these words in Present-Day English exemplifies the contrast between technical and taboo usage (cf. the colloquial expression the shit hit the fan, beside a potentially more formal if less likely. The ordure hit the fan). Ordure and shit refer to the same natural object, but they plainly have developed distinct connotations. It should have become clear how such variation within variational space corresponds to the mutations of biological evolution; and, as in biological evolution, these linguistic mutations are constrained by the setting in which they exist. The main constraint on (phonological, grammatical, lexicological) variational space within a given variety of a language relates to the systemic properties of language in general.

Thus, for instance, analogical change in the history of a language may proceed further than the rest of the system requires, so further regulation becomes necessary. If language is systematic, then the rules of language are interconnected, and change in one can be assumed to have implications for others.

Space can be 'squeezed', that is, variables may start to overlap with each other to an unacceptable extent, introducing loss of information content and subsequent reorganisation; or space can be 'expanded', leading to an excess of redundancy. The interaction between variation and systemic constraints will be returned to frequently in subsequent chapters.

CONTACT BETWEEN LINGUISTIC SYSTEMS

The attentive reader will have noticed a flaw in the argument as presented in the previous section. If variation is constrained by a system, and that system reacts therapeutically, then there will in theory come a point in time when the system reaches an optimum position where all elements of which the system consists are in stasis; the variational spaces for each linguistic item will be stable, and the potential for the implementation of linguistic change will not be realised.

In such a situation, and given the existence of the mechanisms of linguistic evolution sketched so far, change should cease to occur. However, it is a matter of observation that no living language is unchanging. It is therefore necessary to distinguish a third factor in the operation of linguistic change: contact. Contact is most obviously manifested linguistically in the changing lexicon, when words are borrowed into English from other languages, but it can be more subtle: not only words, but also grammatical structures and even sounds can be transferred between languages, or from variety to variety within a language, for all sorts of reasons (e.g. for reasons of social prestige).

Moreover, the effects of linguistic contact need not be simply a matter of transference of forms; languages or varieties can affect each other in more subtle ways. Contact is a crucial factor in linguistic change because no language or variety of language exists in a vacuum. Speech-communities come into contact with other speech-communities in all sorts of situations, and the subsequent interaction between these communities causes linguistic change.

Some languages and varieties of language certainly change more slowly than others, and the reasons for the variable speeds of linguistic change are easy to determine, through the observation of extralinguistic correspondences. Languages such as Icelandic and Lithuanian have changed slowly over time because they are spoken by relatively homogeneous speech-communities which are comparatively isolated-either by geography or by historical hostility-from the groups of people around them. Thus rural varieties of English tend to change slowly in comparison with their urban counterparts not only because people in the countryside have fewer folk to interact with, but also because those folk who are there interact more closely.

In all these cases, there are strong social ties between the users of these languages or varieties, necessary in communities where the environment is hostile or where a strong communal sense is necessary for the efficient functioning of society. In urban settings, such limited change is demonstrated by those who stick closely to one social group without interacting greatly with those outside their immediate circle (e.g. the core members of certain urban 'gangs', who sustain their linguistic norms through exceptionally strong social ties).

Other languages, or varieties of language, change more quickly, and here, too, the social correspondences are well attested. Change is peculiarly liable to occur when large-scale immigration, invasion or social revolution takes place; it also tends to happen more quickly in towns, where large numbers of people, many with quite distinct linguistic systems, interact with each other. The term used to describe the social relationships between such folk is 'weakly tied', that is, having comparatively loose social ties with those around them.

Typically, a person with weak social ties will be 'class-mobile', attempting to leave one class and enter another, or feeling uneasily poised between one social group and another. It is an interesting fact that the modern discipline of dialectology/sociolinguistics has tended to move away from the study of strongly tied individuals (e.g. the notorious NORMS, 'non-mobile older rural males' who have preserved traditional usage because their language tends not to change, reflecting their tight social networks) towards weakly tied persons whose language, because it is liable to show a wider range of variation, exemplifies the processes of linguistic change discussed above.

There is a parallel in biological theory for 'variable-speed' evolution in language: so-called 'punctuationism', which, to put it crudely, holds that evolution takes place more quickly at some periods than at others. Some who have written on these matters have unfairly taken the work of the punctuationists to represent a rejection of Darwinian theory.

However, it has been shown quite conclusively that punctuationism, or more properly the 'theory of punctuated equilibrium', can be comfortably accommodated within the Darwinian paradigm; Dawkins points out that to take punctuationism as a rejection of Darwinian theory 'is as if the discovery that the Earth is not a perfect sphere but a slightly flattened spheroid were given banner treatment under the headline: The three mechanisms of linguistic change distinguished above-variation, systemic regulation, contact-are not to be taken as totally separate causes of the phenomenon; rather, they interact in complex and, except in the most general terms, practically unpredictable ways to produce dynamic change in the history of a given language. To sum up the argument so far: new variants are produced, and are imitated through contact; but they are constrained by the changing intra- and extralinguistic systems of which they are a part. The description of change given above might be considered somewhat mechanical, but it can easily be restated in more human terms. Human beings are social creatures, and not simply transmitters (speakers) or receivers (hearers); they are both.

When humans speak, they are not only producing sounds and grammar and vocabulary; they are also monitoring what they and others say by listening, and evaluating the communicative efficiency of their speech for the purposes for which it is being used: communicative purposes which are not only to do with the conveying and receiving of information, but also to do with such matters as signalling the social circumstances of the interaction taking place.

And what humans hear is constantly being monitored, that is, compared with their earlier experience as speakers and hearers. In any given speech-community there may be broad agreement as to the prototypical core-value of a given linguistic item, but, when speech-communities interact with each other, the overlap will not be exact, and this 'rough fit' is the source of linguistic variation.

Such individual microlinguistic events, the choices of individual speakers, can (although they need not) develop into those macrolinguistic events which we term 'linguistic change'. This principle of monitoring, or feedback as it is sometimes called, is crucial to an understanding of language-change. Individual and group-usages are all systems which overlap to a greater or lesser extent, each system consisting of a range of allowable variation-variation which can be found at every linguistic level.

The range of allowable variation within any individual system makes up the 'givens' from which each new utterance proceeds: the linguistic input to a new speech-act. Givens may be considered to be either inherited or borrowed; speakers use variants which are native to their own variety, or they select variants which are available to them through contact with other varieties or even with other languages. This process whereby givens are transmitted is not of course genetic, for there does not seem to be any genetic transmission of language-specific features.

Rather, the process comes about through immersion in a particular speech-community. The truth of this argument is indicated, for example, by the fact that children of immigrants often adopt not their parents' language or variety but that of their peers in the same age-group. Linguistic givens exist at every level of language-lexicon, grammar, graphology, phonology-and in all they exist as the set of inherited and borrowed choices. They provide the language-setting from which any particular linguistic choice made at a particular time must proceed.

TREES AND WAVES

The last section concluded with a reference to the notions of inheritance and borrowing, and these notions are central to the historical study of language. Two descriptive models have traditionally been used to illustrate the processes of inheritance and borrowing respectively: the tree model and the wave model.

Both models derive from nineteenth-century scholarship, and stem from comparisons with what were (and in some quarters still are) perceived to be more 'mature' sciences: the tree model relates to the phylogenetic tree used in evolutionary biology, and the wave model relates to theories of action and reaction developed for the discipline of physics.

At one time the two models were seen as mutually exclusive, but most linguists since the end of the nineteenth century have considered them to be complementary. These models are relevant in both micro- and macrolinguistic contexts. According to the tree model, children attempt to reproduce the language of their parents; according to the wave model, children borrow linguistic features from their peers.

These models are also relevant on a macro-linguistic scale: languages descend from earlier ancestors (thus French and Spanish descend from Latin), or they borrow from neighbouring languages (thus Finnish, a non-Indo-European language, contains many Indo-European lexical items borrowed from Swedish).

LANGUAGE AND CHAOS

But the two models, even when considered together, lack an important component: they do not allow for the element of apparently chaotic dynamicity in the operation of language, whereby the complex interaction of changing systems produces yet further change.

Relevant here is recently fashionable 'chaos theory'-which, of course, is not so much about the chaotic nature of the world as about the ways in which order emerges from apparently chaotic processes. M.A.K. Halliday is probably the most prominent of those linguists who have used fruitfully the chaotic model of language. Halliday's views on the nature of a 'dynamic open system' are directly relevant to the argument of this book:

Dynamic open systems have the property that they are metastable: that is, they persist only through constant change; and this change takes place through interactive exchanges with their environment. In the course of such interaction, the system exports disorder; and in the process of exporting disorder, and so increasing the entropy of its environment, the system renews itself, gains information, imports or rather creates order and in this way continues to function.

Languages working through time would seem to be a perfect example of such a system. Speaker-innovations constantly interact with their intra-and extralinguistic environment, which forms a system; and these interactions can cause system-wide changes. Thus a theory of historical linguistics must take into account both speaker and system, and have the ability to provide for interactions between the two. The processes involved are dynamic and open, and this insight needs to be built into our practice of linguistic historiography.

These chaotic notions do not conflict with the evolutionary orientation of the first part of this chapter. Chaos theory holds that order comes from the complex interaction of apparently random factors. Of course, this is not to argue, metaphysically, that there is some ultimate intended goal for human language in general or the history of English in particular. Linguistic change may rather be regarded, in a comparison already suggested at the beginning of this chapter, as driven, like biological evolution, by a 'blind watchmaker': apparent direction is the result of interactive reinforcement between variables at every level of language.

This process of interactive reinforcement is also sometimes described, metaphorically, as a 'hidden hand', or a 'conspiracy', or (perhaps most satisfactorily, since no element of consciousness is to be supposed) a 'snowball'. Such snowballs are common in linguistic evolution. Some of the more general issues raised by these last points. In these, the intention has been to establish a theoretical framework for the historical study of English.

This theoretical framework will be tested and exemplified through the examination of a number of major linguistic developments in English during the last two thousand years. In each case examined, outcomes which have been traditionally assigned to one linguistic level-writing-system, phonology, lexicology, grammar-are shown to be the result of interaction between intralinguistic developments (i.e. developments in other parts of the linguistic system, not just restricted to the level in which the development in question is assigned) and extra-linguistic events (i.e. social and historical change).

This interaction, which may be termed dynamic, demonstrates a fact well attested in many of the natural sciences but even now not yet fully accepted in the humanities: that a given event can be the result of more than one cause. It is held here that this perception of multi-factorial causation is crucial for understanding linguistic change.

FORMULATION OF SPEECH

Speech is so familiar a feature of daily life that we rarely pause to define it. It seems as natural to man as walking, and only less so than breathing. Yet it needs but a moment's reflection to convince us that this naturalness of speech is but an illusory feeling. The process of acquiring speech is, in sobre fact, an utterly different sort of thing from the process of learning to walk. In the case of the latter function, culture, in other words, the traditional body of social usage, is not seriously brought into play.

The child is individually equipped, by the complex set of factors that we term biological heredity, to make all the needed muscular and nervous adjustments that result in walking. Indeed, the very conformation of these muscles and of the appropriate parts of the nervous system may be said to be primarily adapted to the movements made in walking and in similar activities. In a very real sense the normal human being is predestined to walk, not because his elders will assist him to learn the art, but because his organism is prepared from birth, or even from the moment of conception, to take on all those expenditures of nervous energy and all those muscular adaptations that result in walking. To put it concisely, walking is an inherent, biological function of man.

Not so language. It is of course true that in a certain sense the individual is predestined to talk, but that is due entirely to the circumstance that he is born not merely in nature, but in the lap of a society that is certain, reasonably certain, to lead him to its traditions. Eliminate society and there is every reason to believe that he will learn to walk, if, indeed, he survives at all. But it is just as certain that he will never learn to talk, that is, to communicate ideas according to the traditional system of a particular society. Or, again, remove the new-born individual from the social environment into which he has come and transplant him to an utterly alien one. He will develop the art of walking in his new environment very much as he would have developed it in the old.

But his speech will be completely at variance with the speech of his native environment. Walking, then, is a general human activity that varies only within circumscribed limits as we pass from individual to individual. Its variability is involuntary and purposeless. Speech is a human activity that varies without assignable limit as we pass from social group to social group, because it is a purely historical heritage of the group, the product of long continued social usage. It varies as all creative effort varies — not as consciously, perhaps, but none the less as truly as do the religions, the beliefs, the customs, and the arts of different peoples.

Walking is an organic, an instinctive, function (not, of course, itself an instinct); speech is a non-instinctive, acquired, "cultural" function. There is one fact that has frequently tended to prevent the recognition of language as a merely conventional system of sound symbols, that has seduced the popular mind into attributing to it an instinctive basis that it does not really possess.

This is the well-known observation that under the stress of emotion, say of a sudden twinge of pain or of unbridled joy, we do involuntarily give utterance to sounds that the hearer interprets as indicative of the emotion itself. But there is all the difference in the world between such involuntary expression of feeling and the normal type of communication of ideas that is speech.

The former kind of utterance is indeed instinctive, but it is nonsymbolic; in other words, the sound of pain or the sound of joy does not, as such, indicate the emotion, it does not stand aloof, as it were, and announce that such and such an emotion is being felt.

What it does is to serve a more or less automatic overflow of the emotional energy; in a sense, it is part and parcel of the emotion itself. Moreover, such instinctive cries hardly constitute communication in any strict sense. They are not addressed to any one, they are merely overheard, if heard at all, as the bark of a dog, the sound of approaching footsteps, or the rustling of the wind are heard.

If they convey certain ideas to the hearer, it is only in the very general sense in which any and every sound or even any phenomenon in our environment may be said to convey an idea to the perceiving mind. If the involuntary cry of pain which is conventionally represented by "Oh!" be looked upon as a true speech symbol equivalent to some such idea as "I am in great pain," it is just as allowable to interpret the appearance of clouds as an equivalent symbol that carries the definite message "It is likely to rain." A definition of language, however, that is so extended as to cover every type of inference becomes utterly meaningless. The mistake must not be made of identifying our conventional interjections (our oh! and ah! and sh!) with the instinctive cries themselves.

These interjections are merely conventional fixations of the natural sounds. They therefore differ widely in various languages in accordance with the specific phonetic genius of each of these. As such they may be considered an integral portion of speech, in the properly cultural sense of the term, being no more identical with the instinctive cries themselves than such words as "cuckoo" and "killdeer" are identical with the cries of the birds they denote or than Rossini's treatment of a storm in the overture to "William Tell" is in fact a storm. In other words, the interjections and sound-imitative words of normal speech are related to their natural prototypes as is art, a purely social or cultural thing, to nature.

It may be objected that, though the interjections differ somewhat as we pass from language to language, they do nevertheless offer striking family resemblances and may therefore be looked upon as having grown up out of a common instinctive base. But their case is nowise different from that, say, of the varying national modes of pictorial representation.

A Japanese picture of a hill both differs from and resembles a typical modern European painting of the same kind of hill. Both are suggested by and both "imitate" the same natural feature. Neither the one nor the other is the same thing as, or, in any intelligible sense, a direct outgrowth of, this natural feature. The two modes of representation are not identical because they proceed from differing historical traditions, are executed with differing pictorial techniques. The interjections of Japanese and English are, just so, suggested by a common natural prototype, the instinctive cries, and are thus unavoidably suggestive of each other.

They differ, now greatly, now but little, because they are builded out of historically diverse materials or techniques, the respective linguistic traditions, phonetic systems, speech habits of the two peoples. Yet the instinctive cries as such are practically identical for all humanity, just as the human skeleton or nervous system is to all intents and purposes a "fixed," that is, an only slightly and "accidentally" variable, feature of man's organism.

Interjections are among the least important of speech elements. Their discussion is valuable mainly because it can be shown that even they, avowedly the nearest of all language sounds to instinctive utterance, are only superficially of an instinctive nature. Were it therefore possible to demonstrate that the whole of language is traceable, in its ultimate historical and psychological foundations, to the interjections, it would still not follow that language is an instinctive activity. But, as a matter of fact, all attempts so to explain the origin of speech have been fruitless.

There is no tangible evidence, historical or otherwise, tending to show that the mass of speech elements and speech processes has evolved out of the interjections. These are a very small and functionally insignificant proportion of the vocabulary of language; at no time and in no linguistic province that we have record of do we see a noticeable tendency towards their elaboration into the primary warp and woof of language. They are never more, at best, than a decorative edging to the ample, complex fabric.

What applies to the interjections applies with even greater force to the sound-imitative words. Such words as "whippoorwill," "to mew," "to caw" are in no sense natural sounds that man has instinctively or automatically reproduced. They are just as truly creations of the human mind, flights of the human fancy, as anything else in language. They do not directly grow out of nature, they are suggested by it and play with it.

Hence the onomatopoetic theory of the origin of speech, the theory that would explain all speech as a gradual evolution from sounds of an imitative character, really brings us no nearer to the instinctive level than is language as we know it to-day. As to the theory itself, it is scarcely more credible than its interjectional counterpart. It is true that a number of words which we do not now feel to have a sound-imitative value can be shown to have once had a phonetic form that strongly suggests their origin as imitations of natural sounds. Such is the English word "to laugh."

For all that, it is quite impossible to show, nor does it seem intrinsically reasonable to suppose, that more than a negligible proportion of the elements of speech or anything at all of its formal apparatus is derivable from an onomatopoetic source. However much we may be disposed on general principles to assign a fundamental importance in the languages of primitive peoples to the imitation of natural sounds, the actual fact of the matter is that these languages show no particular preference for imitative words.

Among the most primitive peoples of aboriginal America, the Athabaskan tribes of the Mackenzie River speak languages in which such words seem to be nearly or entirely absent, while they are used freely enough in languages as sophisticated as English and German. Such an instance shows how little the essential nature of speech is concerned with the mere imitation of things.

The way is now cleared for a serviceable definition of language. Language is a purely human and noninstinctive method of communicating ideas, emotions, and desires by means of a system of voluntarily produced symbols. These symbols are, in the first instance, auditory and they are produced by the so-called "organs of speech."

There is no discernible instinctive basis in human speech as such, however much instinctive expressions and the natural environment may serve as a stimulus for the development of certain elements of speech, however much instinctive tendencies, motor and other, may give a predetermined range or mold to linguistic expression. Such human or animal communication, if "communication" it may be called, as is brought about by involuntary, instinctive cries is not, in our sense, language at all.

I have just referred to the "organs of speech," and it would seem at first blush that this is tantamount to an admission that speech itself is an instinctive, biologically predetermined activity. We must not be misled by the mere term. There are, properly speaking, no organs of speech; there are only organs that are incidentally useful in the production of speech sounds. The lungs, the larynx, the palate, the nose, the tongue, the teeth, and the lips, are all so utilized, but they are no more to be thought of as primary organs of speech than are the fingers to be considered as essentially organs of piano-playing or the knees as organs of prayer.

Speech is not a simple activity that is carried on by one or more organs biologically adapted to the purpose. It is an extremely complex and ever-shifting network of adjustments — in the brain, in the nervous system, and in the articulating and auditory organs — tending towards the desired end of communication.

The lungs developed, roughly speaking, in connection with the necessary biological function known as breathing; the nose, as an organ of smell; the teeth, as organs useful in breaking up food before it was ready for digestion. If, then, these and other organs are being constantly utilized in speech, it is only because any organ, once existent and in so far as it is subject to voluntary control, can be utilized by man for secondary purposes.

Physiologically, speech is an overlaid function, or, to be more precise, a group of overlaid functions. It gets what service it can out of organs and functions, nervous and muscular, that have come into being and are maintained for very different ends than its own. It is true that physiological psychologists speak of the localization of speech in the brain.

This can only mean that the sounds of speech are localized in the auditory tract of the brain, or in some circumscribed portion of it, precisely as other classes of sounds are localized; and that the motor processes involved in speech (such as the movements of the glottal cords in the larynx, the movements of the tongue required to pronounce the vowels, lip movements required to articulate certain consonants, and numerous others) are localized in the motor tract precisely as are all other impulses to special motor activities.

In the same way control is lodged in the visual tract of the brain over all those processes of visual recognition involved in reading. Naturally the particular points or clusters of points of localization in the several tracts that refer to any element of language are connected in the brain by paths of association, so that the outward, or psycho-physical, aspect of language, is of a vast network of associated localizations in the brain and lower nervous tracts, the auditory localizations being without doubt the most fundamental of all for speech.

However, a speech- sound localized in the brain, even when associated with the particular movements of the "speech organs" that are required to produce it, is very far from being an element of language. It must be further associated with some element or group of elements of experience, say a visual image or a class of visual images or a feeling of relation, before it has even rudimentary linguistic significance.

This "element" of experience is the content or "meaning" of the linguistic unit; the associated auditory, motor, and other cerebral processes that lie immediately back of the act of speaking and the act of hearing speech are merely a complicated symbol of or signal for these "meanings," of which more anon. We see therefore at once that language as such is not and cannot be definitely localized, for it consists of a peculiar symbolic relation — physiologically an arbitrary one — between all possible elements of consciousness on the one hand and certain selected elements localized in the auditory, motor, and other cerebral and nervous tracts on the other.

If language can be said to be definitely "localized" in the brain, it is only in that general and rather useless sense in which all aspects of consciousness, all human interest and activity, may be said to be "in the brain." Hence, we have no recourse but to accept language as a fully formed functional system within man's psychic or "spiritual" constitution. We cannot define it as an entity in psychophysical terms alone, however much the psycho-physical basis is essential to its functioning in the individual.

From the physiologist's or psychologist's point of view we may seem to be making an unwarrantable abstraction in desiring to handle the subject of speech without constant and explicit reference to that basis. However, such an abstraction is justifiable. We can profitably discuss the intention, the form, and the history of speech, precisely as we discuss the nature of any other phase of human culture — say art or religion — as an institutional or cultural entity, leaving the organic and psychological mechanisms back of it as something to be taken for granted.

Accordingly, it must be clearly understood that this introduction to the study of speech is not concerned with those aspects of physiology and of physiological psychology that underlie speech. Our study of language is not to be one of the genesis and operation of a concrete mechanism; it is, rather, to be an inquiry into the function and form of the arbitrary systems of symbolism that we term languages.

I have already pointed out that the essence of language consists in the assigning of conventional, voluntarily articulated, sounds, or of their equivalents, to the diverse elements of experience. The word "house" is not a linguistic fact if by it is meant merely the acoustic effect produced on the ear by its constituent consonants and vowels, pronounced in a certain order; nor the motor processes and tactile feelings which make up the articulation of the word; nor the visual perception on the part of the hearer of this articulation; nor the visual perception of the word "house" on the written or printed page; nor the motor processes and tactile feelings which enter into the writing of the word; nor the memory of any or all of these experiences.

It is only when these, and possibly still other, associated experiences are automatically associated with the image of a house that they begin to take on the nature of a symbol, a word, an element of language. But the mere fact of such an association is not enough. One might have heard a particular word spoken in an individual house under such impressive circumstances that neither the word nor the image of the house ever recurs in consciousness without the other becoming present at the same time.

This type of association does not constitute speech. The association must be a purely symbolic one; in other words, the world must denote, tag off, the image, must have no other significance than to serve as a counter to refer to it whenever it is necessary or convenient to do so. Such an association, voluntary and, in a sense, arbitrary as it is, demands a considerable exercise of selfconscious attention. At least to begin with, for habit soon makes the association nearly as automatic as any and more rapid than most.

But we have traveled a little too fast. Were the symbol "house " — whether an auditory, motor, or visual experience or image — attached but to the single image of a particular house once seen, it might perhaps, by an indulgent criticism, be termed an element of speech, yet it is obvious at the outset that speech so constituted would have little or no value for purposes of communication.

The world of our experiences must be enormously simplified and generalized before it is possible to make a symbolic inventory of all our experiences of things and relations; and this inventory is imperative before we can convey ideas. The elements of language, the symbols that ticket off experience, must therefore be associated with whole groups, delimited classes, of experience rather than with the single experiences themselves.

Only so is communication possible, for the single experience lodges in an individual consciousness and is, strictly speaking, incommunicable. To be communicated it needs to be referred to a class which is tacitly accepted by the community as an identity. Thus, the single impression which I have had of a particular house must be identified with all my other impressions of it.

Further, my generalized memory or my "notion" of this house must be merged with the notions that all other individuals who have seen the house have formed of it. The particular experience that we started with has now been widened so as to embrace all possible impressions or images that sentient beings have formed or may form of the house in question. This first simplification of experience is at the bottom of a large number of elements of speech, the so-called proper nouns or names of single individuals or objects. It is, essentially, the type of simplification which underlies, or forms the crude subject of, history and art. But we cannot be content with this measure of reduction of the infinity of experience. We must cut to the bone of things, we must more or less arbitrarily throw whole masses of experience together as similar enough to warrant their being looked upon — mistakenly, but conveniently — as identical. This house and that house and thousands of other phenomena of like character are thought of as having enough in common, in spite of great and obvious differences of detail, to be classed under the same heading.

In other words, the speech element "house" is the symbol, first and foremost, not of a single perception, nor even of the notion of a particular object, but of a "concept" in other words, of a convenient capsule of thought that embraces thousands of distinct experiences and that is ready to take in thousands more. If the single significant elements of speech are the symbols of concepts, the actual flow of speech may be interpreted as a record of the setting of these concepts into mutual relations.

The question has often been raised whether thought is possible without speech; further, if speech and thought be not but two facets of the same psychic process. The question is all the more difficult because it has been hedged about by misunderstandings.

In the first place, it is well to observe that whether or not thought necessitates symbolism, that is speech, the flow of language itself is not always indicative of thought. We have seen that the typical linguistic element labels a concept. It does not follow from this that the use to which language is put is always or even mainly conceptual. We are not in ordinary life so much concerned with concepts as such as with concrete particularities and specific relations.

When I say, for instance, "I had a good breakfast this morning," it is clear that I am not in the throes of laborious thought, that what I have to transmit is hardly more than a pleasurable memory symbolically rendered in the grooves of habitual expression. Each element in the sentence defines a separate concept or conceptual relation or both combined, but the sentence as a whole has no conceptual significance whatever. It is somewhat as though a dynamo capable of generating enough power to run an elevator were operated almost exclusively to feed an electric doorbell.

The parallel is more suggestive than at first sight appears. Language may be looked upon as an instrument capable of running a gamut of psychic uses. Its flow not only parallels that of the inner content of consciousness, but parallels it on different levels, ranging from the state of mind that is dominated by particular images to that in which abstract concepts and their relations are alone at the focus of attention and which is ordinarily termed reasoning. Thus the outward form only of language is constant; its inner meaning, its psychic value or intensity, varies freely with attention or the selective interest of the mind, also, needless to say, with the mind's general development.

From the point of view of language, thought may be defined as the highest latent or potential content of speech, the content that is obtained by interpreting each of the elements in the flow of language as possessed of its very fullest conceptual value. From this it follows at once that language and thought are not strictly coterminous. At best language can but be the outward facet of thought on the highest, most generalized, level of symbolic expression.

To put our viewpoint somewhat differently, language is primarily a pre-rational function. It humbly works up to the thought that is latent in, that may eventually be read into, its classifications and its forms; it is not, as is generally but naïvely assumed, the final label put upon the finished thought. Most people, asked if they can think without speech, would probably answer, "Yes, but it is not easy for me to do so. Still I know it can be done."

Language is but a garment! But what if language is not so much a garment as a prepared road or groove? It is, indeed, in the highest degree likely that language is an instrument originally put to uses lower than the conceptual plane and that thought arises as a refined interpretation of its content. The product grows, in other words, with the instrument, and thought may be no more conceivable, in its genesis and daily practice, without speech than is mathematical reasoning practicable without the lever of an appropriate mathematical symbolism.

No one believes that even the most difficult mathematical proposition is inherently dependent on an arbitrary set of symbols, but it is impossible to suppose that the human mind is capable of arriving at or holding such a proposition without the symbolism. The, writer, for one, is strongly of the opinion that the feeling entertained by so many that they can think, or even reason, without language is an illusion.

The illusion seems to be due to a number of factors. The simplest of these is the failure to distinguish between imagery and thought. As a matter of fact, no sooner do we try to put an image into conscious relation with another than we find ourselves slipping into a silent flow of words. Thought may be a natural domain apart from the artificial one of speech, but speech would seem to be the only road we know of that leads to it. A still more fruitful source of the illusive feeling that language may be dispensed with in thought is the common failure to realise that language is not identical with its auditory symbolism.

The auditory symbolism may be replaced, point for point, by a motor or by a visual symbolism (many people can read, for instance, in a purely visual sense, that is, without the intermediating link of an inner flow of the auditory images that correspond to the printed or written words) or by still other, more subtle and elusive, types of transfer that are not so easy to define.

Hence the contention that one thinks without language merely because he is not aware of a coexisting auditory imagery is very far indeed from being a valid one. One may go so far as to suspect that the symbolic expression of thought may in some cases run along outside the fringe of the conscious mind, so that the feeling of a free, nonlinguistic stream of thought is for minds of a certain type a relatively, but only a relatively, justified one. Psycho-physically, this would mean that the auditory or equivalent visual or motor centres in the brain, together with the appropriate paths of association, that are the cerebral equivalent of speech, are touched off so lightly during the process of thought as not to rise into consciousness at all. This would be a limiting case-thought riding lightly on the submerged crests of speech, instead of jogging along with it, hand in hand.

The modern psychology has shown us how powerfully symbolism is at work in the unconscious mind. It is therefore easier to understand at the present time than it would have been twenty years ago that the most rarefied thought may be but the conscious counterpart of an unconscious linguistic symbolism.

One word more as to the relation between language and thought. The point of view that we have developed does not by any means preclude the possibility of the growth of speech being in a high degree dependent on the development of thought. We may assume that language arose pre-rationally — just how and on what precise level of mental activity we do not know — but we must not imagine that a highly developed system of speech symbols worked itself out before the genesis of distinct concepts and of thinking, the handling of concepts.

We must rather imagine that thought processes set in, as a kind of psychic overflow, almost at the beginning of linguistic expression; further, that the concept, once defined, necessarily reacted on the life of its linguistic symbol, encouraging further linguistic growth. We see this complex process of the interaction of language and thought actually taking place under our eyes.

The instrument makes possible the product, the product refines the instrument. The birth of a new concept is invariably foreshadowed by a more or less strained or extended use of old linguistic material; the concept does not attain to individual and independent life until it has found a distinctive linguistic embodiment. In most cases the new symbol is but a thing wrought from linguistic material already in existence in ways mapped out by crushingly despotic precedents. As soon as the word is at hand, we instinctively feel, with something of a sigh of relief, that the concept is ours for the handling. Not until we own the symbol do we feel that we hold a key to the immediate knowledge or understanding of the concept. Would we be so ready to die for "liberty," to struggle for "ideals," if the words themselves were not ringing within us? And the word, as we know, is not only a key; it may also be a fetter.

Language is primarily an auditory system of symbols. In so far as it is articulated it is also a motor system, but the motor aspect of speech is clearly secondary to the auditory. In normal individuals the impulse to speech first takes effect in the sphere of auditory imagery and is then transmitted to the motor nerves that control the organs of speech. The motor processes and the accompanying motor feelings are not, however, the end, the final resting point.

They are merely a means and a control leading to auditory perception in both speaker and hearer. Communication, which is the very object of speech, is successfully effected only when the hearer's auditory perceptions are translated into the appropriate and intended flow of imagery or thought or both combined. Hence the cycle of speech, in so far as we may look upon it as a purely external instrument, begins and ends in the realm of sounds.

The concordance between the initial auditory imagery and the final auditory perceptions is the social seal or warrant of the successful issue of the process. As we have already seen, the typical course of this process may undergo endless modifications or transfers into equivalent systems without thereby losing its essential formal characteristics.

The most important of these modifications is the abbreviation of the speech process involved in thinking. This has doubtless many forms, according to the structural or functional peculiarities of the individual mind. The least modified form is that known as "talking to one's self" or "thinking aloud." Here the speaker and the hearer are identified in a single person, who may be said to communicate with himself.

More significant is the still further abbreviated form in which the sounds of speech are not articulated at all. To this belong all the varieties of silent speech and of normal thinking. The auditory centres alone may be excited; or the impulse to linguistic expression may be communicated as well to the motor nerves that communicate with the organs of speech but be inhibited either in the muscles of these organs or at some point in the motor nerves themselves; or, possibly, the auditory centres may be only slightly, if at all, affected, the speech process manifesting itself directly in the motor sphere.

There must be still other types of abbreviation. How common is the excitation of the motor nerves in silent speech, in which no audible or visible articulations result, is shown by the frequent experience of fatigue in the speech organs, particularly in the larynx, after unusually stimulating reading or intensive thinking.

All the modifications so far considered are directly patterned on the typical process of normal speech. Of very great interest and importance is the possibility of transferring the whole system of speech symbolism into other terms than those that are involved in the typical process. This process, as we have seen, is a matter of sounds and of movements intended to produce these sounds. The sense of vision is not brought into play. But let us suppose that one not only hears the articulated sounds but sees the articulations themselves as they are being executed by the speaker.

Clearly, if one can only gain a sufficiently high degree of adroitness in perceiving these movements of the speech organs, the way is opened for a new type of speech symbolism — that in which the sound is replaced by the visual image of the articulations that correspond to the sound. This sort of system has no great value for most of us because we are already possessed of the auditory-motor system of which it is at best but an imperfect translation, not all the articulations being visible to the eye.

However, it is well known what excellent use deaf-mutes can make of "reading from the lips" as a subsidiary method of apprehending speech. The most important of all visual speech symbolisms is, of course, that of the written or printed word, to which, on the motor side, corresponds the system of delicately adjusted movements which result in the writing or typewriting or other graphic method of recording speech.

The significant feature for our recognition in these new types of symbolism, apart from the fact that they are no longer a by-product of normal speech itself, is that each element (letter or written word) in the system corresponds to a specific element (sound or sound-group or spoken word) in the primary system. Written language is thus a point-to-point equivalence, to borrow a mathematical phrase, to its spoken counterpart.

The written forms are secondary symbols of the spoken ones — symbols of symbols — yet so close is the correspondence that they may, not only in theory but in the actual practice of certain eye-readers and, possibly, in certain types of thinking, be entirely substituted for the spoken ones. Yet the auditory-motor associations are probably always latent at the least, that is, they are unconsciously brought into play. Even those who read and think without the slightest use of sound imagery are, at last analysis, dependent on it.

They are merely handling the circulating medium, the money, of visual symbols as a convenient substitute for the economic goods and services of the fundamental auditory symbols. The possibilities of linguistic transfer are practically unlimited. A familiar example is the Morse telegraph code, in which the letters of written speech are represented by a conventionally fixed sequence of longer or shorter ticks.

Here the transfer takes place from the written word rather than directly from the sounds of spoken speech. The letter of the telegraph code is thus a symbol of a symbol of a symbol. It does not, of course, in the least follow that the skilled operator, in order to arrive at an understanding of a telegraphic message, needs to transpose the individual sequence of ticks into a visual image of the word before he experiences its normal auditory image.

The precise method of reading off speech from the telegraphic communication undoubtedly varies widely with the individual. It is even conceivable, if not exactly likely, that certain operators may have learned to think directly, so far as the purely conscious part of the process of thought is concerned, in terms of the tick-auditory symbolism or, if they happen to have a strong natural bent toward motor symbolism, in terms of the correlated tactile-motor symbolism developed in the sending of telegraphic messages.

Still another interesting group of transfers are the different gesture languages, developed for the use of deaf-mutes, of Trappist monks vowed to perpetual silence, or of communicating parties that are within seeing distance of each other but are out of earshot. Some of these systems are one-to-one equivalences of the normal system of speech; others, like military gesture-symbolism or the gesture language of the Plains Indians of North America (understood by tribes of mutually unintelligible forms of speech) are imperfect transfers, limiting themselves to the rendering of such grosser speech elements as are an imperative minimum under difficult circumstances.

In these latter systems, as in such still more imperfect symbolisms as those used at sea or in the woods, it may be contended that language no longer properly plays a part but that the ideas are directly conveyed by an utterly unrelated symbolic process or by a quasiinstinctive imitativeness. Such an interpretation would be erroneous. The intelligibility of these vaguer symbolisms can hardly be due to anything but their automatic and silent translation into the terms of a fuller flow of speech. We shall no doubt conclude that all voluntary communication of ideas, aside from normal speech, is either a transfer, direct or indirect, from the typical symbolism of language as spoken and heard or, at the least, involves the intermediary of truly linguistic symbolism.

This is a fact of the highest importance. Auditory imagery and the correlated motor imagery leading to articulation are, by whatever devious ways we follow the process, the historic fountain-head of all speech and of all thinking. One other point is of still greater importance.

The ease with which speech symbolism can be transferred from one sense to another, from technique to technique, itself indicates that the mere sounds of speech are not the essential fact of language, which lies rather in the classification, in the formal patterning, and in the relating of concepts. Once more, language, as a structure, is on its inner face the mold of thought. It is this abstracted language, rather more than the physical facts of speech, that is to concern us in our inquiry. There is no more striking general fact about language than its universality.

One may argue as to whether a particular tribe engages in activities that are worthy of the name of religion or of art, but we know of no people that is not possessed of a fully developed language. The lowliest South African Bushman speaks in the forms of a rich symbolic system that is in essence perfectly comparable to the speech of the cultivated Frenchman.

It goes without saying that the more abstract concepts are not nearly so plentifully represented in the language of the savage, nor is there the rich terminology and the finer definition of nuances that reflect the higher culture. Yet the sort of linguistic development that parallels the historic growth of culture and which, in its later stages, we associate with literature is, at best, but a superficial thing.

The fundamental groundwork of language – the development of a clear-cut phonetic system, the specific association of speech elements with concepts, and the delicate provision for the formal expression of all manner of relations – all this meets us rigidly perfected and systematized in every language known to us.

Many primitive languages have a formal richness, a latent luxuriance of expression that eclipses anything known to the languages of modern civilization. Even in the mere matter of the inventory of speech the layman must be prepared for strange surprises. Popular statements as to the extreme poverty of expression to which primitive languages are doomed are simply myths.

Scarcely less impressive than the universality of speech is its almost incredible diversity. Those of us that have studied French or German, or, better yet, Latin or Greek, know in what varied forms a thought may run. The formal divergences between the English plan and the Latin plan, however, are comparatively slight in the perspective of what we know of more exotic linguistic patterns. The universality and the diversity of speech lead to a significant inference.

We are forced to believe that language is an immensely ancient heritage of the human race, whether or not all forms of speech are the historical outgrowth of a single pristine form. It is doubtful if any other cultural asset of man, be it the art of drilling for fire or of chipping stone, may lay claim to a greater age. I am inclined to believe that it antedated even the lowliest developments of material culture, that these developments, in fact, were not strictly possible until language, the tool of significant expression, had itself taken shape.

ELEMENTS OF SPEECH

We have more than once referred to the "elements of speech," by which we understood, roughly speaking, what are ordinarily called "words." We must now look more closely at these elements and acquaint ourselves with the stuff of language. The very simplest element of speech – and by "speech" we shall henceforth mean the auditory system of speech symbolism, the flow of spoken words – is the individual sound, though, as we shall see later on, the sound is not itself a simple structure but the resultant of a series of independent, yet closely correlated, adjustments in the organs of speech.

And yet the individual sound is not, properly considered, an element of speech at all, for speech is a significant function and the sound as such has no significance. It happens occasionally that the single sound is an independently significant element (such as French a "has" and à "to" or Latin i "go!"), but such cases are fortuitous coincidences between individual sound and significant word.

The coincidence is apt to be fortuitous not only in theory but in point of actual historic fact; thus, the instances cited are merely reduced forms of originally fuller phonetic groups – Latin habet and ad and Indo-European ei respectively. If language is a structure and if the significant elements of language are the bricks of the structure, then the sounds of speech can only be compared to the unformed and unburnt clay of which the bricks are fashioned. In this chapter we shall have nothing further to do with sounds as sounds.

The true, significant elements of language are generally sequences of sounds that are either words, significant parts of words, or word groupings. What distinguishes each of these elements is that it is the outward sign of a specific idea, whether of a single concept or image or of a number of such concepts or images definitely connected into a whole. The single word may or may not be the simplest significant element we have to deal with.

The English words sing, sings, singing, singer each conveys a perfectly definite and intelligible idea, though the idea is disconnected and is therefore functionally of no practical value. We recognize immediately that these words are of two sorts. The first word, sing, is an indivisible phonetic entity conveying the notion of a certain specific activity. The other words all involve the same fundamental notion but, owing to the addition of other phonetic elements, this notion is given a particular twist that modifies or more closely defines it. They represent, in a sense, compounded concepts that have flowered from the fundamental one.

We may, therefore, analyse the words sings, singing, and singer as binary expressions involving a fundamental concept, a concept of subject matter (sing), and a further concept of more abstract order — one of person, number, time, condition, function, or of several of these combined. If we symbolize such a term as sing by the algebraic formula A, we shall have to symbolize such terms as sings and singer by the formula A + B. The element A may be either a complete and independent word (sing) or the fundamental substance, the so-called root or stem or "radical element" (sing-) of a word.

The element b (-s, -ing, -er) is the indicator of a subsidiary and, as a rule, a more abstract concept; in the widest sense of the word "form," it puts upon the fundamental concept a formal limitation. We may term it a "grammatical element" or affix. As we shall see later on, the grammatical element or the grammatical increment, as we had better put it, need not be suffixed to the radical element. It may be a prefixed element (like the un- of unsingable), it may be inserted into the very body of the stem (like the n of the Latin vinco "I conquer" as contrasted with its absence in vici "I have conquered"), it may be the complete or partial repetition of the stem, or it may consist of some modification of the inner form of the stem (change of vowel, as in sung and song; change of consonant as in dead and death; change of accent; actual abbreviation).

Each and every one of these types of grammatical element or modification has this peculiarity, that it may not, in the vast majority of cases, be used independently but needs to be somehow attached to or welded with a radical element in order to convey an intelligible notion. We had better, therefore, modify our formula, A + b, to A + (b), the round brackets symbolizing the incapacity of an element to stand alone. The grammatical element, moreover, is not only non-existent except as associated with a radical one, it does not even, as a rule, obtain its measure of significance unless it is associated with a particular class of radical elements.

Thus, the -s of English he hits symbolizes an utterly different notion from the -s of books, merely because hit and book are differently classified as to function. We must hasten to observe, however, that while the radical element may, on occasion, be identical with the word, it does not follow that it may always, or even customarily, be used as a word.

Thus, the hort"garden" of such Latin forms as hortus, horti, and horto is as much of an abstraction, though one yielding a more easily apprehended significance, than the -ing of singing. Neither exists as an independently intelligible and satisfying element of speech. Both the radical element, as such, and the grammatical element, therefore, is reached only by a process of abstraction. It seemed proper to symbolize singer as A + (b); hort-us must be symbolized as (A) + (b).

So far, the first speech element that we have found which we can say actually "exists" is the word. Before defining the word, however, we must look a little more closely at the type of word that is illustrated by sing. Are we, after all, justified in identifying it with a radical element? Does it represent a simple correspondence between concept and linguistic expression?

Is the element sing-, that we have abstracted from sings, singing, and singer and to which we may justly ascribe a general unmodified conceptual value, actually the same linguistic fact as the word sing? It would almost seem absurd to doubt it, yet a little reflection only is needed to convince us that the doubt is entirely legitimate. The word sing cannot, as a matter of fact, be freely used to refer to its own conceptual content.

The existence of such evidently related forms as sang and sung at once shows that it cannot refer to past time, but that, for at least an important part of its range of usage, it is limited to the present. On the other hand, the use of sing as an "infinitive" (in such locutions as to sing and he will sing) does indicate that there is a fairly strong tendency for the word sing to represent the full, untrammeled amplitude of a specific concept.

Yet if sing were, in any adequate sense, the fixed expression of the unmodified concept, there should be no room for such vocalic aberrations as we find in sang and sung and song, nor should we find sing specifically used to indicate present time for all persons but one (third person singular *sings*). The truth of the matter is that sing is a kind of twilight word, trembling between the status of a true radical element and that of a modified word of the type of singing. Though it has no outward sign to indicate that it conveys more than a generalized idea, we do feel that there hangs about it a variable mist of added value.

The formula A does not seem to represent it so well as A + (0). We might suspect sing of belonging to the A + (b) type, with the reservation that the (b) had vanished. This report of the "feel" of the word is far from fanciful, for historical evidence does, in all earnest, show that sing is in origin a number of quite distinct words, of type A + (b), that have pooled their separate values. The (b) of each of these has gone as a tangible phonetic element; its force, however, lingers on in weakened measure. The sing of I sing is the correspondent of the Anglo-Saxon singe; the infinitive sing, of singan; the imperative sing of sing. Ever since the breakdown of English forms that set in about the time of the Norman Conquest, our language has been straining towards the creation of simple concept-words, unalloyed by formal connotations, but it has not yet succeeded in this, apart, possibly, from isolated adverbs and other elements of that sort.

Were the typical unanalyzable word of the language truly a pure concept-word (type A) instead of being of a strangely transitional type (type A + [0]), our sing and work and house and thousands of others would compare with the genuine radical words of numerous other languages. Such a radicalword, to take a random example, is the Nootka word hamot "bone."

Our English correspondent is only superficially comparable. Hamot means "bone" in a quite indefinite sense; to our English word clings the notion of singularity. The Nootka Indian can convey the idea of plurality, in one of several ways, if he so desires, but he does not need to; hamot may do for either singular or plural, should no interest happen to attach to the distinction.

As soon as we say "bone" (aside from its secondary usage to indicate material), we not merely specify the nature of the object but we imply, whether we will or no, that there is but one of these objects to be considered. And this increment of value makes all the difference.

We now know of four distinct formal types of word: A (Nootka hamot); A + (0) (sing,bone); A + (b) (singing); (A) + (b) (Latin hortus). There is but one other type that is fundamentally possible: A + B, the union of two (or more) independently occurring radical elements into a single term. Such a word is the compound fire-engine or a Sioux form equivalent to eat-stand (i.e., "to eat while standing").

It frequently happens, however, that one of the radical elements becomes functionally so subordinated to the other that it takes on the character of a grammatical element. We may symbolize this by A + b, a type that may gradually, by loss of external connection between the subordinated element b and its independent counterpart B merge with the commoner type A + (b). A word like beautiful is an example of A + b, the -ful barely preserving the impress of its lineage. A word like homely, on the other hand, is clearly of the type A + (b), for no one but a linguistic student is aware of the connection between the -ly and the independent word *like.*

In actual use, of course, these five (or six) fundamental types may be indefinitely complicated in a number of ways The (0) may have a multiple value; in other words, the inherent formal modification of the basic notion of the word may affect more than one category. In such a Latin word as cor "heart," for instance, not only is a concrete concept conveyed, but there cling to the form, which is actually shorter than its own radical element (cord-), the three distinct, yet intertwined, formal concepts of singularity, gender classification (neuter), and case (subjective-objective).

The complete grammatical formula for cor is, then, A + (0) + (0) + (0), though the merely external, phonetic formula would be (A) —, (A) indicating the abstracted "stem" cord-, the minus sign a loss of material. The significant thing about such a word as cor is that the three conceptual limitations are not merely expressed by implication as the word sinks into place in a sentence; they are tied up, for good and all, within the very vitals of the word and cannot be eliminated by any possibility of usage.

Other complications result from a manifolding of parts. In a given word there may be several elements of the order A (we have already symbolized this by the type A + B), of the order (A), of the order b, and of the order (b). Finally, the various types may be combined among themselves in endless ways. A comparatively simple language like English, or even Latin, illustrates but a modest proportion of these theoretical possibilities.

But if we take our examples freely from the vast storehouse of language, from languages exotic as well as from those that we are more familiar with, we shall find that there is hardly a possibility that is not realized in actual usage. One example will do for thousands, one complex type for hundreds of possible types. I select it from Paiute, the language of the Indians of the arid plateaus of southwestern Utah. The word wii-to-kuchum-punku-rügani-yugwi-va-ntü-m(ü) is of unusual length even for its own language, but it is no psychological monster for all that. It means "they who are going to sit and cut up with a knife a black cow (or bull)," or, in the order of the Indian elements, "knife-black-buffalo-pet-cut up-sit(plur.)-future-participle-animate plur."

The formula for this word, in accordance with our symbolism, would be (F) + (E) + C + d + A + B + (g) + (h) + (i) + (0). It is the plural of the future participle of a compound verb "to sit and cut up" — A + B. The elements (g) — which denotes futurity —, (h) — a participial suffix —, and (i) — indicating the animate plural — are grammatical elements which convey nothing when detached.

The formula (0) is intended to imply that the finished word conveys, in addition to what is definitely expressed, a further relational idea, that of subjectivity; in other words, the form can only be used as the subject of a sentence, not in an objective or other syntactic relation.

The radical element A ("to cut up"), before entering into combination with the coördinate element B ("to sit"), is itself compounded with two nominal elements or element-groups — an instrumentally used stem (F) ("knife"), which may be freely used as the radical element of noun forms but cannot be employed as an absolute noun in its given form, and an objectively used group — (E) + C + d ("black cow or bull"). This group in turn consists of an adjectival radical element (E) ("black"), which cannot be independently employed (the absolute notion of "black" can be rendered only as the participle of a verb: "black-be-ing"), and the compound noun C + d ("buffalo-pet").

The radical element C properly means "buffalo," but the element d, properly an independently occurring noun meaning "horse" (originally "dog" or "domesticated animal" in general), is regularly used as a quasi-subordinate element indicating that the animal denoted by the stem to which it is affixed is owned by a human being. It will be observed that the whole complex (F) + (E) + C + d + A + B is functionally no more than a verbal base, corresponding to the sing- of an English form like singing; that this complex remains verbal in force on the addition of the temporal element (g) — this (g), by the way, must not be understood as appended to B alone, but to the whole basic complex as a unit — and that the elements (h) + (i) + (0) transform the verbal expression into a formally well-defined noun. It is high time that we decided just what is meant by a word. Our first impulse, no doubt, would have been to define the word as the symbolic, linguistic counterpart of a single concept.

We now know that such a definition is impossible. In truth it is impossible to define the word from a functional standpoint at all, for the word may be anything from the expression of a single concept — concrete or abstract or purely relational (as in of or by or and) — to the expression of a complete thought (as in Latin dico "I say" or, with greater elaborateness of form, in a Nootka verb form denoting "I have been accustomed to eat twenty round objects [e.g., apples] while engaged in [doing so and so]"). In the latter case the word becomes identical with the sentence.

The word is merely a form, a definitely molded entity that takes in as much or as little of the conceptual material of the whole thought as the genius of the language cares to allow. Thus it is that while the single radical elements and grammatical elements, the carriers of isolated concepts, are comparable as we pass from language to language, the finished words are not.

Radical (or grammatical) element and sentence — these are the primary functional units of speech, the former as an abstracted minimum, and the latter as the esthetically satisfying embodiment of a unified thought. The actual formal units of speech, the words, may on occasion identify themselves with either of the two functional units; more often they mediate between the two extremes, embodying one or more radical notions and also one or more subsidiary ones. We may put the whole matter in a nutshell by saying that the radical and grammatical elements of language, abstracted as they are from the realities of speech, respond to the conceptual world of science, abstracted as it is from the realities of experience, and that the word, the existent unit of living speech, responds to the unit of actually apprehended experience, of history, of art.

The sentence is the logical counterpart of the complete thought only if it be felt as made up of the radical and grammatical elements that lurk in the recesses of its words. It is the psychological counterpart of experience, of art, when it is felt, as indeed it normally is, as the finished play of word with word. As the necessity of defining thought solely and exclusively for its own sake becomes more urgent, the word becomes increasingly irrelevant as a means.

We can therefore easily understand why the mathematician and the symbolic logician are driven to discard the word and to build up their thought with the help of symbols which have, each of them, a rigidly unitary value. But is not the word, one may object, as much of an abstraction as the radical element? Is it not as arbitrarily lifted out of the living sentence as is the minimum conceptual element out of the word?

Some students of language have, indeed, looked upon the word as such an abstraction, though with very doubtful warrant, it seems to me. It is true that in particular cases, especially in some of the highly synthetic languages of aboriginal America, it is not always easy to say whether a particular element of language is to be interpreted as an independent word or as part of a larger word. These transitional cases, puzzling as they may be on occasion, do not, however, materially weaken the case for the psychological validity of the word.

Linguistic experience, both as expressed in standardized, written form and as tested in daily usage, indicates overwhelmingly that there is not, as a rule, the slightest difficulty in bringing the word to consciousness as a psychological reality. No more convincing test could be desired than this, that the naive Indian, quite unaccustomed to the concept of the written word, has nevertheless no serious difficulty in dictating a text to a linguistic student word by word; he tends, of course, to run his words together as in actual speech, but if he is called to a halt and is made to understand what is desired, he can readily isolate the words as such, repeating them as units.

He regularly refuses, on the other hand, to isolate the radical or grammatical element, on the ground that it "makes no sense." What, then, is the objective criterion of the word? The speaker and hearer feel the word, let us grant, but how shall we justify their feeling? If function is not the ultimate criterion of the word, what is? It is easier to ask the question than to answer it. The best that we can do is to say that the word is one of the smallest, completely satisfying bits of isolated "meaning" into which the sentence resolves itself.

It cannot be cut into without a disturbance of meaning, one or the other or both of the severed parts remaining as a helpless wait on our hands. In practice this unpretentious criterion does better servicc than might be supposed. In such a sentence as It is unthinkable, it is simply impossible to group the elements into any other and smaller "words" than the three indicated.

Think or thinkable might be isolated, but as neither un- nor -able nor is-un yields a measurable satisfaction; we are compelled to leave unthinkable as an integral whole, a miniature bit of art. Added to the "feel" of the word are frequently, but by no means invariably, certain external phonetic characteristics. Chief of these is accent.

In many, perhaps in most, languages the single word is marked by a unifying accent, an emphasis on one of the syllables, to which the rest are subordinated. The particular syllable that is to be so distinguished is dependent, needless to say, on the special genius of the language.

The importance of accent as a unifying feature of the word is obvious in such English examples as unthinkable, characterizing. The long Paiute word that we have analyzed is marked as a rigid phonetic unit by several features, chief of which are the accent on its second syllable (wii'"knife") and the slurring ("unvoicing," to use the technical phonetic term) of its final vowel (-mü, animate plural). Such features as accent, cadence, and the treatment of consonants and vowels within the body of a word are often useful as aids in the external demarcation of the word, but they must by no means be interpreted, as is sometimes done, as themselves responsible for its psychological existence.

They at best but strengthen a feeling of unity that is already present on other grounds. We have already seen that the major functional unit of speech, the sentence, has, like the word, a psychological as well as a merely logical or abstracted existence.

Its definition is not difficult. It is the linguistic expression of a proposition. It combines a subject of discourse with a statement in regard to this subject. Subject and "predicate" may be combined in a single word, as in Latin dico; each may be expressed independently, as in the English equivalent, I say; each or either may be so qualified as to lead to complex propositions of many sorts.

No matter how many of these qualifying elements (words or functional parts of words) are introduced, the sentence does not lose its feeling of unity so long as each and every one of them falls in place as contributory to the definition of either the subject of discourse or the core of the predicate.

Such a sentence as The mayor of New York is going to deliver a speech of welcome in French is readily felt as a unified statement, incapable of reduction by the transfer of certain of its elements, in their given form, to the preceding or following sentences. The contributory ideas of New York, of welcome, and in French may be eliminated without hurting the idiomatic flow of the sentence. The mayor is going to deliver a speech is a perfectly intelligible proposition. But further than this we cannot go in the process of reduction. We cannot say, for instance, Mayor is going to deliver.

The reduced sentence resolves itself into the subject of discourse — the mayor — and the predicate — is going to deliver a speech. It is customary to say that the true subject of such a sentence is mayor, the true predicate is going or even are, the other elements being strictly subordinate. Such an analysis, however, is purely schematic and is without psychological value. It is much better frankly to recognize the fact that either or both of the two terms of the sentence-proposition may be incapable of expression in the form of single words.

There are languages that can convey all that is conveyed by The-mayor is-going-to-deliver-a-speech in two words, a subject word and a predicate word, but English is not so highly synthetic. The point that we are really making here is that underlying the finished sentence is a living sentence type, of fixed formal characteristics.

These fixed types or actual sentence-ground works may be freely overlaid by such additional matter as the speaker or writer cares to put on, but they are themselves as rigidly "given" by tradition as are the radical and grammatical elements abstracted from the finished word.

New words may be consciously created from these fundamental elements on the analogy of old ones, but hardly new types of words. In the same way new sentences are being constantly created, but always on strictly traditional lines. The enlarged sentence, however, allows as a rule of considerable freedom in the handling of what may be called "unessential" parts. It is this margin of freedom which gives us the opportunity of individual style.

The habitual association of radical elements, grammatical elements, words, and sentences with concepts or groups of concepts related into wholes is the fact itself of language. It is important to note that there is in all languages a certain randomness of association. Thus, the idea of "hide" may be also expressed by the word "conceal," the notion of "three times" also by "thrice." The multiple expression of a single concept is universally felt as a source of linguistic strength and variety, not as a needless extravagance.

More irksome is a random correspondence between idea and linguistic expression in the field of abstract and relational concepts, particularly when the concept is embodied in a grammatical element. Thus, the randomness of the expression of plurality in such words as books, oxen, sheep, and geese is felt to be rather more, I fancy, an unavoidable and traditional predicament than a welcome luxuriance.

It is obvious that a language cannot go beyond a certain point in this randomness. Many languages go incredibly far in this respect, it is true, but linguistic history shows conclusively that sooner or later the less frequently occurring associations are ironed out at the expense of the more vital ones. In other words, all languages have an inherent tendency to economy of expression. Were this tendency entirely inoperative, there would be no grammar.

The fact of grammar, a universal trait of language, is simply a generalized expression of the feeling that analogous concepts and relations are most conveniently symbolized in analogous forms. Were a language ever completely "grammatical," it would be a perfect engine of conceptual expression. Unfortunately, or luckily, no language is tyrannically consistent. All grammars leak.

Up to the present we have been assuming that the material of language reflects merely the world of concepts and, on what I have ventured to call the "prerational" plane, of images, which are the raw material of concepts. We have, in other words, been assuming that language moves entirely in the ideational or cognitive sphere. It is time that we amplified the picture.

The volitional aspect of consciousness also is to some extent explicitly provided for in language. Nearly all languages have special means for the expression of commands (in the imperative forms of the verb, for example) and of desires, unattained or unattainable (Would he might come! or Would he were here!) The emotions, on the whole, seem to be given a less adequate outlet. Emotion, indeed, is proverbially inclined to speechlessness.

Most, if not all, the interjections are to be put to the credit of emotional expression, also, it may be, a number of linguistic elements expressing certain modalities, such as dubitative or potential forms, which may be interpreted as reflecting the emotional states of hesitation or doubt — attenuated fear. On the whole, it must be admitted that ideation reigns supreme in language, that volition and emotion come in as distinctly secondary factors. This, after all, is perfectly intelligible. The world of image and concept, the endless and ever-shifting picture of objective reality, is the unavoidable subject-matter of human communication, for it is only, or mainly, in terms of this world that effective action is possible. Desire, purpose, emotion are the personal colour of the objective world; they are applied privately by the individual soul and are of relatively little importance to the neighboring one.

All this does not mean that volition and emotion are not expressed. They are, strictly speaking, never absent from normal speech, but their expression is not of a truly linguistic nature. The nuances of emphasis, tone, and phrasing, the varying speed and continuity of utterance, the accompanying bodily movements, all these express something of the inner life of impulse and feeling, but as these means of expression are, at last analysis, but modified forms of the instinctive utterance that man shares with the lower animals, they cannot be considered as forming part of the essential cultural conception of language, however much they may be inseparable from its actual life.

And this instinctive expression of volition and emotion is, for the most part, sufficient, often more than sufficient, for the purposes of communication. There are, it is true, certain writers on the psychology of language who deny its prevailingly cognitive character but attempt, on the contrary, to demonstrate the origin of most linguistic elements within the domain of feeling! Confess that I am utterly unable to follow them.

What there is of truth in their contentions may be summed up, it seems to me, by saying that most words, like practically all elements of consciousness, have an associated feeling-tone, a mild, yet none the less real and at times insidiously powerful, derivative of pleasure or pain.

This feeling-tone, however, is not as a rule an inherent value in the word itself; it is rather a sentimental growth on the word's true body, on its conceptual kernel. Not only may the feeling-tone change from one age to another (this, of course, is true of the conceptual content as well), but it varies remarkably from individual to individual according to the personal associations of each, varies, indeed, from time to time in a single individual's consciousness as his experiences mold him and his moods change.

To be sure, there are socially accepted feeling-tones, or ranges of feeling-tone, for many words over and above the force of individual association, but they are exceedingly variable and elusive things at best. They rarely have the rigidity of the central, primary fact. We all grant, for instance, that storm, tempest, and hurricane, quite aside from their slight differences of actual meaning, have distinct feeling-tones, tones that are felt by all sensitive speakers and readers of English in a roughly equivalent fashion.

Storm, we feel, is a more general and a decidedly less "magnificent" word than the other two; tempest is not only associated with the sea but is likely, in the minds of many, to have obtained a softened glamour from a specific association with Shakespeare's great play; hurricane has a greater forthrightness, a director ruthlessness than its synonyms. Yet the individual's feelingtones for these words are likely to vary enormously.

To some tempest and hurricane may seem "soft," literary words, the simpler storm having a fresh, rugged value which the others do not possess (think of storm and stress). If we have browsed much in our childhood days in books of the Spanish Main, hurricane is likely to have a pleasurably bracing tone; if we have had the misfortune to be caught in one, we are not unlikely to feel the word as cold, cheerless, sinister.

The feeling-tones of words are of no use, strictly speaking, to science; the philosopher, if he desires to arrive at truth rather than merely to persuade, finds them his most insidious enemies. But man is rarely engaged in pure science, in solid thinking.

Generally his mental activities are bathed in a warm current of feeling and he seizes upon the feeling-tones of words as gentle aids to the desired excitation. They are naturally of great value to the literary artist. It is interesting to note, however, that even to the artist they are a danger. A word whose customary feeling-tone is too unquestioningly accepted becomes a plushy bit of furniture, a cliché. Every now and then the artist has to fight the feeling-tone, to get the word to mean what it nakedly and conceptually should mean, depending for the effect of feeling on the creative power of an individual juxtaposition of concepts or images.

Chapter 5

Forms in Language

GRAMMATICAL CONCEPT

English grammar displays minimal inflection compared with most other Indo-European languages. This is caused by deflexion. For example, Modern English, unlike Modern German or Dutch and the Romance languages, lacks grammatical gender and adjectival agreement. Case marking has almost disappeared from the language and mainly survives in pronouns. The patterning of strong (e.g. *speak/spoke/spoken*) versus weak verbs inherited from Germanic has declined in importance and the remnants of inflection (such as plural marking) have become more regular.

At the same time as inflection has declined in importance in English, the language has become more analytic, and developed a greater reliance on features such as modal verbs and word order to convey grammatical information. Auxiliary verbs are used to mark constructions such as questions, negatives, the passive voice and progressive tenses.

The question of form in language presents itself under two aspects. We may either consider the formal methods employed by a language, its "grammatical processes," or we may ascertain the distribution of concepts with reference to formal expression. What are the formal patterns of the language? And what types of concepts make up the content of these formal patterns?

The two points of view are quite distinct. The English word unthinkingly is, broadly speaking, formally parallel to the word reformers, each being built up on a radical element which may occur as an independent verb (think, form), this radical element being preceded by an element (un-, re-) that conveys a definite and fairly concrete significance but that cannot be used independently, and followed by two elements (-ing, -ly; -er, -s) that limit the application of the radical concept in a relational sense.

This formal pattern — (b) + A + (c) + (d) -is a characteristic feature of the language. A countless number of functions may be expressed by it; in other words, all the possible ideas conveyed by such prefixed and suffixed elements, while tending to fall into minor groups, do not necessarily form natural, functional systems. There is no logical reason, for instance, why the numeral function of -s should be formally expressed in a manner that is analogous to the expression of the idea conveyed by -ly. It is perfectly conceivable that in another language the concept of manner (-ly) may be treated according to an entirely different pattern from that of plurality.

The former might have to be expressed by an independent word (say, thus unthinking), the latter by a prefixed element (say, plural -reform -er). There are, of course, an unlimited number of other possibilities. Even within the confines of English alone the relative independence of form and function can be made obvious. Thus, the negative idea conveyed by uncan be just as adequately expressed by a suffixed element (-less) in such a word as thoughtlessly.

Such a twofold formal expression of the negative function would be inconceivable in certain languages, say Eskimo, where a suffixed element would alone be possible. Again, the plural notion conveyed by the -s of reformers is just as definitely expressed in the word geese, where an utterly distinct method is employed.

Furthermore, the principle of vocalic change (goose — geese) is by no means confined to the expression of the idea of plurality; it may also function as an indicator of difference of time (e.g., sing — sang, throw — threw). But the expression in English of past time is not by any means always bound up with a change of vowel. In the great majority of cases the same idea is expressed by means of a distinct suffix (die-d, worked). Functionally, died and sang are analogous; so are reformers and geese. Formally, we must arrange these words quite otherwise.

Both die-d and re-form-er-s employ the method of suffixing grammatical elements; both sang and geese have grammatical form by virtue of the fact that their vowels differ from the vowels of other words with which they are closely related in form and meaning (goose; sing, sung). Every language possesses one or more formal methods for indicating the relation of a secondary concept to the main concept of the radical element.

Some of these grammatical processes, like suffixing, are exceedingly wide-spread; others, like vocalic change, are less common but far from rare; still others, like accent and consonantal change, are somewhat exceptional as functional processes. Not all languages are as irregular as English in the assignment of functions to its stock of grammatical processes. As a rule, such basic concepts as those of plurality and time are rendered by means of one or other method alone, but the rule has so many exceptions that we cannot safely lay it down as a principle.

Wherever we go we are impressed by the fact that pattern is one thing, the utilization of pattern quite another. A few further examples of the multiple expressions of identical functions in other languages than English may help to make still more vivid this idea of the relative independence of form and function.

In Hebrew, as in other Semitic languages, the verbal idea as such is expressed by three, less often by two or four, characteristic consonants. Thus, the group sh-m-r expresses the idea of "guarding," the group g-n-b that of "stealing," n-t-n that of "giving." Naturally these consonantal sequences are merely abstracted from the actual forms.

The consonants are held together in different forms by characteristic vowels that vary according to the idea that it is desired to express. Prefixed and suffixed elements are also frequently used. The method of internal vocalic change is exemplified in shamar "he has guarded," shomer "guarding," shamur "being guarded," shmor "(to) guard." Analogously, ganab "he has stolen" goneb "stealing," ganub "being stolen," gnob "(to) steal." But not all infinitives are formed according to the type of shmor and gnob or of other types of internal vowel change.

Certain verbs suffix a t-element for the infinitive, e.g., teneth "to give," heyo-th "to be." Again, the pronominal ideas may be expressed by independent words (e.g., anoki "I"), by prefixed elements (e.g., e-shmor "I shall guard"), or by suffixed elements (e.g., shamar-ti "I have guarded"). In Nass, an Indian language of British. Columbia, plurals are formed by four distinct methods.

Most nouns (and verbs) are reduplicated in the plural, that is, part of the radical element is repeated, e.g., gyat "person," gyigyat "people." A second method is the use of certain characteristic prefixes, e.g., an'on "hand," ka-an'on "hands"; wai "one paddles," lu-wai "several paddle." Still other plurals are formed by means of internal vowel change, e.g., gwula "cloak," gwila "cloaks." Finally, a fourth class of plurals is constituted by such nouns as suffix a grammatical element, e.g., waky "brother," wakykw "brothers."

From such groups of examples as these — and they might be multiplied ad nauseam — we cannot but conclude that linguistic form may and should be studied as types of patterning, apart from the associated functions. We are the more justified in this procedure as all languages evince a curious instinct for the development of one or more particular grammatical processes at the expense of others, tending always to lose sight of any explicit functional value that the process may have had in the first instance, delighting, it would seem, in the sheer play of its means of expression.

It does not matter that in such a case as the English goose — geese, foul — defile, sing — sang — sung we can prove that we are dealing with historically distinct processes, that the vocalic alternation of sing and sang, for instance, is centuries older as a specific type of grammatical process than the outwardly parallel one of goose and geese. It remains true that there is (or was) an inherent tendency in English, at the time such forms as geese came into being, for the utilization of vocalic change as a significant linguistic method. Failing the precedent set by such already existing types of vocalic alternation as sing — sang — sung, it is highly doubtful if the detailed conditions that brought about the evolution of forms like teeth and geese from tooth and goose would have been potent enough to allow the native linguistic feeling to win through to an acceptance of these new types of plural formation as psychologically possible.

This feeling for form as such, freely expanding along predetermined lines and greatly inhibited in certain directions by the lack of controlling types of patterning, should be more clearly understood than it seems to be. A general survey of many diverse types of languages is needed to give us the proper perspective on this point. We saw that every language has an inner phonetic system of definite pattern. We now learn that it has also a definite feeling for patterning on the level of grammatical formation.

Both of these submerged and powerfully controlling impulses to definite form operate as such, regardless of the need for expressing particular concepts or of giving consistent external shape to particular groups of concepts. It goes without saying that these impulses can find realization only in concrete functional expression. We must say something to be able to say it in a certain manner.

Let us now take up a little more systematically, however briefly, the various grammatical processes that linguistic research has established. They may be grouped into six main types: word order; composition; affixation, including the use of prefixes, suffixes, and infixes; internal modification of the radical or grammatical element, whether this affects a vowel or a consonant; reduplication; and accentual differences, whether dynamic (stress) or tonal (pitch). There are also special quantitative processes, like vocalic lengthening or shortening and consonantal doubling, but these may be looked upon as particular sub-types of the process of internal modification.

Possibly still other formal types exist, but they are not likely to be of importance in a general survey. It is important to bear in mind that a linguistic phenomenon cannot be looked upon as illustrating a definite "process" unless it has an inherent functional value. The consonantal change in English, for instance, of book-s and bag-s (s in the former, z in the latter) is of no functional significance.

It is a purely external, mechanical change induced by the presence of a preceding voiceless consonant, k, in the former case, of a voiced consonant, g, in the latter. This mechanical alternation is objectively the same as that between the noun house and the verb to house. In the latter case, however, it has an important grammatical function, that of transforming a noun into a verb. The two alternations belong, then, to entirely different psychological categories. Only the latter is a true illustration of consonantal modification as a grammatical process.

The simplest, at least the most economical, method of conveying some sort of grammatical notion is to juxtapose two or more words in a definite sequence without making any attempt by inherent modification of these words to establish a connection between them. Let us put down two simple English words at random, say sing praise. This conveys no finished thought in English, nor does it clearly establish a relation between the idea of singing and that of praising.

Nevertheless, it is psychologically impossible to hear or see the two words juxtaposed without straining to give them some measure of coherent significance. The attempt is not likely to yield an entirely satisfactory result, but what is significant is that as soon as two or more radical concepts are put before the human mind in immediate sequence it strives to bind them together with connecting values of some sort. In the case of sing praise different individuals are likely to arrive at different provisional results.

Some of the latent possibilities of the juxtaposition, expressed in currently satisfying form, are: sing praise (to him)! or singing praise, praise expressed in a song or to sing and praise or one who sings a song of praise (compare such English compounds as killjoy, i.e., one who kills joy) or he sings a song of praise (to him). The theoretical possibilities in the way of rounding out these two concepts into a significant group of concepts or even into a finished thought are indefinitely numerous.

None of them will quite work in English, but there are numerous languages where one or other of these amplifying processes is habitual. It depends entirely on the genius of the particular language what function is inherently involved in a given sequence of words. Some languages, like Latin, express practically all relations by means of modifications within the body of the word itself. In these, sequence is apt to be a rhetorical rather than a strictly grammatical principle. Whether I say in Latin hominem femina or femina hominem videt or hominem videt femina or videt femina hominem makes little or no difference beyond, possibly, a rhetorical or stylistic one. The woman sees the man is the identical significance of each of these sentences.

In Chinook, an Indian language of the Columbia River, one can be equally free, for the relation between the verb and the two nouns is as inherently fixed as in Latin. The difference between the two languages is that, while Latin allows the nouns to establish their relation to each other and to the verb, Chinook lays the formal burden entirely on the verb, the full content of which is more or less adequately rendered by she-him-sees. Eliminate the Latin case suffixes (-a and -em) and the Chinook pronominal prefixes (she-him-) and we cannot afford to be so indifferent to our word order. We need to husband our resources.

In other words, word order takes on a real functional value. Latin and Chinook are at one extreme. Such languages as Chinese, Siamese, and Annamite, in which each and every word, if it is to function properly, falls into its assigned place, are at the other extreme. But the majority of languages fall between these two extremes.

In English, for instance, it may make little grammatical difference whether I say yesterday the man saw the dog or the man saw the dog yesterday, but it is not a matter of indifference whether I say yesterday the man saw the dog or yesterday the dog saw the man or whether I say he is here or is he here? In the one case, of the latter group of examples, the vital distinction of subject and object depends entirely on the placing of certain words of the sentence, in the latter a slight difference of sequence makes all the difference between statement and question.

It goes without saying that in these cases the English principle of word order is as potent a means of expression as is the Latin use of case suffixes or of an interrogative particle. There is here no question of functional poverty, but of formal economy. We have already seen something of the process of composition, the uniting into a single word of two or more radical elements. Psychologically this process is closely allied to that of word order in so far as the relation between the elements is implied, not explicitly stated. It differs from the mere juxtaposition of words in the sentence in that the compounded elements are felt as constituting but parts of a single word-organism.

Such languages as Chinese and English, in which the principle of rigid sequence is well developed, tend not infrequently also to the development of compound words. It is but a step from such a Chinese word sequence as jin tak "man virtue," i.e., "the virtue of men," to such more conventionalized and psychologically unified juxtapositions as t'ien tsz "heaven son," i.e., "emperor," or shui fu "water man," i.e., "water carrier."

In the latter case we may as well frankly write shui-fu as a single word, the meaning of the compound as a whole being as divergent from the precise etymological values of its component elements as is that of our English word typewriter from the merely combined values of type and writer. In English the unity of the word typewriter is further safeguarded by a predominant accent on the first syllable and by the possibility of adding such a suffixed element as the plural -s to the whole word. Chinese also unifies its compounds by means of stress.

However, then, in its ultimate origins the process of composition may go back to typical sequences of words in the sentence, it is now, for the most part, a specialized method of expressing relations. French has as rigid a word order as English but does not possess anything like its power of compounding words into more complex units. On the other hand, classical Greek, in spite of its relative freedom in the placing of words, has a very considerable bent for the formation of compound terms.

It is curious to observe how greatly languages differ in their ability to make use of the process of composition. One would have thought on general principles that so simple a device as gives us our typewriter and blackbird and hosts of other words would be an all but universal grammatical process. Such is not the case. There are a great many languages, like Eskimo and Nootka and, aside from paltry exceptions, the Semitic languages, that cannot compound radical elements.

What is even stranger is the fact that many of these languages are not in the least averse to complex word formations, but may on the contrary effect a synthesis that far surpasses the utmost that Greek and Sanskrit are capable of. Such a Nootka word, for instance, as "when, as they say, he had been absent for four days" might be expected to embody at least three radical elements corresponding to the concepts of "absent," "four," and "day."

As a matter of fact the Nootka word is utterly incapable of composition in our sense. It is invariably built up out of a single radical element and a greater or less number of suffixed elements, some of which may have as concrete significance as the radical element itself. In the particular case we have cited the radical element conveys the idea of "four," the notions of "day" and "absent" being expressed by suffixes that are as inseparable from the radical nucleus of the word as is an English element like -er from the sing or hunt of such words as singer and hunter.

The tendency to word synthesis is, then, by no means the same thing as the tendency to compounding radical elements, though the latter is not infrequently a ready means for the synthetic tendency to work with. There is a bewildering variety of types of composition. These types vary according to function, the nature of the compounded elements, and order.

In a great many languages composition is confined to what we may call the delimiting function, that is, of the two or more compounded elements one is given a more precisely qualified significance by the others, which contribute nothing to the formal build of the sentence. In English, for instance, such compounded elements as red in redcoat or over in overlook merely modify the significance of the dominant coat or look without in any way sharing, as such, in the predication that is expressed by the sentence.

Some languages, however, such as Iroquois and Nahuatl, employ the method of composition for much heavier work than this. In Iroquois, for instance, the composition of a noun, in its radical form, with a following verb is a typical method of expressing case relations, particularly of the subject or object. Imeat-eat, for instance, is the regular Iroquois method of expressing the sentence I am eating meat. In other languages similar forms may express local or instrumental or still other relations.

Such English forms as killjoy and marplot also illustrate the compounding of a verb and a noun, but the resulting word has a strictly nominal, not a verbal, function. We cannot say he marplots. Some languages allow the composition of all or nearly all types of elements. Paiute, for instance, may compound noun with noun, adjective with noun, verb with noun to make a noun, noun with verb to make a verb, adverb with verb, verb with verb. Yana, an Indian language of California, can freely compound noun with noun and verb with noun, but not verb with verb.

On the other hand, Iroquois can compound only noun with verb, never noun and noun as in English or verb and verb as in so many other languages. Finally, each language has its characteristic types of order of composition. In English the qualifying element regularly precedes; in certain other languages it follows.

Sometimes both types are used in the same language, as in Yana, where "beef" is "bitter-venison" but "deerliver" is expressed by "liver-deer." The compounded object of a verb precedes the verbal element in Paiute, Nahuatl, and Iroquois, follows it in Yana, Tsimshian, and the Algonkin languages. Of all grammatical processes affixing is incomparably the most frequently employed. There are languages, like Chinese and Siamese, that make no grammatical use of elements that do not at the same time possess an independent value as radical elements, but such languages are uncommon. Of the three types of affixing-the use of prefixes, suffixes, and infixes – suffixing is much the commonest.

Indeed, it is a fair guess that suffixes do more of the formative work of language than all other methods combined. It is worth noting that there are not a few affixing languages that make absolutely no use of prefixed elements but possess a complex apparatus of suffixes.

Such are Turkish, Hottentot, Eskimo, Nootka, and Yana. Some of these, like the three last mentioned, have hundreds of suffixed elements, many of them of a concreteness of significance that would demand expression in the vast majority of languages by means of radical elements.

The reverse case, the use of prefixed elements to the complete exclusion of suffixes, is far less common. A good example is Khmer (or Cambodgian), spoken in French CochinChina, though even here there are obscure traces of old suffixes that have ceased to function as such and are now felt to form part of the radical element.

A considerable majority of known languages are prefixing and suffixing at one and the same time, but the relative importance of the two groups of affixed elements naturally varies enormously. In some languages, such as Latin and Russian, the suffixes alone relate the word to the rest of the sentence, the prefixes being confined to the expression of such ideas as delimit the concrete significance of the radical element without influencing its bearing in the proposition.

A Latin form like remittebantur "they were being sent back" may serve as an illustration of this type of distribution of elements. The prefixed element re- "back" merely qualifies to a certain extent the inherent significance of the radical element mitt- "send," while the suffixes -eba-, -nt-, and -ur convey the less concrete, more strictly formal, notions of time, person, plurality, and passivity. On the other hand, there are languages, like the Bantu group of Africa or the Athabaskan languages of North America, in which the grammatically significant elements precede, those that follow the radical element forming a relatively dispensable class. The Hupa word te-s-e-ya-te "I will go," for example, consists of a radical element -ya- "to go," three essential prefixes and a formally subsidiary suffix.

The element te- indicates that the act takes place here and there in space or continuously over space; practically, it has no clear-cut significance apart from such verb stems as it is customary to connect it with. The second prefixed element, -s-, is even less easy to define. All we can say is that it is used in verb forms of "definite" time and that it marks action as in progress rather than as beginning or coming to an end.

The third prefix, -e-, is a pronominal element, "I," which can be used only in "definite" tenses. It is highly important to understand that the use of -eis conditional on that of -s- or of certain alternative prefixes and that te- also is in practice linked with -s-. The group te-s-e-ya is a firmly knit grammatical unit. The suffix -te, which indicates the future, is no more necessary to its formal balance than is the prefixed re- of the Latin word; it is not an element that is capable of standing alone but its function is materially delimiting rather than strictly formal.

It is not always, however, that we can clearly set off the suffixes of a language as a group against its prefixes. In probably the majority of languages that use both types of affixes each group has both delimiting and formal or relational functions. The most that we can say is that a language tends to express similar functions in either the one or the other manner. If a certain verb expresses a certain tense by suffixing, the probability is strong that it expresses its other tenses in an analogous fashion and that, indeed, all verbs have suffixed tense elements.

Similarly, we normally expect to find the pronominal elements, so far as they are included in the verb at all, either consistently prefixed or suffixed. But these rules are far from absolute. We have already seen that Hebrew prefixes its pronominal elements in certain cases, suffixes them in others. In Chimariko, an Indian language of California, the position of the pronominal affixes depends on the verb; they are prefixed for certain verbs, suffixed for others.

It will not be necessary to give many further examples of prefixing and suffixing. One of each category will suffice to illustrate their formative possibilities. The idea expressed in English by the sentence I came to give it to her is rendered in Chinook by i-n-i-a-l-u-d-am. This word — and it is a thoroughly unified word with a clear-cut accent on the first a — consists of a radical element, -d- "to give," six functionally distinct, if phonetically frail, prefixed elements, and a suffix.

Of the prefixes, i- indicates recently past time; n-, the pronominal subject "I"; -i-, the pronominal object "it"; -a-, the second pronominal object "her"; -l-, a prepositional element indicating that the preceding pronominal prefix is to be understood as an indirect object (-her-to-, i.e., "to her"); and -u-, an element that it is not easy to define satisfactorily but which, on the whole, indicates movement away from the speaker. The suffixed -am modifies the verbal content in a local sense; it adds to the notion conveyed by the radical element that of "arriving" or "going (or coming) for that particular purpose."

It is obvious that in Chinook, as in Hupa, the greater part of the grammatical machinery resides in the prefixes rather than in the suffixes. A reverse case, one in which the grammatically significant elements cluster, as in Latin, at the end of the word is yielded by Fox, one of the better known Algonkin languages of the Mississippi Valley.

We may take the form eh-kiwi-n-a-m-oht-ati-wa-ch(i) "then they together kept (him) in flight from them." The radical element here is kiwi-, a verb stem indicating the general notion of "indefinite movement round about, here and there." The prefixed element *eh-* is hardly more than an adverbial particle indicating temporal subordination; it may be conveniently rendered as "then." Of the seven suffixes included in this highly-wrought word, -n- seems to be merely a phonetic element serving to connect the verb stem with the following -

a-; -a- is a "secondary stem" denoting the idea of " flight, to flee"; -m- denotes causality with reference to an animate object; -o(ht)- indicates activity done for the subject (the socalled "middle" or "medio-passive" voice of Greek); -(a)ti- is a reciprocal element, "one another"; -wa-ch(i) is the third person animate plural (-wa-, plural; -chi, more properly personal) of so-called "conjunctive" forms.

The word may be translated more literally (and yet only approximately as to grammatical feeling) as "then they (animate) caused some animate being to wander about in flight from one another of themselves." Eskimo, Nootka, Yana, and other languages have similarly complex arrays of suffixed elements, though the functions performed by them and their principles of combination differ widely.

We have reserved the very curious type of affixation known as "infixing" for separate illustration. It is utterly unknown in English, unless we consider the -n- of stand (contrast stood) as an infixed element. The earlier Indo-European languages, such as Latin, Greek and Sanskrit, made a fairly considerable use of infixed nasals to differentiate the present tense of a certain class of verbs from other forms (contrast Latin vinc-o "I conquer" with vic-i "I conquered"; Greek lamb-an-o "I take" with e-lab-on "I took").

There are, however, more striking examples of the process, examples in which it has assumed a more clearly defined function than in these Latin and Greek cases. It is particularly prevalent in many languages of southeastern Asia and of the Malay archipelago. Good examples from Khmer (Cambodgian) are tmeu "one who walks" and daneu "walking" (verbal noun), both derived from deu "to walk." Further examples may be quoted from Bontoc Igorot, a Filipino language.

IDEA

Thus, an infixed -in- conveys the idea of the product of an accomplished action, e.g., kayu "wood," kinayu "gathered wood." Infixes are also freely used in the Bontoc Igorot verb. Thus, an infixed -um- is characteristic of many intransitive verbs with personal pronominal suffixes, e.g., sad- "to wait," sumid-ak "I wait"; kineg "silent," kuminek-ak "I am silent." In other verbs it indicates futurity, e.g., tengao- "to celebrate a holiday," tumengao-ak "I shall have a holiday." The past tense is frequently indicated by an infixed -in-; if there is already an infixed -um-, the two elements combine to -in-m-, e.g., kinminek-ak "I am silent."

Obviously the infixing process has in this (and related) languages the same vitality that is possessed by the commoner prefixes and suffixes of other languages. The process is also found in a number of aboriginal American languages. The Yana plural is sometimes formed by an infixed element, e.g., k'uruwi "medicine-men," k'uwi "medicineman"; in Chinook an infixed -l- is used in certain verbs to indicate repeated activity, e.g., ksik'ludelk "she keeps looking at him," iksik'lutk "she looked at him" (radical element -tk).

A peculiarly interesting type of infixation is found in the Siouan languages, in which certain verbs insert the pronominal elements into the very body of the radical element, e.g., Sioux *cheti* "to build a fire," *chewati* "I build a fire"; *shuta* "to miss," *shuunta-pi* "we miss." A subsidiary but by no means unimportant grammatical process is that of internal vocalic or consonantal change.

In some languages, as in English (sing, sang, sung, song; goose, geese), the former of these has become one of the major methods of indicating fundamental changes of grammatical function. At any rate, the process is alive enough to lead our children into untrodden ways. We all know of the growing youngster who speaks of having brung something, on the analogy of such forms as sung and flung. In Hebrew, as we have seen, vocalic change is of even greater significance than in English. What is true of Hebrew is of course true of all other Semitic languages.

A few examples of so-called "broken" plurals from Arabic will supplement the Hebrew verb forms that I have given in another connection. The noun balad "place" has the plural form bilad; gild "hide" forms the plural gulud; ragril "man," the plural rigal; shibbak "window," the plural shababik. Very similar phenomena are illustrated by the Hamitic languages of Northern Africa, e.g., Shilh izbil "hair," plural izbel; a-slem "fish," plural i-slim-en; sn "to know," sen "to be knowing"; rmi "to become tired," rumni "to be tired"; ttss "to fall asleep," ttoss "to sleep."

Strikingly similar to English and Greek alternations of the type sing — sang and leip-o "I leave," leloip-a "I have left," are such Somali cases as al "I am," il "I was"; i-dah-a "I say," i-di "I said," deh "say!" Vocalic change is of great significance also in a number of American Indian languages. In the Athabaskan group many verbs change the quality or quantity of the vowel of the radical element as it changes its tense or mode. The Navaho verb for "I put (grain) into a receptacle" is bi-hi-sh-ja, in which -ja is the radical element; the past tense, bi-hi-ja', has a long a-vowel, followed by the "glottal stop"; the future is bi-h-de-sh-ji with complete change of vowel.

In other types of Navaho verbs the vocalic changes follow different lines, e.g., yah-a-ni-ye "you carry (a pack) into (a stable)"; past, yah-i-ni-yin (with long i in -yin; -n is here used to indicate nasalization); future, yah-a-di-yehl (with long e). In another Indian language, Yokuts, vocalic modifications affect both noun and verb forms.

Thus, buchong "son" forms the plural bochang-i (contrast the objective buchong-a); enash "grandfather," the plural inash-a; the verb engtyim "to sleep" forms the continuative ingetym-ad "to be sleeping" and the past ingetymash. Consonantal change as a functional process is probably far less common than vocalic modifications, but it is not exactly rare. There is an interesting group of cases in English, certain nouns and corresponding verbs differing solely in that the final consonant is voiceless or voiced.

Examples are wreath (with th as in think), but to wreathe (with th as in then); house, but to house (with s pronounced like z). That we have a distinct feeling for the interchange as a means of distinguishing the noun from the verb is indicated by the extension of the principle by many Americans to such a noun as rise (e.g., the rise of democracy) — pronounced like rice — in contrast to the verb to rise (s like z).

In the Celtic languages the initial consonants undergo several types of change according to the grammatical relation that subsists between the word itself and the preceding word. Thus, in modern Irish, a word like bo "ox" may under the appropriate circumstances, take the forms bho (pronounce wo) or mo (e.g., an bo "the ox" as a subject, but tir na mo "land of the oxen," as a possessive plural).

In the verb the principle has as one of its most striking consequences the "aspiration" of initial consonants in the past tense. If a verb begins with t, say, it changes the t to th (now pronounced h) in forms of the past; if it begins with g, the consonant changes, in analogous forms, to gh (pronounced like a voiced spirant g or like y, according to the nature of the following vowel). In modern Irish the principle of consonantal change, which began in the oldest period of the language as a secondary consequence of certain phonetic conditions, has become one of the primary grammatical processes of the language.

Perhaps as remarkable as these Irish phenomena are the consonantal interchanges of Ful, an African language of the Soudan. Here we find that all nouns belonging to the personal class form the plural by changing their initial g, j, d, b, k, ch, and p to y (or w), y, r, w, h, s and f respectively; e.g., jim-o "companion," yim-'be "companions"; pio-o "beater," fio-'be "beaters." Curiously enough, nouns that belong to the class of things form their singular and plural in exactly reverse fashion, e.g., yola-re "grass-grown place," jola-je "grass-grown places"; fitan-du "soul," pital-i "souls."

In Nootka, to refer to but one other language in which the process is found, the t or tl of many verbal suffixes becomes hl in forms denoting repetition, e.g., hita-'ato "to fall out," hita-'ahl "to keep falling out"; mat-achisht-utl "to fly on to the water," mat-achisht-ohl "to keep flying on to the water." Further, the hl of certain elements changes to a peculiar h-sound in plural forms, e.g., yak-ohl "sore-faced," yak-oh "sore-faced (people)."

Nothing is more natural than the prevalence of reduplication, in other words, the repetition of all or part of the radical element. The process is generally employed, with self-evident symbolism, to indicate such concepts as distribution, plurality, repetition, customary activity, increase of size, added intensity, continuance. Even in English it is not unknown, though it is not generally accounted one of the typical formative devices of our language.

Such words as goody-goody and to poohpooh have become accepted as part of our normal vocabulary, but the method of duplication may on occasion be used more freely than is indicated by such stereotyped examples. Such locutions as a big big man or Let it cool till it's thick thick are far more common, especially in the speech of women and children, than our linguistic text-books would lead one to suppose.

In a class by themselves are the really enormous number of words, many of them sound-imitative or contemptuous in psychological tone, that consist of duplications with either change of the vowel or change of the initial consonant-words of the type sing-song, riff-raff, wishy-washy, harum-skarum, roly-poly.

Words of this type are all but universal. Such examples as the Russian ChudoYudo (a dragon), the Chinese ping-pang "rattling of rain on the roof," the Tibetan kyang-kyong "lazy," and the Manchu porpon parpan "blear-eyed" are curiously reminiscent, both in form and in psychology, of words nearer home. But it can hardly be said that the duplicative process is of a distinctively grammatical significance in English. We must turn to other languages for illustration.

Such cases as Hottentot go-go "to look at carefully" (from go "to see"), Somali fenfen "to gnaw at on all sides" (from fen "to gnaw at"), Chinook iwi iwi "to look about carefully, to examine" (from iwi "to appear"), or Tsimshian am'am "several (are) good" (from am "good") do not depart from the natural and fundamental range of significance of the process.

A more abstract function is illustrated in Ewe, in which both infinitives and verbal adjectives are formed from verbs by duplication; e.g., yi "to go," yiyi "to go, act of going"; wo "to do," wowo "done"; mawomawo "not to do" (with both duplicated verb stem and duplicated negative particle).

Causative duplications are characteristic of Hottentot, e.g., gamgam "to cause to tell" (from gam "to tell"). Or the process may be used to derive verbs from nouns, as in Hottentot khoe-khoe "to talk Hottentot" (from khoe-b "man, Hottentot"), or as in Kwakiutl metmat "to eat clams" (radical element *met-* "clam").

The most characteristic examples of reduplication are such as repeat only part of the radical element. It would be possible to demonstrate the existence of a vast number of formal types of such partial duplication, according to whether the process makes use of one or more of the radical consonants, preserves or weakens or alters the radical vowel, or affects the beginning, the middle, or the end of the radical element. The functions are even more exuberantly developed than with simple duplication, though the basic notion, at least in origin, is nearly always one of repetition or continuance.

Examples illustrating this fundamental function can be quoted from all parts of the globe. Initially reduplicating are, for instance, Shilh ggen "to be sleeping" (from gen "to sleep"); Ful pepeu-'do "liar" (i.e., "one who always lies"), plural fefeu-'be (from fewa "to lie"); Bontoc Igorot anak "child," ananak "children"; kamu-ek "I hasten," kakamu-ek "I hasten more"; Tsimshian gyad "person," gyigyad "people"; Nass gyibayuk "to fly," gyigyibayuk "one who is flying."

Psychologically comparable, but with the reduplication at the end, are Somali ur "body," plural urar; Hausa suna "name," plural sunana-ki; Washo gusu "buffalo," gususu "buffaloes"; Takelma himi-d- "to talk to," himim-d- "to be accustomed to talk to." Even more commonly than simple duplication, this partial duplication of the radical element has taken on in many languages functions that seem in no way related to the idea of increase.

The best known examples are probably the initial reduplication of our older IndoEuropean languages, which helps to form the perfect tense of many verbs (e.g., Sanskrit dadarsha "I have seen," Greek leloipa "I have left," Latin tetigi "I have touched," Gothic lelot "I have let"). In Nootka reduplication of the radical element is often employed in association with certain suffixes; e.g., hluch- "woman" forms hluhluch-'ituht "to dream of a woman," hluhluchk'ok "resembling a woman." Psychologically similar to the Greek and Latin examples are many Takelma cases of verbs that exhibit two forms of the stem, one employed in the present or past, the other in the future and in certain modes and verbal derivatives.

The former has final reduplication, which is absent in the latter; e.g., *al-yebeb-i'n* "I show (or showed) to him," al*yeb-in* "I shall show him." We come now to the subtlest of all grammatical processes, variations in accent, whether of stress or pitch. The chief difficulty in isolating accent as a functional process is that it is so often combined with alternations in vocalic quantity or quality or complicated by the presence of affixed elements that its grammatical value appears as a secondary rather than as a primary feature.

In Greek, for instance, it is characteristic of true verbal forms that they throw the accent back as far as the general accentual rules will permit, while nouns may be more freely accented. There is thus a striking accentual difference between a verbal form like eluthemen "we were released," accented on the second syllable of the word, and its participial derivative lutheis "released," accented on the last.

The presence of the characteristic verbal elements e- and -men in the first case and of the nominal -s in the second tends to obscure the inherent value of the accentual alternation. This value comes out very neatly in such English doublets as to refund and a refund, to extract and an extract, to come down and a come down, to lack luster and lack-luster eyes, in which the difference between the verb and the noun is entirely a matter of changing stress.

In the Athabaskan languages there are not infrequently significant alternations of accent, as in Navaho ta-di-gis "you wash yourself" (accented on the second syllable), ta-di-gis "he washes himself" (accented on the first). Pitch accent may be as functional as stress and is perhaps more often so. The mere fact, however, that pitch variations are phonetically essential to the language, as in Chinese (e.g., feng "wind" with a level tone, feng "to serve" with a falling tone) or as in classical Greek (e.g., lab-on "having taken" with a simple or high tone on the suffixed participial -on, gunaik-on "of women" with a compound or falling tone on the case suffix -on) does not necessarily constitute a functional, or perhaps we had better say grammatical, use of pitch.

In such cases the pitch is merely inherent in the radical element or affix, as any vowel or consonant might be. It is different with such Chinese alternations as chung (level) "middle" and chung (falling) "to hit the middle"; mai (rising) "to buy" and mai (falling) "to sell"; pei (falling) "back" and pei (level) "to carry on the back." Examples of this type are not exactly common in Chinese and the language cannot be said to possess at present a definite feeling for tonal differences as symbolic of the distinction between noun and verb. There are languages, however, in which such differences are of the most fundamental grammatical importance.

They are particularly common in the Soudan. In Ewe, for instance, there are formed from subo "to serve" two reduplicated forms, an infinitive subosubo "to serve," with a low tone on the first two syllables and a high one on the last two, and an abjectival subosubo "serving," in which all the syllables have a high tone. Even more striking are cases furnished by Shilluk, one of the languages of the headwaters of the Nile.

The plural of the noun often differs in tone from the singular, e.g., yit (high) "ear" but yit (low) "ears." In the pronoun three forms may be distinguished by tone alone; e "he" has a high tone and is subjective, -e "him" (e.g., a chwol-e "he called him") has a low tone and is objective, -e "his" (e.g., wod-e "his house") has a middle tone and is possessive.

From the verbal element gwed- "to write" are formed gwed-o "(he) writes" with a low tone, the passive gwet "(it was) written" with a falling tone, the imperative gwet "write!" with a rising tone, and the verbal noun gwet "writing" with a middle tone. In aboriginal America also pitch accent is known to occur as a grammatical process. A good example of such a pitch language is Tlingit, spoken by the Indians of the southern coast of Alaska. In this language many verbs vary the tone of the radical element according to tense; hun "to sell," sin "to hide," tin "to see," and numerous other radical elements, if low-toned, refer to past time, if hightoned, to the future.

Another type of function is illustrated by the Takelma forms hel "song," with falling pitch, but hel "sing!" with a rising inflection; parallel to these forms are sel (falling) "black paint," sel (rising) "paint it!" All in all it is clear that pitch accent, like stress and vocalic or consonantal modifications, is far less infrequently employed as a grammatical process than our own habits of speech would prepare us to believe probable.

Because English is so widely spoken, it has often been referred to as a "global language", the *lingua franca* of the modern era. While English is not an official language in many countries, it is currently the language most often taught as a second language around the world. Some linguists believe that it is no longer the exclusive cultural sign of "native English speakers", but is rather a language that is absorbing aspects of cultures worldwide as it continues to grow.

It is, by international treaty, the official language for aerial and maritime communications, as well as one of the official languages of the European Union, the United Nations, and most international athletic organisations, including the International Olympic Committee. Books, magazines, and newspapers written in English are available in many countries around the world.

English is also the most commonly used language in the sciences. In 1997, the Science Citation Index reported that 95% of its articles were written in English, even though only half of them came from authors in English-speaking countries.

Chapter 6

Concept of Grammar

VOCABULARY

Germanic words (generally words of German or to a lesser extent Scandinavian origin) which include all the basics such as pronouns and conjunctions tend to be shorter than the Latinate words of English, and more common in ordinary speech. The longer Latinate words are regarded by many as more elegant or educated.

However, the excessive use of Latinate or Romance words is considered by some to be either pretentious (as in the stereotypical policeman's talk of "apprehending the suspect") or an attempt to obfuscate an issue. George Orwell's essay "Politics and the English Language" gives a thorough treatment of this feature of English. An English speaker is often able to choose between Germanic and Latinate synonyms: "come" or "arrive"; "sight" or "vision"; "freedom" or "liberty." Often there is a choice between a Germanic word (oversee), a Latin word (supervise), and a French word derived from the same Latin word (survey).

The richness of the language arises from the variety of different meanings and nuances such synonyms have from each other, enabling the speaker to express fine variations or shades of thought. Familiarity with the etymology of groups of synonyms can give English speakers greater control over their linguistic register.

An exception to this and a peculiarity perhaps unique to English is that the nouns for meats are commonly different from, and unrelated to, those for the animals from which they are produced, the animal commonly having a Germanic name and the meat having a French-derived one. Examples include: deer and venison; cow and beef; or swine/pig and pork. This is assumed to be a result of the aftermath of the Norman invasion, where a French-speaking elite were the consumers of the meat, produced by English-speaking lower classes. In everyday speech, the majority of words will normally be Germanic.

If a speaker wishes to make a forceful point in an argument in a very blunt way, Germanic words will usually be chosen. A majority of Latinate words (or at least a majority of content words) will normally be used in more formal speech and writing, such as a courtroom or an encyclopedia article. However, there are other Latinate words that are used normally in everyday speech and do not sound formal; these are mainly words for concepts that no longer have Germanic words, and are generally assimilated better and in many cases do not appear Latinate. For instance, the words *mountain, valley, river, aunt, uncle, push* and *stay* are all Latinate.

English is noted for the vast size of its active vocabulary and its fluidity. English easily accepts technical terms into common usage and imports new words and phrases that often come into common usage. Examples of this phenomenon include: cookie, Internet and URL (technical terms), as well as genre, uber, lingua franca and amigo (imported words/phrases, from French, German, modern Latin, and Spanish, respectively).

In addition, slang often provides new meanings for old words and phrases. In fact, this fluidity is so pronounced that a distinction often needs to be made between formal forms of English and contemporary usage. We have seen that the single word expresses either a simple concept or a combination of concepts so interrelated as to form a psychological unity. We have, furthermore, briefly reviewed from a strictly formal standpoint the main processes that are used by all known languages to affect the fundamental concepts – those embodied in unanalyzable words or in the radical elements of words – by the modifying or formative influence of subsidiary concepts. In this chapter we shall look a little more closely into the nature of the world of concepts, in so far as that world is reflected and systematized in linguistic structure. Let us begin with a simple sentence that involves various kinds of concepts — the farmer kills the duckling. A rough and ready analysis discloses here the presence of three distinct and fundamental concepts that are brought into connection with each other in a number of ways.

These three concepts are "farmer" (the subject of discourse), "kill" (defining the nature of the activity which the sentence informs us about), and "duckling" (another subject of discourse that takes an important though somewhat passive part in this activity). We can visualize the farmer and the duckling and we have also no difficulty in constructing an image of the killing. In other words, the elements farmer, kill, and duckling define concepts of a concrete order.

But a more careful linguistic analysis soon brings us to see that the two subjects of discourse, however simply we may visualize them, are not expressed quite as directly, as immediately, as we feel them. A "farmer" is in one sense a perfectly unified concept, in another he is "one who farms." The concept conveyed by the radical element (farm-) is not one of personality at all but of an industrial activity (to farm), itself based on the concept of a particular type of object (a farm). Similarly, the concept of duckling is at one remove from that which is expressed by the radical element of the word, duck. This element, which may occur as an independent word, refers to a whole class of animals, big and little, while duckling is limited in its application to the young of that class.

The word farmer has an "agentive" suffix -er that performs the function of indicating the one that carries out a given activity, in this case that of farming. It transforms the verb to farm into an agentive noun precisely as it transforms the verbs to sing, to paint, to teach into the corresponding agentive nouns singer, painter, teacher. The element -ling is not so freely used, but its significance is obvious. It adds to the basic concept the notion of smallness (as also in gosling, fledgeling) or the somewhat related notion of "contemptible" (as in weakling, princeling, hireling). The agentive -er and the diminutive -ling both convey fairly concrete ideas (roughly those of "doer" and "little"), but the concreteness is not stressed. They do not so much define distinct concepts as mediate between concepts.

The -er of farmer does not quite say "one who (farms)" it merely indicates that the sort of person we call a "farmer" is closely enough associated with activity on a farm to be conventionally thought of as always so occupied. He may, as a matter of fact, go to town and engage in any pursuit but farming, yet his linguistic label remains "farmer."

Language here betrays a certain helplessness or, if one prefers, a stubborn tendency to look away from the immediately suggested function, trusting to the imagination and to usage to fill in the transitions of thought and the details of application that distinguish one concrete concept (to farm) from another "derived" one (farmer). It would be impossible for any language to express every concrete idea by an independent word or radical element.

The concreteness of experience is infinite, the resources of the richest language are strictly limited. It must perforce throw countless concepts under the rubric of certain basic ones, using other concrete or semi-concrete ideas as functional mediators. The ideas expressed by these mediating elements — they may be independent words, affixes, or modifications of the radical element-may be called "derivational" or "qualifying." Some concrete concepts, such as kill, are expressed radically; others, such as farmer and duckling, are expressed derivatively.

MODES OF CORRESPONDENCE

Corresponding to these two modes of expression we have two types of concepts and of linguistic elements, radical (farm, kill, duck) and derivational (-er, -ling). When a word (or unified group of words) contains a derivational element (or word) the concrete significance of the radical element (farm-, duck-) tends to fade from consciousness and to yield to a new concreteness (farmer, duckling) that is synthetic in expression rather than in thought. In our sentence the concepts of farm and duck are not really involved at all; they are merely latent, for formal reasons, in the linguistic expression.

Returning to this sentence, we feel that the analysis of farmer and duckling are practically irrelevant to an understanding of its content and entirely irrelevant to a feeling for the structure of the sentence as a whole. From the standpoint of the sentence the derivational elements -er and -ling are merely details in the local economy of two of its terms (farmer, duckling) that it accepts as units of expression.

This indifference of the sentence as such to some part of the analysis of its words is shown by the fact that if we substitute such radical words as man and chick for farmer and duckling, we obtain a new material content, it is true, but not in the least a new structural mold. We can go further and substitute another activity for that of "killing," say "taking." The new sentence, the man takes the chick, is totally different from the first sentence in what it conveys, not in how it conveys it. We feel instinctively, without the slightest attempt at conscious analysis, that the two sentences fit precisely the same pattern, that they are really the same fundamental sentence, differing only in their material trappings.

In other words, they express identical relational concepts in an identical manner. The manner is here threefold — the use of an inherently relational word (the) in analogous positions, the analogous sequence (subject; predicate, consisting of verb and object) of the concrete terms of the sentence, and the use of the suffixed element -s in the verb.

Change any of these features of the sentence and it becomes modified, slightly or seriously, in some purely relational, non-material regard. If the is omitted (farmer kills duckling, man takes chick), the sentence becomes impossible; it falls into no recognized formal pattern and the two subjects of discourse seem to hang incompletely in the void.

We feel that there is no relation established between either of them and what is already in the minds of the speaker and his auditor. As soon as a the is put before the two nouns, we feel relieved. We know that the farmer and duckling which the sentence tells us about are the same farmer and duckling that we had been talking about or hearing about or thinking about some time before.

If I meet a man who is not looking at and knows nothing about the farmer in question, I am likely to be stared at for my pains if I announce to him that "the farmer [what farmer?] kills the duckling [didn't know he had any, whoever he is]." If the fact nevertheless seems interesting enough to communicate, I should be compelled to speak of "a farmer up my way" and of "a duckling of his." These little words, the and a, have the important function of establishing a definite or an indefinite reference.

If I omit the first the and also leave out the suffixed -s, I obtain an entirely new set of relations. Farmer, kill the duckling implies that I am now speaking to the farmer, not merely about him; further, that he is not actually killing the bird, but is being ordered by me to do so. The subjective relation of the first sentence has become a vocative one, one of address, and the activity is conceived in terms of command, not of statement. We conclude, therefore, that if the farmer is to be merely talked about, the little the must go back into its place and the -s must not be removed.

The latter element clearly defines, or rather helps to define, statement as contrasted with command. I find, moreover, that if I wish to speak of several farmers, I cannot say the farmers kills the duckling, but must say the farmers kill the duckling. Evidently -s involves the notion of singularity in the subject. If the noun is singular, the verb must have a form to correspond; if the noun is plural, the verb has another, corresponding form.

Comparison with such forms as I kill and you kill shows, moreover, that the -s has exclusive reference to a person other than the speaker or the one spoken to. We conclude, therefore, that it connotes a personal relation as well as the notion of singularity. And comparison with a sentence like the farmer killed the duckling indicates that there is implied in this overburdened -s a distinct reference to present time. Statement as such and personal reference may well be looked upon as inherently relational concepts. Number is evidently felt by those who speak English as involving a necessary relation, otherwise there would be no reason to express the concept twice, in the noun and in the verb. Time also is clearly felt as a relational concept; if it were not, we should be allowed to say the farmer killed-s to correspond to the farmer kill-s. Of the four concepts inextricably interwoven in the -s suffix, all are felt as relational, two necessarily so. The distinction between a truly relational concept and one that is so felt and treated, though it need not be in the nature of things, will receive further attention in a moment.

Finally, I can radically disturb the relational cut of the sentence by changing the order of its elements. If the positions of farmer and kills are interchanged, the sentence reads kills the farmer the duckling, which is most naturally interpreted as an unusual but not unintelligible mode of asking the question, does the farmer kill the duckling? In this new sentence the act is not conceived as necessarily taking place at all. It may or it may not be happening, the implication being that the speaker wishes to know the truth of the matter and that the person spoken to is expected to give him the information.

The interrogative sentence possesses an entirely different "modality" from the declarative one and implies a markedly different attitude of the speaker towards his companion. An even more striking change in personal relations is effected if we interchange the farmer and the duckling. The duckling kills the farmer involves precisely the same subjects of discourse and the same type of activity as our first sentence, but the roles of these subjects of discourse are now reversed. The duckling has turned, like the proverbial worm, or, to put it in grammatical terminology, what was "subject" is now "object," what was object is now subject.

ANALYSING YOUR SENTENCE

The following tabular statement analyzes the sentence from the point of view of the concepts expressed in it and of the grammatical processes employed for their expression.

- Concrete Concepts
  - *First subject of discourse*: Farmer
  - *Second subject of discourse*: Duckling
  - *Activity*: Kill
- Analyzable into
  - Radical Concepts
    - (a) *Verb*: (to) Farm
    - (b) *Noun*: Duck
    - (c) *Verb*: Kill
  - Derivational Concepts
    - (a) *Agentive*: expressed by suffix -er
    - (b) *Diminutive*: expressed by suffix -ling
- Relational Concepts
  - Modality.
  - *Declarative*: expressed by sequence of "subject" plus verb; and implied by suffixed *-s*
- Personal relations
  - Subjectivity of farmer: expressed by position of farmer before kills; and by suffixed *-s*
  - Objectivity of duckling: expressed by position of duckling after kills
- Number
  - Singularity of first subject of discourse: expressed by lack of plural suffix in farmer; and by suffix -s in following verb
  - Singularity of second subject of discourse: expressed by lack of plural suffix in *duckling*
- Time
  - *Present*: expressed by lack of preterit suffix in verb; and by suffixed-*s*

In this short sentence of five words there are expressed, therefore, thirteen distinct concepts, of which three are radical and concrete, two derivational, and eight relational. Perhaps the most striking result of the analysis is a renewed realization of the curious lack of accord in our language between function and form.

The method of suffixing is used both for derivational and for relational elements; independent words or radical elements express both concrete ideas (objects, activities, qualities) and relational ideas (articles like the and a; words defining case relations, like of, to, for, with, by; words defining local relations, like in, on, at); the same relational concept may be expressed more than once (thus, the singularity of farmer is both negatively expressed in the noun and positively in the verb); and one element may convey a group of interwoven concepts rather than one definite concept alone (thus the -s of kills embodies no less than four logically independent relations).

Our analysis may seem a bit labored, but only because we are so accustomed to our own well-worn grooves of expression that they have come to be felt as inevitable. Yet destructive analysis of the familiar is the only method of approach to an understanding of fundamentally different modes of expression. When one has learned to feel what is fortuitous or illogical or unbalanced in the structure of his own language, he is already well on the way towards a sympathetic grasp of the expression of the various classes of concepts in alien types of speech. Not everything that is "outlandish" is intrinsically illogical or far-fetched. It is often precisely the familiar that a wider perspective reveals as the curiously exceptional.

From a purely logical standpoint it is obvious that there is no inherent reason why the concepts expressed in our sentence should have been singled out, treated, and grouped as they have been and not otherwise. The sentence is the outgrowth of historical and of unreasoning psychological forces rather than of a logical synthesis of elements that have been clearly grasped in their individuality.

This is the case, to a greater or less degree, in all languages, though in the forms of many we find a more coherent, a more consistent, reflection than in our English forms of that unconscious analysis into individual concepts which is never entirely absent from speech; however it may be complicated with or overlaid by the more irrational factors. A cursory examination of other languages, near and far, would soon show that some or all of the thirteen concepts that our sentence happens to embody may not only be expressed in different form but that they may be differently grouped among themselves; that some among them may be dispensed with; and that other concepts, not considered worth expressing in English idiom, may be treated as absolutely indispensable to the intelligible rendering of the proposition. First as to a different method of handling such concepts as we have found expressed in the English sentence.

If we turn to German, we find that in the equivalent sentence the definiteness of reference expressed by the English the is unavoidably coupled with three other concepts — number case (der is subjective; das is subjective or objective, by elimination therefore objective), and gender, a new concept of the relational order that is not in this case explicitly involved in English (der is masculine, das is neuter).

Indeed, the chief burden of the expression of case, gender, and number is in the German sentence borne by the particles of reference rather than by the words that express the concrete concepts to which these relational concepts ought logically to attach themselves. In the sphere of concrete concepts too it is worth noting that the German splits up the idea of "killing" into the basic concept of "dead" (tot) and the derivational one of "causing to do (or be) so and so" (by the method of vocalic change, tot-); the German tot-et (analytically tot- + vowel change + -et) "causes to be dead" is, approximately, the formal equivalent of our dead-en-s, though the idiomatic application of this latter word is different.

Wandering still further afield, we may glance at the Yana method of expression. Literally translated, the equivalent Yana sentence would read something like "kill-s he farmer he to duck-ling," in which "he" and "to" are rather awkward English renderings of a general third personal pronoun (he, she, it, or they) and an objective particle which indicates that the following noun is connected with the verb otherwise than as subject. The suffixed element in "kill-s" corresponds to the English suffix with the important exceptions that it makes no reference to the number of the subject and that the statement is known to be true, that it is vouched for by the speaker.

Number is only indirectly expressed in the sentence in so far as there is no specific verb suffix indicating plurality of the subject nor specific plural elements in the two nouns. Had the statement been made on another's authority, a totally different "tense-modal" suffix would have had to be used. The pronouns of reference ("he") imply nothing by themselves as to number, gender, or case.

Gender, indeed, is completely absent in Yana as a relational category. The Yana sentence has already illustrated the point that certain of our supposedly essential concepts may be ignored; both the Yana and the German sentence illustrate the further point that certain concepts may need expression for which an English-speaking person, or rather the English-speaking habit, finds no need whatever.

One could go on and give endless examples of such deviations from English form, but we shall have to content ourselves with a few more indications. In the Chinese sentence "Man kill duck," which may be looked upon as the practical equivalent of "The man kills the duck," there is by no means present for the Chinese consciousness that childish, halting, empty feeling which we experience in the literal English translation.

The three concrete concepts — two objects and an action — are each directly expressed by a monosyllabic word which is at the same time a radical element; the two relational concepts — "subject" and "object" — are expressed solely by the position of the concrete words before and after the word of action. And that is all.

Definiteness or indefiniteness of reference, number, personality as an inherent aspect of the verb, tense, not to speak of gender — all these are given no expression in the Chinese sentence, which, for all that, is a perfectly adequate communication — provided, of course, there is that context, that background of mutual understanding that is essential to the complete intelligibility of all speech.

Nor does this qualification impair our argument, for in the English sentence too we leave unexpressed a large number of ideas which are either taken for granted or which have been developed or are about to be developed in the course of the conversation. Nothing has been said, for example, in the English, German, Yana, or Chinese sentence as to the place relations of the farmer, the duck, the speaker, and the listener. Are the farmer and the duck both visible or is one or the other invisible from the point of view of the speaker, and are both placed within the horizon of the speaker, the listener, or of some indefinite point of reference "off yonder"?

In other words, to paraphrase awkwardly certain latent "demon-strative" ideas, does this farmer (invisible to us but standing behind a door not far away from me, you being seated yonder well out of reach) kill that duckling (which belongs to you)? or does that farmer (who lives in your neighborhood and whom we see over there) kill that duckling (that belongs to him)?

This type of demonstrative elaboration is foreign to our way of thinking, but it would seem very natural, indeed unavoidable, to a Kwakiutl Indian. What, then, are the absolutely essential concepts in speech, the concepts that must be expressed if language is to be a satisfactory means of communication? Clearly we must have, first of all, a large stock of basic or radical concepts, the concrete wherewithal of speech. We must have objects, actions, qualities to talk about, and these must have their corresponding symbols in independent words or in radical elements.

No proposition, however abstract its intent, is humanly possible without a tying on at one or more points to the concrete world of sense. In every intelligible proposition at least two of these radical ideas must be expressed, though in exceptional cases one or even both may be understood from the context. And, secondly, such relational concepts must be expressed as moor the concrete concepts to each other and construct a definite, fundamental form of proposition.

In this fundamental form there must be no doubt as to the nature of the relations that obtain between the concrete concepts. We must know what concrete concept is directly or indirectly related to what other, and how. If we wish to talk of a thing and an action, we must know if they are coordinately related to each other (e.g., "He is fond of wine and gambling"); or if the thing is conceived of as the starting point, the "doer" of the action, or, as it is customary to say, the "subject" of which the action is predicated; or if, on the contrary, it is the end point, the "object" of the action. If I wish to communicate an intelligible idea about a farmer, a duckling, and the act of killing, it is not enough to state the linguistic symbols for these concrete ideas in any order, higgledypiggledy, trusting that the hearer may construct some kind of a relational pattern out of the general probabilities of the case.

The fundamental syntactic relations must be unambiguously expressed. I can afford to be silent on the subject of time and place and number and of a host of other possible types of concepts, but I can find no way of dodging the issue as to who is doing the killing. There is no known language that can or does dodge it, any more than it succeeds in saying something without the use of symbols for the concrete concepts. We are thus once more reminded of the distinction between essential or unavoidable relational concepts and the dispensable type.

The former are universally expressed, the latter are but sparsely developed in some languages, elaborated with a bewildering exuberance in others. But what prevents us from throwing in these "dispensable" or "secondary" relational concepts with the large, floating group of derivational, qualifying concepts that we have already discussed? Is there, after all is said and done, a fundamental difference between a qualifying concept like the negative in unhealthy and a relational one like the number concept in books? If unhealthy may be roughly paraphrased as not healthy, may not books be just as legitimately paraphrased, barring the violence to English idiom, as several book?

There are, indeed, languages in which the plural, if expressed at all, is conceived of in the same sobre, restricted, one might almost say casual, spirit in which we feel the negative in unhealthy. For such languages the number concept has no syntactic significance whatever, is not essentially conceived of as defining a relation, but falls into the group of derivational or even of basic concepts. In English, however, as in French, German, Latin, Greek — indeed in all the languages that we have most familiarity with — the idea of number is not merely appended to a given concept of a thing. It may have something of this merely qualifying value, but its force extends far beyond.

It infects much else in the sentence, molding other concepts, even such as have no intelligible relation to number, into forms that are said to correspond to or "agree with" the basic concept to which it is attached in the first instance. If "a man falls" but "men fall" in English, it is not because of any inherent change that has taken place in the nature of the action or because the idea of plurality inherent in "men" must, in the very nature of ideas, relate itself also to the action performed by these men.

What we are doing in these sentences is what most languages, in greater or less degree and in a hundred varying ways, are in the habit of doing — throwing a bold bridge between the two basically distinct types of concept, the concrete and the abstractly relational, infecting the latter, as it were, with the colour and grossness of the former. By a certain violence of metaphor the material concept is forced to do duty for (or intertwine itself with) the strictly relational.

The case is even more obvious if we take gender as our text. In the two English phrases, "The white woman that comes" and "The white men that come," we are not reminded that gender, as well as number, may be elevated into a secondary relational concept. It would seem a little far-fetched to make of masculinity and femininity, crassly material, philosophically accidental concepts that they are, a means of relating quality and person, person and action, nor would it easily occur to us, if we had not studied the classics, that it was anything but absurd to inject into two such highly attenuated relational concepts as are expressed by "the" and "that" the combined notions of number and sex.

Yet all this, and more, happens in Latin. Illa alba femina quae venit and illi albi homines qui veniunt, conceptually translated, amount to this: that-one-feminine-doer one-feminine-white-doer feminine-doing-one woman which-one-feminine-doer other -one-nowcome; and: that-several-masculine-doer several-masculine-white-doer masculine-doing-several-man which-several-masculine-doer other-several-now-come. Each word involves no less than four concepts, a radical concept (either properly concrete — white, man, woman, come-or demonstrative — that, which) and three relational concepts, selected from the categories of case, number, gender, person, and tense.

Logically, only case (the relation of woman or men to a following verb, of which to its antecedent, of that and white to woman or men, and of which to come) imperatively demands expression, and that only in connection with the concepts directly affected (there is, for instance, no need to be informed that the whiteness is a doing or doer's whiteness). The- other relational concepts are either merely parasitic (gender throughout; number in the demonstrative, the adjective, the relative, and the verb) or irrelevant to the essential syntactic form of the sentence (number in the noun; person; tense).

An intelligent and sensitive Chinaman, accustomed as he is to cut to the very bone of linguistic form, might well say of the Latin sentence, "How pedantically imaginative!" It must be difficult for him, when first confronted by the illogical complexities of our European languages, to feel at home in an attitude that so largely confounds the subjectmatter of speech with its formal pattern or, to be more accurate, that turns certain fundamentally concrete concepts to such attenuated relational uses. I have exaggerated somewhat the concreteness of our subsidiary or rather non-syntactical relational concepts in order that the essential facts might come out in bold relief. It goes without saying that a Frenchman has no clear sex notion in his mind when he speaks of un arbre. ("a-masculine tree") or of une pomme ("a-feminine apple").

ROLE OF LINGUISTIC IN LITERATURE

In both the French and English instances the primary ideas of sex and time have become diluted by form-analogy and by extensions into the relational sphere, the concepts ostensibly indicated being now so vaguely delimited that it is rather the tyranny of usage than the need of their concrete expression that sways us in the selection of this or that form.

If the thinning out process continues long enough, we may eventually be left with a system of forms on our hands from which all the colour of life has vanished and which merely persist by inertia, duplicating each other's secondary, syntactic functions with endless prodigality. Hence, in part, the complex conjugational systems of so many languages, in which differences of form are attended by no assignable differences of function.

There must have been a time, for instance, though it antedates our earliest documentary evidence, when the type of tense formation represented by drove or sank differed in meaning, in however slightly nuanced a degree, from the type (killed, worked) which has now become established in English as the prevailing preterit formation, very much as we recognize a valuable distinction at present between both these types and the "perfect" (has driven, has killed) but may have ceased to do so at some point in the future.

Now form lives longer than its own conceptual content. Both are ceaselessly changing, but, on the whole, the form tends to linger on when the spirit has flown or changed its being. Irrational form, form for form's sake – however we term this tendency to hold on to formal distinctions once they have come to be – is as natural to the life of language as is the retention of modes of conduct that have long outlived the meaning they once had.

There is another powerful tendency which makes for a formal elaboration that does not strictly correspond to clear-cut conceptual differences. This is the tendency to construct schemes of classification into which all the concepts of language must be fitted.

Once we have made up our minds that all things are either definitely good or bad or definitely black or white, it is difficult to get into the frame of mind that recognizes that any particular thing may be both good and bad (in other words, indifferent) or both black and white (in other words, gray), still more difficult to realise that the good-bad or black-white categories may not apply at all. Language is in many respects as unreasonable and stubborn about its classifications as is such a mind. It must have its perfectly exclusive pigeon-holes and will tolerate no flying vagrants.

Any concept that asks for expression must submit to the classificatory rules of the game, just as there are statistical surveys in which even the most convinced atheist must perforce be labeled Catholic, Protestant, or Jew or get no hearing. In English we have made up our minds that all action must be conceived of in reference to three standard times. If, therefore, we desire to state a proposition that is as true tomorrow as it was yesterday, we have to pretend that the present moment may be elongated fore and aft so as to take in all eternity.

In French we know once for all that an object is masculine or feminine, whether it be living or not; just as in many American and East Asiatic languages it must be understood to belong to a certain form-category (say, ring-round, ball-round, long and slender, cylindrical, sheet-like, in mass like sugar) before it can be enumerated (e.g., "two ball-class potatoes," "three sheetclass carpets") or even said to "be" or "be handled in a definite way" (thus, in the Athabaskan languages and in Yana, "to carry" or "throw" a pebble is quite another thing than to carry or throw a log, linguistically no less than in terms of muscular experience).

Such instances might be multiplied at will. It is almost as though at some period in the past the unconscious mind of the race had made a hasty inventory of experience, committed itself to a premature classification that allowed of no revision, and saddled the inheritors of its language with a science that they no longer quite believed in nor had the strength to overthrow.

Dogma, rigidly prescribed by tradition, stiffens into formalism. Linguistic categories make up a system of surviving dogma – dogma of the unconscious. They are often but half real as concepts; their life tends ever to languish away into form for form's sake. There is still a third cause for the rise of this nonsignificant form, or rather of non-significant differences of form. This is the mechanical operation of phonetic processes, which may bring about formal distinctions that have not and never had a corresponding functional distinction.

Much of the irregularity and general formal complexity of our declensional and conjugational systems is due to this process. The plural of hat is hats, the plural of self is selves. In the former case we have a true -s symbolizing plurality, in the latter a z-sound coupled with a change in the radical element of the word of f to v. Here we have not a falling together of forms that originally stood for fairly distinct concepts — as we saw was presumably the case with such parallel forms as drove and worked — but a merely mechanical manifolding of the same formal element without a corresponding growth of a new concept.

This type of form development, therefore, while of the greatest interest for the general history of language, does not directly concern us now in our effort to understand the nature of grammatical concepts and their tendency to degenerate into purely formal counters. We may now conveniently revise our first classification of concepts as expressed in language and suggest the following scheme:

- Basic (Concrete) Concepts (such as objects, actions, qualities): normally expressed by independent words or radical elements; involve no relation as such
- Derivational Concepts (less concrete, as a rule, than I, more so than III): normally expressed by affixing non-radical elements to radical elements or by inner modification of these; differ from type I in defining ideas that are irrelevant to the proposition as a whole but that give a radical element a particular increment of significance and that are thus inherently related in a specific way to concepts of type I
- Concrete Relational Concepts (still more abstract, yet not entirely devoid of a measure of concreteness): normally expressed by affixing non-radical elements

to radical elements, but generally at a greater remove from these than is the case with elements of type II, or by inner modification of radical elements; differ fundamentally from type II in indicating or implying relations that transcend the particular word to which they are immediately attached, thus leading over to

- Pure Relational Concepts (purely abstract): normally expressed by affixing non-radical elements to radical elements (in which case these concepts are frequently intertwined with those of type III) or by their inner modification, by independent words, or by position; serve to relate the concrete elements of the proposition to each other, thus giving it definite syntactic form.

The nature of these four classes of concepts as regards their concreteness or their power to express syntactic relations may be thus symbolized:

I Basic Concepts
II Derivational Concepts
III Concrete Relational Concepts
IV Pure Relational Concepts

These schemes must not be worshipped as fetiches. In the actual work of analysis difficult problems frequently arise and we may well be in doubt as to how to group a given set of concepts. This is particularly apt to be the case in exotic languages, where we may be quite sure of the analysis of the words in a sentence and yet not succeed in acquiring that inner "feel" of its structure that enables us to tell infallibly what is "material content" and what is "relation."

Concepts of class I are essential to all speech, also concepts of class IV. Concepts II and III are both common, but not essential; particularly group III, which represents, in effect, a psychological and formal confusion of types II and IV or of types I and IV, is an avoidable class of concepts.

Logically there is an impassable gulf between I and IV, but the illogical, metaphorical genius of speech has wilfully spanned the gulf and set up a continuous gamut of concepts and forms that leads imperceptibly from the crudest of materialities ("house" or "John Smith") to the most subtle of relations. It is particularly significant that the unanalyzable independent word belongs in most cases to either group I or group IV, rather less commonly to II or III. It is possible for a concrete concept, represented by a simple word, to lose its material significance entirely and pass over directly into the relational sphere without at the same time losing its independence as a word.

This happens, for instance, in Chinese and Cambodgian when the verb "give" is used in an abstract sense as a mere symbol of the "indirect objective" relation (e.g., Cambodgian "We make story this give all that person who have child," i.e., "We have made this story *for* all those that have children").

There are, of course, also not a few instances of transitions between groups I and II and I and III, as well as of the less radical one between II and III. To the first of these transitions belongs that whole class of examples in which the independent word, after passing through the preliminary stage of functioning as the secondary or qualifying element in a compound, ends up by being a derivational affix pure and simple, yet without losing the memory of its former independence.

Such an element and concept is the full of teaspoonfull, which hovers psychologically between the status of an independent, radical concept (compare full) or of a subsidiary element in a compound (cf. brim-full) and that of a simple suffix (cf. dutiful) in which the primary concreteness is no longer felt. In general, the more highly synthetic our linguistic type, the more difficult and even arbitrary it becomes to distinguish groups I and II.

Not only is there a gradual loss of the concrete as we pass through from group I to group IV, there is also a constant fading away of the feeling of sensible reality within the main groups of linguistic concepts themselves. In many languages it becomes almost imperative, therefore, to make various sub-classifications, to segregate, for instance, the more concrete from the more abstract concepts of group II. Yet we must always beware of reading into such abstracter groups that purely formal, relational feeling that we can hardly help associating with certain of the abstracter concepts which, with us, fall in group III, unless, indeed, there is clear evidence to warrant such a reading in.

An example or two should make clear these all-important distinctions. In Nootka we have an unusually large number of derivational affixes (expressing concepts of group II). Some of these are quite material in content (e.g., "in the house," "to dream of"), others, like an element denoting plurality and a diminutive affix, are far more abstract in content. The former type are more closely welded with the radical element than the latter, which can only be suffixed to formations that have the value of complete words. If, therefore, I wish to say "the small fires in the house" — and I can do this in one word — I must form the word "fire-in-the-house," to which elements corresponding to "small," our plural, and "the" are appended.

The element indicating the definiteness of reference that is implied in our "the" comes at the very end of the word. So far, so good. "Fire-in-thehouse-the" is an intelligible correlate of our "the housefire." But is the Nootka correlate of "the small fires in the house" the true equivalent of an English "the house-firelets"? By no means. First of all, the plural element precedes the diminutive in Nootka: "fire-in-thehouse-plural-small-the," in other words "the house-fireslet," which at once reveals the important fact that the plural concept is not as abstractly, as relationally, felt as in English. A more adequate rendering would be "the house-fire-several-let," in which, however, "several" is too gross a word, "-let" too choice an element ("small" again is too gross).

In truth we cannot carry over into English the inherent feeling of the Nootka word, which seems to hover somewhere between "the house-firelets" and "the house-fire-several-small." But what more than anything else cuts off all possibility of comparison between the English -s of "house-firelets" and the "-several-small" of the Nootka word is this, that in Nootka neither the plural nor the diminutive affix corresponds or refers to anything else in the sentence. In English "the house-firelets burn" (not "burns"), in Nootka neither verb, nor adjective, nor anything else in the proposition is in the least concerned with the plurality or the diminutiveness of the fire. Hence, while Nootka recognizes a cleavage between concrete and less concrete concepts within group II, the less concrete do not transcend the group and lead us into that abstracter air into which our plural -s carries us. But at any rate, the reader may object, it is something that the Nootka plural affix is set apart from the concreter group of affixes; and may not the Nootka diminutive have a slenderer, a more elusive content than our -let or -ling or the German -chen or -lein?

Can such a concept as that of plurality ever be classified with the more material concepts of group II? Indeed it can be. In Yana the third person of the verb makes no formal distinction between singular and plural. Nevertheless the plural concept can be, and nearly always is, expressed by the suffixing of an element (-ba-) to the radical element of the verb. "It burns in the east" is rendered by the verb ya-hau-si "burn-east-s." "They burn in the east" is ya-bahau-si.

Note that the plural affix immediately follows the radical element (*ya*-), disconnecting it from the local element (-hau-). It needs no labored argument to prove that the concept of plurality is here hardly less concrete than that of location "in the east," and that the Yana form corresponds in feeling not so much to our "They burn in the east" (ardunt oriente) as to a "Burn-severaleast-s, it plurally burns in the east," an expression which we cannot adequately assimilate for lack of the necessary form-grooves into which to run it.

But can we go a step farther and dispose of the category of plurality as an utterly material idea, one that would make of "books" a "plural book," in which the "plural," like the "white" of "white book," falls contentedly into group I? Our "many books" and "several books" are obviously not cases in point. Even if we could say "many book" and "several book" (as we can say "many a book" and "each book"), the plural concept would still not emerge as clearly as it should for our argument; "many" and "several" are contaminated by certain notions of quantity or scale that are not essential to the idea of plurality itself. We must turn to central and eastern Asia for the type of expression we are seeking. In Tibetan, for instance, nga-s mi mthong "I-by man see, by me a man is seen, I see a man" may just as well be understood to mean "I see men," if there happens to be no reason to emphasize the fact of plurality.

If the fact is worth expressing, however, I can say nga-s mi rnams mthong "by me man plural see," where rnams is the perfect conceptual analogue of -s in books, divested of all relational strings. Rnams follows its noun as would any other attributive word — "man plural" (whether two or a million) like "man white." No need to bother about his plurality any more than about his whiteness unless we insist on the point.

What is true of the idea of plurality is naturally just as true of a great many other concepts. They do not necessarily belong where we who speak English are in the habit of putting them. They may be shifted towards I or towards IV, the two poles of linguistic expression. Nor dare we look down on the Nootka Indian and the Tibetan for their material attitude towards a concept which to us is abstract and relational, lest we invite the reproaches of the Frenchman who feels a subtlety of relation in femme blanche and homme blanc that he misses in the coarser-grained white woman and white man.

But the Bantu Negro, were he a philosopher, might go further and find it strange that we put in group II a category, the diminutive, which he strongly feels to belong to group III and which he uses, along with a number of other classificatory concepts, to relate his subjects and objects, attributes and predicates, as a Russian or a German handles his genders and, if possible, with an even greater finesse.

It is because our conceptual scheme is a sliding scale rather than a philosophical analysis of experience that we cannot say in advance just where to put a given concept. We must dispense, in other words, with a well-ordered classification of categories. What boots it to put tense and mode here or number there when the next language one handles puts tense a peg "lower down" (towards I), mode and number a peg "higher up" (towards IV)? Nor is there much to be gained in a summary work of this kind from a general inventory of the types of concepts generally found in groups II, III, and IV. There are too many possibilities.

It would be interesting to show what are the most typical noun-forming and verb-forming elements of group II; how variously nouns may be classified (by gender; personal and non-personal; animate and inanimate; by form; common and proper); how the concept of number is elaborated (singular and plural; singular, dual, and plural; singular, dual, trial, and plural; single, distributive, and collective); what tense distinctions may be made in verb or noun (the "past," for instance, may be an indefinite past, immediate, remote, mythical, completed, prior); how delicately certain languages have developed the idea of "aspect" (momentaneous, durative, continuative, inceptive, cessative, durative-inceptive, iterative, momentaneous-iterative, durative-iterative, resultative, and still others); what modalities may be recognized (indicative, imperative, potential, dubitative, optative, negative, and a host of others); what distinctions of person are possible (is "we," for instance, conceived of as a plurality of "I" or is it as distinct from "I" as either is from "you" or "he"? — both attitudes are illustrated in language; moreover, does "we" include, you to whom I speak or not? — "inclusive" and "exclusive" forms); what may be the general scheme of orientation, the so-called demonstrative categories ("this" and "that" in an endless procession of nuances); how frequently the form ex-presses the source or nature of the speaker's knowledge (known by actual experience, by hearsay, by inference); how the syntactic relations may be expressed in the noun (subjective and objective; agentive, instrumental, and person affected; various types of "genitive" and indirect relations) and, correspondingly, in the verb (active and passive; active and static; transitive and intransitive; impersonal, reflexive, reciprocal, indefinite as to object, and many other special limitations on the starting-point and end-point of the flow of activity).

These details, important as many of them are to an understanding of the "inner form" of language, yield in general significance to the more radical group-distinctions that we have set up. It is enough for the general reader to feel that language struggles towards two poles of linguistic expression — material content and relation — and that these poles tend to be connected by a long series of transitional concepts.

In dealing with words and their varying forms we have had to anticipate much that concerns the sentence as a whole. Every language has its special method or methods of binding words into a larger unity. The importance of these methods is apt to vary with the complexity of the individual word. The more synthetic the language, in other words, the more clearly the status of each word in the sentence is indicated by its own resources, the less need is there for looking beyond the word to the sentence as a whole.

The Latin agit "(he) acts" needs no outside help to establish its place in a proposition. Whether I say agit dominus "the master acts" or sic femina agit "thus the woman acts," the net result as to the syntactic feel of the agit is practically the same. It can only be a verb, the predicate of a proposition, and it can only be conceived as a statement of activity carried out by a person (or thing) other than you or me. It is not so with such a word as the English act. Act is a syntactic waif until we have defined its status in a proposition — one thing in "they act abominably," quite another in "that was a kindly act." The Latin sentence speaks with the assurance of its individual members; the English word needs the prompting of its fellows. Roughly speaking, to be sure.

And yet to say that a sufficiently elaborate word-structure compensates for external syntactic methods is perilously close to begging the question. The elements of the word are related to each other in a specific way and follow each other in a rigorously determined sequence. This is tantamount to saying that a word which consists of more than a radical element is a crystallization of a sentence or of some portion of a sentence, that a form like agit is roughly the psychological equivalent of a form like age is "act he."

Breaking down, then, the wall that separates word and sentence, we may ask: What, at last analysis, are the fundamental methods of relating word to word and element to element, in short, of passing from the isolated notions symbolized by each word and by each element to the unified proposition that corresponds to a thought? The answer is simple and is implied in the preceding remarks. The most fundamental and the most powerful of all relating methods is the method of order. Let us think of some more or less concrete idea, say a colour, and set down its symbol — red; of another concrete idea, say a person or object, setting down its symbol — dog; finally, of a third concrete idea, say an action, setting down its symbol — run.

It is hardly possible to set down these three symbols — red dog run — without relating them in some way, for example (the) red dog run(s). I am far from wishing to state that the proposition has always grown up in this analytic manner, merely that the very process of juxtaposing concept to concept, symbol to symbol, forces some kind of relational "feeling," if nothing else, upon us.

To certain syntactic adhesions we are very sensitive, for example, to the attributive relation of quality (red dog) or the subjective relation (dog run) or the objective relation (kill dog), to others we are more indifferent, for example, to the attributive relation of circumstance (to-day red dog run or red dog to-day run or red dog run to-day, all of which are equivalent propositions or propositions in embryo).

Words and elements, then, once they are listed in a certain order, tend not only to establish some kind of relation among themselves but are attracted to each other in greater or in less degree. It is presumably this very greater or less that ultimately leads to those firmly solidified groups of elements (radical element or elements plus one or more grammatical elements) that we have studied as complex words.

They are in all likelihood nothing but sequences that have shrunk together and away from other sequences or isolated elements in the flow of speech. While they are fully alive, in other words, while they are functional at every point, they can keep themselves at a psychological distance from their neighbours. As they gradually lose much of their life, they fall back into the embrace of the sentence as a whole and the sequence of independent words regains the importance it had in part transferred to the crystallized groups of elements. Speech is thus constantly tightening and loosening its sequences. In its highly integrated forms (Latin, Eskimo) the "energy" of sequence is largely locked up in complex word formations, it becomes transformed into a kind of potential energy that may not be released for millennia. In its more analytic forms (Chinese, English). This energy is mobile, ready to hand for such service as we demand of it.

There can be little doubt that stress has frequently played a controlling influence in the formation of element-groups or complex words out of certain sequences in the sentence. Such an English word as withstand is merely an old sequence with stand, i.e., "against stand," in which the unstressed adverb was permanently drawn to the following verb and lost its independence as a significant element.

In the same way French futures of the type irai "(I) shall go" are but the resultants of a coalescence of originally independent words: ir a'i "to-go I-have," under the influence of a unifying accent. But stress has done more than articulate or unify sequences that in their own right imply a syntactic relation. Stress is the most natural means at our disposal to emphasize a linguistic contrast, to indicate the major element in a sequence. Hence we need not be surprised to find that accent too, no less than sequence, may serve as the unaided symbol of certain relations.

Such a contrast as that of g' between ("one who goes between") and to go between' may be of quite secondary origin in English, but there is every reason to believe that analogous distinctions have prevailed at all times in linguistic history. A sequence like see' man might imply some type of relation in which see qualifies the following word, hence "a seeing man" or "a seen (or visible) man," or is its predication, hence "the man sees" or "the man is seen," while a sequence like see man' might indicate that the accented word in some way limits the application of the first, say as direct object, hence "to see a man" or "(he) sees the man."

Such alternations of relation, as symbolized by varying stresses, are important and frequent in a number of languages.

It is a somewhat venturesome and yet not an altogether unreasonable speculation that sees in word order and stress the primary methods for the expression of all syntactic relations and looks upon the present relational value of specific words and elements as but a secondary condition due to a transfer of values.

Thus, we may surmise that the Latin -m of words like feminam, dominum, and civem did not originally denote that "woman," "master," and "citizen" were objectively related to the verb of the proposition but indicated something far more concrete, that the objective relation was merely implied by the position or accent of the word (radical element) immediately preceding the -m, and that gradually, as its more concrete significance faded away, it took over a syntactic function that did not originally belong to it.

This sort of evolution by transfer is traceable in many instances. Thus, the of in an English phrase like "the law of the land" is now as colorless in content, as purely a relational indicator as the "genitive" suffix -is in the Latin lex urbis "the law of the city." We know, however, that it was originally an adverb of considerable concreteness of meaning, "away, moving from," and that the syntactic relation was originally expressed by the case form of the second noun.

As the case form lost its vitality, the adverb took over its function. If we are actually justified in assuming that the expression of all syntactic relations is ultimately traceable to these two unavoidable, dynamic features of speech — sequence and stress — an interesting thesis results: — All of the actual content of speech, its clusters of vocalic and consonantal sounds, is in origin limited to the concrete; relations were originally not expressed in outward form but were merely implied and articulated with the help of order and rhythm.

In other words, relations were intuitively felt and could only "leak out" with the help of dynamic factors that themselves move on an intuitional plane. There is a special method for the expression of relations that has been so often evolved in the history of language that we must glance at it for a moment. This is the method of "concord" or of like signaling. It is based on the same principle as the password or label.

All persons or objects that answer to the same countersign or that bear the same imprint are thereby stamped as somehow related. It makes little difference, once they are so stamped, where they are to be found or how they behave themselves. They are known to belong together. We are familiar with the principle of concord in Latin and Greek.

Many of us have been struck by such relentless rhymes as vidi illum bonum dominum "I saw that good master" or quarum dearum saevarum "of which stern goddesses." Not that sound-echo, whether in the form of rhyme or of alliteration is necessary to concord, though in its most typical and original forms concord is nearly always accompanied by sound repetition.

The essence of the principle is simply this, that words (elements) that belong together, particularly if they are syntactic equivalents or are related in like fashion to another word or element, are outwardly marked by the same or functionally equivalent affixes. The application of the principle varies considerably according to the genius of the particular language.

In Latin and Greek, for instance, there is concord between noun and qualifying word (adjective or demonstrative) as regards gender, number, and case, between verb and subject only as regards number, and no concord between verb and object. In Chinook there is a more far-reaching concord between noun, whether subject or object, and verb. Every noun is classified according to five categories — masculine, feminine, neuter, dual, and plural. "Woman" is feminine, "sand" is neuter, "table" is masculine.

If, therefore, I wish to say "The woman put the sand on the table," I must place in the verb certain class or gender prefixes that accord with corresponding noun prefixes. The sentence reads then, "The (fem.)-woman she (fem.)-it (neut.)-it (masc.)-on-put the (neut.)-sand the (masc.)-table." If "sand" is qualified as "much" and "table" as "large," these new ideas are expressed as abstract nouns, each with its inherent class-prefix ("much" is neuter or feminine, "large" is masculine) and with a possessive prefix referring to the qualified noun.

ROLE OF GRAMMAR

Adjective thus calls to noun, noun to verb. "The woman put much sand on the large table," therefore, takes the form: "The (fem.)-woman she (fem.)-it (neut.)-it (masc.)-on-put the (fem.) -thereof (neut.) -quantity the (neut.)-sand the (masc.)-thereof (masc.)argeness the (masc.)-table." The classification of "table" as masculine is thus three times insisted on — in the noun, in the adjective, and in the verb.

In the Bantu languages, the principle of concord works very much as in Chinook. In them also nouns are classified into a number of categories and are brought into relation with adjectives, demonstratives, relative pronouns, and verbs by means of prefixed elements that call off the class and make up a complex system of concordances.

In such a sentence as "That fierce lion who came here is dead," the class of "lion," which we may call the animal class, would be referred to by concording prefixes no less than six times, — with the demonstrative ("that"), the qualifying adjective, the noun itself, the relative pronoun,- the subjective prefix to the verb of the relative clause, and the subjective prefix to the verb of the main clause ("is dead").

We recognize in this insistence on external clarity of reference the same spirit as moves in the more familiar illum bonum dominum. Psychologically the methods of sequence and accent lie at the opposite pole to that of concord. Where they are all for implication, for subtlety of feeling, concord is impatient of the least ambiguity but must have its well-certificated tags at every turn. Concord tends to dispense with order. In Latin and Chinook the independent words are free in position, less so in Bantu.

In both Chinook and Bantu, however, the methods of concord and order are equally important for the differentiation of subject and object, as the classifying verb prefixes refer to subject, object, or indirect object according to the relative position they occupy. These examples again bring home to us the significant fact that at some point or other order asserts itself in every language as the most fundamental of relating principles.

The observant reader has probably been surprised that all this time we have had so little to say of the timehonored "parts of speech." The reason for this is not far to seek. Our conventional classification of words into parts of speech is only a vague, wavering approximation to a consistently worked out inventory of experience.

]We imagine, to begin with, that all "verbs" are inherently concerned with action as such, that a "noun" is the name of some definite object or personality that can be pictured by the mind, that all qualities are necessarily expressed by a definite group of words to which we may appropriately apply the term "adjective." As soon as we test our vocabulary, we discover that the parts of speech are far from corresponding to so simple an analysis of reality.

We say "it is red" and define "red" as a quality-word or adjective. We should consider it strange to think of an equivalent of "is red" in which the whole predication (adjective and verb of being) is conceived of as a verb in precisely the same way in which we think of "extends" or "lies" or "sleeps" as a verb. Yet as soon as we give the "durative" notion of being red an inceptive or transitional turn, we can avoid the parallel form "it becomes red, it turns red" and say "it reddens."

No one denies that "reddens" is as good a verb as "sleeps" or even "walks." Yet "it is red" is related to "it reddens" very much as is "he stands" to "he stands up" or "he rises." It is merely a matter of English or of general Indo-European idiom that we cannot say "it reds" in the sense of "it is red." There are hundreds of languages that can. Indeed there are many that can express what we should call an adjective only by making a participle out of a verb.

"Red" in such languages is merely a derivative "being red," as our "sleeping" or "walking" are derivatives of primary verbs. Just as we can verbify the idea of a quality in such cases as "reddens," so we can represent a quality or an action to ourselves as a thing. We speak of "the height of a building" or "the fall of an apple" quite as though these ideas were parallel to "the roof of a building" or "the skin of an apple," forgetting that the nouns (height, fall) have not ceased to indicate a quality and an act when we have made them speak with the accent of mere objects.

And just as there are languages that make verbs of the great mass of adjectives, so there are others that make nouns of them. In Chinook, as we have seen, "the big table" is "the-table its-bigness"; in Tibetan the same idea may be expressed by "the table of bigness," very much as we may say "a man of wealth" instead of "a rich man."

But are there not certain ideas that it is impossible to render except by way of such and such parts of speech? What can be done with the "to" of "he came to the house"? Well, we can say "he reached the house" and dodge the preposition altogether, giving the verb a nuance that absorbs the idea of local relation carried by the "to." But let us insist on giving independence to this idea of local relation. Must we not then hold to the preposition? No, we can make a noun of it.

We can say something like "he reached the proximity of the house" or "he reached the house-locality." Instead of saying "he looked into the glass" we may say "he scrutinized the glass-interior." Such expressions are stilted in English because they do not easily fit into our formal grooves, but in language after language we find that local relations are expressed in just this way.

The local relation is nominalized. And so we might go on examining the various parts of speech and showing how they not merely grade into each other but are to an astonishing degree actually convertible into each other. The upshot of such an examination would be to feel convinced that the "part of speech" reflects not so much our intuitive analysis of reality as our ability to compose that reality into a variety of formal patterns.

A part of speech outside of the limitations of syntactic form is but a will o' the wisp. For this reason no logical scheme of the parts of speech — their number, nature, and necessary confines — is of the slightest interest to the linguist. Each language has its own scheme. Yet we must not be too destructive. It is well to remember that speech consists of a series of propositions. There must be something to talk about and something must be said about this subject of discourse once it is selected. This distinction is of such fundamental importance that the vast majority of languages have emphasized it by creating some sort of formal barrier between the two terms of the proposition.

The subject of discourse is a noun. As the most common subject of discourse is either a person or a thing, the noun clusters about concrete concepts of that order. As the thing predicated of a subject is generally an activity in the widest sense of the word, a passage from one moment of existence to another, the form which has been set aside for the business of predicating, in other words, the verb, clusters about concepts of activity.

No language wholly fails to distinguish noun and verb, though in particular cases the nature of the distinction may be an elusive one. It is different with the other parts of speech. Not one of them is imperatively required for the life of language.

Chapter 7

Effect of Languages

RELATIONSHIP AMONG LANGUAGES

Languages, like cultures, are rarely sufficient unto themselves. The necessities of intercourse bring the speakers of one language into direct or indirect contact with those of neighboring or culturally dominant languages. The intercourse may be friendly or hostile.

It may move on the humdrum plane of business and trade relations or it may consist of a borrowing or interchange of spiritual goods — art, science, religion. It would be difficult to point to a completely isolated language or dialect, least of all among the primitive peoples. The tribe is often so small that intermarriages with alien tribes that speak other dialects or even totally unrelated languages are not uncommon.

It may even be doubted whether intermarriage, intertribal trade, and general cultural interchanges are not of greater relative significance on primitive levels than on our own. Whatever the degree or nature of contact between neighboring peoples, it is generally sufficient to lead to some kind of linguistic interinfluencing. Frequently the influence runs heavily in one direction.

The language of a people that is looked upon as a centre of culture is naturally far more likely to exert an appreciable influence on other languages spoken in its vicinity than to be influenced by them. Chinese has flooded the vocabularies of Corean, Japanese, and Annamite for centuries, but has received nothing in return. In the Western Europe of medieval and modern times French has exercised a similar, though probably a less overwhelming, influence. English borrowed an immense number of words from the French of the Norman invaders, later also from the court French of Isle de France, appropriated a certain number of affixed elements of derivational value (e.g., -ess of princess, -ard of drunkard, -ty of royalty), may have been somewhat stimulated in its general analytic drift by contact with French, and even allowed French to modify its phonetic pattern slightly (e.g., initial v and j in words like veal and judge; in words of Anglo-Saxon origin v and j can only occur after vowels, e.g., over, hedge). But English has exerted practically no influence on French.

The simplest kind of influence that one language may exert on another is the "borrowing" of words. When there is cultural borrowing there is always the likelihood that the associated words may be borrowed too. When the early Germanic peoples of northern Europe first learned of wine-culture and of paved streets from their commercial or warlike contact with the Romans, it was only natural that they should adopt the Latin words for the strange beverage (vinum, English wine, German Wein) and the unfamiliar type of road (strata [via], English street, German Strasse).

Later, when Christianity was introduced into England, a number of associated words, such as bishop and angel, found their way into English. And so the process has continued uninterruptedly down to the present day, each cultural wave bringing to the language a new deposit of loanwords. The careful study of such loan-words constitutes an interesting commentary on the history of culture. One can almost estimate the role which various peoples have played in the development and spread of cultural ideas by taking note of the extent to which their vocabularies have filtered into those of other peoples.

When we realise that an educated Japanese can hardly frame a single literary sentence without the use of Chinese resources, that to this day Siamese and Burmese and Cambodgian bear the unmistakable imprint of dhism centuries ago, or that whether we argue for or against the teaching of Latin and Greek our argument is sure to be studded with words that have come to us from Rome and Athens, we get some inkling of what early Chinese culture and Buddhism and classical Mediterranean civilization have meant in the world's history.

There are just five languages that have had an overwhelming significance as carriers of culture. They are classical Chinese, Sanskrit, Arabic, Greek, and Latin. In comparison with these even such culturally important languages as Hebrew and French sink into a secondary position. It is a little disappointing to learn that the general cultural influence of English has so far been all but negligible. The English language itself is spreading because the English have colonized immense territories.

But there is nothing to show that it is anywhere entering into the lexical heart of other languages as French has colored the English complexion or as Arabic has permeated Persian and Turkish. This fact alone is significant of the power of nationalism, cultural as well as political, during the last century. There are now psychological resistances to borrowing, or rather to new sources of borrowing that were not greatly alive in the Middle Ages or during the Renaissance.

Are there resistances of a more intimate nature to the borrowing of words? It is generally assumed that the nature and extent of borrowing depend entirely on the historical facts of culture relation; that if German, for instance, has borrowed less copiously than English from Latin and French it is only because Germany has had less intimate relations than England with the culture spheres of classical Rome and France.

This is true to a considerable extent, but it is not the whole truth. We must not exaggerate the physical importance of the Norman invasion nor underrate the significance of the fact that Germany's central geographical position made it peculiarly sensitive to French influences all through the Middle Ages, to humanistic influences in the latter fifteenth and early sixteenth centuries, and again to the powerful French influences of the seventeenth and eighteenth centuries.

It seems very probable that the psychological attitude of the borrowing language itself towards linguistic material has much to do with its receptivity to foreign words. English has long been striving for the completely unified, unanalyzed word, regardless of whether it is monosyllabic or polysyllabic.

WORD GENERALISM

Such words as credible, certitude, intangible are entirely welcome in English because each represents a unitary, well-nuanced idea and because their formal analysis (cred-ible, certitude, in-tang-ible) is not a necessary act of the unconscious mind (cred-, cert-, and tang- have no real existence in English comparable to that of good- in goodness).

A word like intangible, once it is acclimated, is nearly as simple a psychological entity as any radical monosyllable (say vague, thin, grasp). In German, however, polysyllabic words strive to analyse themselves into significant elements. Hence vast numbers of French and Latin words, borrowed at the height of certain cultural influences, could not maintain themselves in the language.

Latin-German words like kredibel "credible" and French-German words like reussieren "to succeed" offered nothing that the unconscious mind could assimilate to its customary method of feeling and handling words. It is as though this unconscious mind said: "I am perfectly willing to accept *kredibel* if you will just tell me what you mean by *kred-*."

Hence German has generally found it easier to create new words out of its own resources, as the necessity for them arose. The psychological contrast between English and German as regards the treatment of foreign material is a contrast that may be studied in all parts of the world. The Athabaskan languages of America are spoken by peoples that have had astonishingly varied cultural contacts, yet nowhere do we find that an Athabaskan dialect has borrowed at all freely from a neighboring language.

These languages have always found it easier to create new words by compounding afresh elements ready to hand. They have for this reason been highly resistant to receiving the linguistic impress of the external cultural experiences of their speakers. Cambodgian and Tibetan offer a highly instructive contrast in their reaction to Sanskrit influence. Both are analytic languages, each totally different from the highlywrought, inflective language of India. Cambodgian is isolating, but, unlike Chinese, it contains many polysyllabic words whose etymological analysis does not matter. Like English, therefore, in its relation to French and Latin, it welcomed immense numbers of Sanskrit loan-words, many of which are in common use to-day.

There was no psychological resistance to them. Classical Tibetan literature was a slavish adaptation of Hindu Buddhist literature and nowhere has Buddhism implanted itself more firmly than in Tibet, yet it is strange how few Sanskrit words have found their way into the language. Tibetan was highly resistant to the polysyllabic words of Sanskrit because they could not automatically fall into significant syllables, as they should have in order to satisfy the Tibetan feeling for form. Tibetan was therefore driven to translating the great majority of these Sanskrit words into native equivalents.

The Tibetan craving for form was satisfied, though the literally translated foreign terms must often have done violence to genuine Tibetan idiom. Even the proper names of the Sanskrit originals were carefully translated, element for element, into Tibetan; e.g., Suryagarbha "Sun-bosomed" was carefully Tibetanized into Nyi-mai snying-po "Sun-of heart-the, the heart (or essence) of the sun." The study of how a language reacts to the presence of foreign words – rejecting them, translating them, or freely accepting them – may throw much valuable light on its innate formal tendencies.

The borrowing of foreign words always entails their phonetic modification. There are sure to be foreign sounds or accentual peculiarities that do not fit the native phonetic habits. They are then so changed as to do as little violence as possible to these habits. Frequently we have phonetic compromises. Such an English word as the recently introduced camouflage, as now ordinarily pronounced, corresponds to the typical phonetic usage of neither English nor French.

The aspirated k, the obscure vowel of the second syllable, the precise quality of the l and of the last a, and, above ail, the strong accent on the first syllable, are all the results of unconscious assimilation to our English habits of pronunciation.

They differentiate our camouflage clearly from the same word as pronounced by the French. On the other hand, the long, heavy vowel in the third syllable and the final position of the "zh" sound (like z in azure) are distinctly un-English, just as, in Middle English, the initial j and v must have been felt at first as not strictly in accord with English usage, though the strangeness has worn off by now. In all four of these cases — initial j, initial v, final "zh," and unaccented a of father — English has not taken on a new sound but has merely extended the use of an old one.

Occasionally a new sound is introduced, but it is likely to melt away before long. In Chaucer's day the old Anglo-Saxon ü (written y) had long become unrounded to i, but a new set of ü-vowels had come in from the French (in such words as due, value, nature). The new ü did not long hold its own; it became diphthongized to iu and was amalgamated with the native iw of words like new and slew. Eventually this diphthong appears as yu, with change of stress — dew (from Anglo-Saxon deaw) like due (Chaucerian dü). Facts like these show how stubbornly a language resists radical tampering with its phonetic pattern.

Nevertheless, we know that languages do influence each other in phonetic respects, and that quite aside from the taking over of foreign sounds with borrowed words. One of the most curious facts that linguistics has to note is the occurrence of striking phonetic parallels in totally unrelated or very remotely related languages of a restricted geographical area. These parallels become especially impressive when they are seen contrastively from a wide phonetic perspective. Here are a few examples.

The Germanic languages as a whole have not developed nasalized vowels. Certain Upper German (Suabian) dialects, however, have now nasalized vowels in lieu of the older vowel + nasal consonant (n). Is it only accidental that these dialects are spoken in proximity to French, which makes abundant use of nasalized vowels? Again, there are certain general phonetic features that mark off Dutch and Flemish in contrast, say, to North German and Scandinavian dialects.

One of these is the presence of unaspirated voiceless stops (p, t, k), which have a precise, metallic quality reminiscent of the corresponding French sounds, but which contrast with the stronger, aspirated stops of English, North German, and Danish.

Even if we assume that the unaspirated stops are more archaic, that they are the unmodified descendants of the old Germanic consonants, is it not perhaps a significant historical fact that the Dutch dialects, neighbours of French, were inhibited from modifying these consonants in accordance with what seems to have been a general Germanic phonetic drift?

Even more striking than these instances is the peculiar resemblance, in certain special phonetic respects, of Russian and other Slavic languages to the unrelated Ural-Altaic languages of the Volga region. The peculiar, dull vowel, for instance, known in Russian as "yeri" has Ural-Altaic analogues, but is entirely wanting in Germanic, Greek, Armenian, and IndoIranian, the nearest Indo-European congeners of Slavic.

We may at least suspect that the Slavic vowel is not historically unconnected with its Ural-Altaic parallels. One of the most puzzling cases of phonetic parallelism is afforded by a large number of American Indian languages spoken west of the Rockies.

Even at the most radical estimate there are at least four totally unrelated linguistic stocks represented in the region from southern Alaska to central California. Nevertheless all, or practically all, the languages of this immense area have some important phonetic features in common.

Chief of these is the presence of a "glottalized" series of stopped consonants of very distinctive formation and of quite unusual acoustic effect. In the northern part of the area all the languages, whether related or not, also possess various voiceless l-sounds and a series of "velar" (backguttural) stopped consonants which are etymologically distinct from the ordinary k-series. It is difficult to believe that three such peculiar phonetic features as I have mentioned could have evolved independently in neighboring groups of languages.

How are we to explain these and hundreds of similar phonetic convergences? In particular cases we may really be dealing with archaic similarities due to a genetic relationship that it is beyond our present power to demonstrate. But this interpretation will not get us far.

It must be ruled entirely out of court, for instance, in two of the three European examples I have instanced; both nasalized vowels and the Slavic "yeri" are demonstrably of secondary origin in Indo-European. However we envisage the process in detail, we cannot avoid the inference that there is a tendency for speech sounds or certain distinctive manners of articulation to spread over a continuous area in somewhat the same way that elements of culture ray out from a geographical centre.

We may suppose that individual variations arising at linguistic borderlands — whether by the unconscious suggestive influence of foreign speech habits or by the actual transfer of foreign sounds into the speech of bilingual individuals — have gradually been incorporated into the phonetic drift of a language.

So long as its main phonetic concern is the preservation of its sound patterning, not of its sounds as such, there is really no reason why a language may not unconsciously assimilate foreign sounds that have succeeded in worming their way into its gamut of individual variations, provided always that these new variations (or reinforced old variations) are in the direction of the native drift.

A simple illustration will throw light on this conception. Let us suppose that two neighboring and unrelated languages, A and B, each possess voiceless lsounds (compare Welsh ll). We surmise that this is not an accident. Perhaps comparative study reveals the fact that in language A the voiceless l-sounds correspond to a sibilant series in other related languages, that an old alternation s: sh has been shifted to the new alternation I (voiceless): s. Does it follows that the voiceless l of language

B has had the same history? Not in the least. Perhaps B has a strong tendency toward audible breath release at the end of a word, so that the final l, like a final vowel, was originally followed by a marked aspiration. Individuals perhaps tended to anticipate a little the voiceless release and to "unvoice" the latter part of the final l-sound (very much as the l of English words like felt tends to be partly voiceless in anticipation of the voicelessness of the t).

Yet this final l with its latent tendency to unvoicing might never have actually developed into a fully voiceless l had not the presence of voiceless l-sounds in A acted as an unconscious stimulus or suggestive push toward a more radical change in the line of B's own drift. Once the final voiceless l emerged, its alternation in related words with medial voiced l is very likely to have led to its analogical spread. The result would be that both A and B have an important phonetic trait in common.

Eventually their phonetic systems, judged as mere assemblages of sounds, might even become completely assimilated to each other, though this is an extreme case hardly ever realized in practice. The highly significant thing about such phonetic interinfluencings is the strong tendency of each language to keep its phonetic pattern intact. So long as the respective alignments of the similar sounds is different, so long as they have differing "values" and "weights" in the unrelated languages, these languages cannot be said to have diverged materially from the line of their inherent drift.

In phonetics, as in vocabulary, we must be careful not to exaggerate the importance of interlinguistic influences. I have already pointed out in passing that English has taken over a certain number of morphological elements from French. English also uses a number of affixes that are derived from Latin and Greek.

Some of these foreign elements, like the -ize of materialize or the -able of breakable, are even productive to-day. Such examples as these are hardly true evidences of a morphological influence exerted by one language on another. Setting aside the fact that they belong to the sphere of derivational concepts and do not touch the central morphological problem of the expression of relational ideas, they have added nothing to the structural peculiarities of our language.

English was already prepared for the relation of pity to piteous by such a native pair as luck and lucky; material and materialize merely swelled the ranks of a form pattern familiar from such instances as wide and widen. In other words, the morphological influence exerted by foreign languages on English, if it is to be gauged by such examples as I have cited, is hardly different in kind from the mere borrowing of words. The introduction of the suffix -ize made hardly more difference to the essential build of the language than did the mere fact that it incorporated a given number of words.

FUTURE OF ENGLISH

Had English evolved a new future on the model of the synthetic future in French or had it borrowed from Latin and Greek their employment of reduplication as a functional device (Latin tango: tetigi; Greek leipo: leloipa), we should have the right to speak of true morphological influence. But such far-reaching influences are not demonstrable. Within the whole course of the history of the English language we can hardly point to one important morphological change that was not determined by the native drift, though here and there we may surmise that this drift was hastened a little by the suggestive influence of French forms.

It is important to realise the continuous, self-contained morphological development of English and the very modest extent to which its fundamental build has been affected by influences from without. The history of the English language has sometimes been represented as though it relapsed into a kind of chaos on the arrival of the Normans, who proceeded to play nine-pins with the Anglo-Saxon tradition.

Students are more conservative today. That a far-reaching analytic development may take place without such external foreign influence as English was subjected to is clear from the history of Danish, which has gone even further than English in certain leveling tendencies. English may be conveniently used as an a fortiori test. It was flooded with French loan-words during the later Middle Ages, at a time when its drift toward the analytic type was especially strong. It was therefore changing rapidly both within and on the surface.

The wonder, then, is not that it took on a number of external morphological features, mere accretions on its concrete inventory, but that, exposed as it was to remolding influences, it remained so true to its own type and historic drift. The experience gained from the study of the English language is strengthened by all that we know of documented linguistic history. Nowhere do we find any but superficial morphological interinfluencings.

We may infer one of several things from this: – That a really serious morphological influence is not, perhaps, impossible, but that its operation is so slow that it has hardly ever had the chance to incorporate itself in the relatively small portion of linguistic history that lies open to inspection; or that there are certain favorable conditions that make for profound morphological disturbances from without, say a peculiar instability of linguistic type or an unusual degree of cultural contact, conditions that do not happen to be realized in our documentary material; or, finally, that we have not the right to assume that a language may easily exert a remolding morphological influence on another.

Meanwhile we are confronted by the baffling fact that important traits of morphology are frequently found distributed among widely differing languages within a large area, so widely differing, indeed, that it is customary to consider them genetically unrelated. Sometimes we may suspect that the resemblance is due to a mere convergence that a similar morphological feature has grown up independently in unrelated languages.

Yet certain morphological distributions are too specific in character to be so lightly dismissed. There must be some historical factor to account for them. Now it should be remembered that the concept of a "linguistic stock" is never definitive in an exclusive sense. We can only say, with reasonable certainty, that such and such languages are descended from a common source, but we cannot say that such and such other languages are not genetically related. All we can do is to say that the evidence for relationship is not cumulative enough to make the inference of common origin absolutely necessary.

May it not be, then, that many instances of morphological similarity between divergent languages of a restricted area are merely the last vestiges of a community of type and phonetic substance that the destructive work of diverging drifts has now made unrecognizable? There is probably still enough lexical and morphological resemblance between modern English and Irish to enable us to make out a fairly conclusive case for their genetic relationship on the basis of the present-day descriptive evidence alone.

It is true that the case would seem weak in comparison to the case that we can actually make with the help of the historical and the comparative data that we possess. It would not be a bad case nevertheless. In another two or three millennia, however, the points of resemblance are likely to have become so obliterated that English and Irish, in the absence of all but their own descriptive evidence, will have to be set down as "unrelated" languages.

They will still have in common certain fundamental morphological features, but it will be difficult to know how to evaluate them. Only in the light of the contrastive perspective afforded by still more divergent languages, such as Basque and Finnish, will these vestigial resemblances receive their true historic value. I cannot but suspect that many of the more significant distributions of morphological similarities are to be explained as just such vestiges.

The theory of "borrowing" seems totally inadequate to explain those fundamental features of structure, hidden away in the very core of the linguistic complex, that have been pointed out as common, say, to Semitic and Hamitic, to the various Soudanese languages, to Malayo-Polynesian and Mon-Khmer and Munda, to Athabaskan and Tlingit and Haida. We must not allow ourselves to be frightened away by the timidity of the specialists, who are often notably lacking in the sense of what I have called "contrastive perspective." Attempts have sometimes been made to explain the distribution of these fundamental structural features by the theory of diffusion. We know that myths, religious ideas, types of social organization, industrial devices, and other features of culture may spread from point to point, gradually making themselves at home in cultures to which they were at one time alien. We also know that words may be diffused no less freely than cultural elements, that sounds also may be "borrowed," and that even morphological elements may be taken over. We may go further and recognize that certain languages have, in all probability, taken on structural features owing to the suggestive influence of neighboring languages.

Chapter 8

Role of Language and Literature

WRITTEN ENGLISH

A version of the language almost universally agreed upon by educated English speakers around the world is called formal written English. It takes virtually the same form no matter where in the English-speaking world it is written. In spoken English, by contrast, there are a vast number of differences between dialects, accents, and varieties of slang, colloquial and regional expressions. In spite of this, local variations in the formal written version of the language are quite limited, being restricted largely to the spelling differences between British and American English.

Languages are more to us than systems of thought transference. They are invisible garments that drape themselves about our spirit and give a predetermined form to all its symbolic expression. When the expression is of unusual significance, we call it literature. Art is so personal an expression that we do not like to feel that it is bound to predetermined form of any sort.

The possibilities of individual expression are infinite, language in particular is the most fluid of mediums. Yet some limitation there must be to this freedom, some resistance of the medium. In great art there is the illusion of absolute freedom. The formal restraints imposed by the material — paint, black and white, marble, piano tones, or whatever it may be — are not perceived; it is as though there were a limitless margin of elbow-room between the artist's fullest utilization of form and the most that the material is innately capable of.

The artist has intuitively surrendered to the inescapable tyranny of the material, made its brute nature fuse easily with his conception.

The material "disappears" precisely because there is nothing in the artist's conception to indicate that any other material exists. For the time being, he, and we with him, move in the artistic medium as a fish moves in the water, oblivious of the existence of an alien atmosphere. No sooner, however, does the artist transgress the law of his medium than we realise with a start that there is a medium to obey.

Language is the medium of literature as marble or bronze or clay are the materials of the sculptor. Since every language has its distinctive peculiarities, the innate formal limitations — and possibilities — of one literature are never quite the same as those of another. The literature fashioned out of the form and substance of a language has the colour and the texture of its matrix.

The literary artist may never be conscious of just how he is hindered or helped or otherwise guided by the matrix, but when it is a question of translating his work into another language, the nature of the original matrix manifests itself at once. All his effects have been calculated, or intuitively felt, with reference to the formal "genius" of his own language; they cannot be carried over without loss or modification. Croce is therefore perfectly right in saying that a work of literary art can never be translated.

Nevertheless literature does get itself translated, sometimes with astonishing adequacy. This brings up the question whether in the art of literature there are not intertwined two distinct kinds or levels of art — a generalized, non-linguistic art, which can be transferred without loss into an alien linguistic medium, and a specifically linguistic art that is not transferable. I believe the distinction is entirely valid, though we never get the two levels pure in practice.

Literature moves in language as a medium, but that medium comprises two layers, the latent content of language — our intuitive record of experience — and the particular conformation of a given language — the specific how of our record of experience. Literature that draws its sustenance mainly — never entirely — from the lower level, say a play of Shakespeare's, is translatable without too great a loss of character. If it moves in the upper rather than in the lower level — a fair example is a lyric of Swinburne's — it is as good as untranslatable. Both types of literary expression may be great or mediocre.

There is really no mystery in the distinction. It can be clarified a little by comparing literature with science. A scientific truth is impersonal, in its essence it is untinctured by the particular linguistic medium in which it finds expression. It can as readily deliver its message in Chinese as in English.

Nevertheless it must have some expression, and that expression must needs be a linguistic one. Indeed the apprehension of the scientific truth is itself a linguistic process, for thought is nothing but language denuded of its outward garb. The proper medium of scientific expression is therefore a generalized language that may be defined as a symbolic algebra of which all known languages are translations.

One can adequately translate scientific literature because the original scientific expression is itself a translation. Literary expression is personal and concrete, but this does not mean that its significance is altogether bound up with the accidental qualities of the medium.

A truly deep symbolism, for instance, does not depend on the verbal associations of a particular language but rests securely on an intuitive basis that underlies all linguistic expression. The artist's "intuition," to use Croce's term, is immediately fashioned out of a generalized human experience — thought and feeling — of which his own individual experience is a highly personalized selection.

The thought relations in this deeper level have no specific linguistic vesture; the rhythms are free, not bound, in the first instance, to the traditional rhythms of the artist's language. Certain artists whose spirit moves largely in the non-linguistic (better, in the generalized linguistic) layer even find a certain difficulty in getting themselves expressed in the rigidly set terms of their accepted idiom. One feels that they are unconsciously striving for a generalized art language, a literary algebra, that is related to the sum of all known languages as a perfect mathematical symbolism is related to all the roundabout reports of mathematical relations that normal speech is capable of conveying.

Their art expression is frequently strained, it sounds at times like a translation from an unknown original — which, indeed, is precisely what it is. These artists — Whitmans and Brownings — impress us rather by the greatness of their spirit than the felicity of their art.

Their relative failure is of the greatest diagnostic value as an index of the pervasive presence in literature of a larger, more intuitive linguistic medium than any particular language. Nevertheless, human expression being what it is, the greatest — or shall we say the most satisfying — literary artists, the Shakespeares and Heines, are those who have known subconsciously to fit or trim the deeper intuition to the provincial accents of their daily speech. In them there is no effect of strain.

Their personal "intuition" appears as a completed synthesis of the absolute art of intuition and the innate, specialized art of the linguistic medium. With Heine, for instance, one is under the illusion that the universe speaks German. The material "disappears."

Every language is itself a collective art of expression. There is concealed in it a particular set of esthetic factors — phonetic, rhythmic, symbolic, morphological-which it does not completely share with any other language. These factors may either merge their potencies with those of that unknown, absolute language to which I have referred — this is·the method of Shakespeare and Heine — or they may weave a private, technical art fabric of their own, the innate art of the language intensified or sublimated.

The latter type, the more technically "literary" art of Swinburne and of hosts of delicate "minor" poets, is too fragile for endurance. It is built out of spiritualized material, not out of spirit. The successes of the Swinburnes are as valuable for diagnostic purposes as the semi-failures of the Brownings. They show to what extent literary art may lean on the collective art of the language itself.

The more extreme technical practitioners may so over-individualize this collective art as to make it almost unendurable, One is not always thankful to have one's flesh and blood frozen to ivory. An artist must utilize the native esthetic resources of his speech.

He may be thankful if the given palette of colours is rich, if the springboard is light. But he deserves no special credit for felicities that are the language's own. We must take for granted this language with all its qualities of flexibility or rigidity and see the artist's work in relation to it. A cathedral on the lowlands is higher than a stick on Mont Blanc.

In other words, we must not commit the folly of admiring a French sonnet because the vowels are more sonorous than our own or of condemning Nietzsche's prose because it harbors in its texture combinations of consonants that would affright on English soil. To so judge literature would be tantamount to loving "Tristan und Isolde" because one is fond of the timbre of horns. There are certain things that one language can do supremely well which it would be almost vain for another to attempt. Generally there are compensations.

The vocalism of English is an inherently drabber thing than the vowel scale of French, yet English compensates for this drawback by its greater rhythmical alertness. It is even doubtful if the innate sonority of a phonetic system counts for as much, as esthetic determinant, as the relations between the sounds, the total gamut of their similarities and contrasts. As long as the artist has the wherewithal to lay out his sequences and rhythms, it matters little what are the sensuous qualities of the elements of his material.

The phonetic groundwork of a language, however, is only one of the features that give its literature a certain direction. Far more important are its morphological peculiarities. It makes a great deal of difference for the development of style if the language can or cannot create compound words, if its structure is synthetic or analytic, if the words of its sentences have considerable freedom of position or are compelled to fall into a rigidly determined sequence. The major characteristics of style, in so far as style is a technical matter of the building and placing of words, are given by the language itself, quite as inescapably, indeed, as the general acoustic effect of verse is given by the sounds and natural accents of the language.

These necessary fundamentals of style are hardly felt by the artist to constrain his individuality of expression. They rather point the way to those stylistic developments that most suit the natural bent of the language. It is not in the least likely that a truly great style can seriously oppose itself to the basic form patterns of the language. It not only incorporates them, it builds on them.

The merit of such a style as W. H. Hudson's or George Moore's is that it does with ease and economy what the language is always trying to do. Carlylese, though individual and vigorous, is yet not style; it is a Teutonic mannerism. Nor is the prose of Milton and his contemporaries strictly English; it is semi-Latin done into magnificent English words.

It is strange how long it has taken the European literatures to learn that style is not an absolute, a something that is to be imposed on the language from Greek or Latin models, but merely the language itself, running in its natural grooves, and with enough of an individual accent to allow the artist's personality to be felt as a presence, not as an acrobat. We understand more clearly now that what is effective and beautiful in one language is a vice in another.

Latin and Eskimo, with their highly inflected forms, lend themselves to an elaborately periodic structure that would be boring in English. English allows, even demands, a looseness that would be insipid in Chinese. And Chinese, with its unmodified words and rigid sequences, has a compactness of phrase, a terse parallelism, and a silent suggestiveness that would be too tart, too mathematical, for the English genius.

While we cannot assimilate the luxurious periods of Latin nor the pointilliste style of the Chinese classics, we can enter sympathetically into the spirit of these alien techniques. I believe that any English poet of to-day would be thankful for the concision that a Chinese poetaster attains without effort. Here is an example: Wu-river stream mouth evening sun sink, North look Liao-Tung, not see home. Steam whistle several noise, sky-earth boundless, Float float one reed out Middle-Kingdom.

These twenty-eight syllables may be clumsily interpreted: "At the mouth of the Yangtsze River, as the sun is about to sink, I look north toward Liao-Tung but do not see my home. The steam-whistle shrills several times on the boundless expanse where meet sky and earth. The steamer, floating gently like a hollow reed, sails out of the Middle Kingdom." But we must not envy Chinese its terseness unduly.

Our more sprawling mode of expression is capable of its own beauties, and the more compact luxuriance of Latin style has its loveliness too. There are almost as many natural ideals of literary style as there are languages. Most of these are merely potential, awaiting the hand of artists who will never come. And yet in the recorded texts of primitive tradition and song there are many passages of unique vigour and beauty. The structure of the language often forces an assemblage of concepts that impresses us as a stylistic discovery. Single Algonkin words are like tiny imagist poems.

We must be careful not to exaggerate a freshness of content that is at least half due to our freshness of approach, but the possibility is indicated none the less of utterly alien literary styles, each distinctive with its disclosure of the search of the human spirit for beautiful form.

Probably nothing better illustrates the formal dependence of literature on language than the prosodic aspect of poetry. Quantitative verse was entirely natural to the Greeks, not merely because poetry grew up in connection with the chant and the dance, but because alternations of long and short syllables were keenly live facts in the daily economy of the language.

The tonal accents, which were only secondarily stress phenomena, helped to give the syllable its quantitative individuality. When the Greek metres were carried over into Latin verse, there was comparativly little strain, for Latin too was characterized by an acute awareness of quantitative distinctions. However, the Latin accent was more markedly stressed than that of Greek. Probably, therefore, the purely quantitative metres modeled after the Greek were felt as a shade more artificial than in the language of their origin. The attempt to cast English verse into Latin and Greek molds has never been successful. The dynamic basis of English is not quantity, but stress, the alternation of accented and unaccented syllables.

This fact gives English verse an entirely different slant and has determined the development of its poetic forms, is still responsible for the evolution of new forms. Neither stress nor syllabic weight is a very keen psychologic factor in the dynamics of French.

The syllable has great inherent sonority and does not fluctuate significantly as to quantity and stress. Quantitative or accentual metrics would be as artificial in French as stress metrics in classical Greek or quantitative or purely syllabic metrics in English. French prosody was compelled to develop on the basis of unit syllable-groups. Assonance, later rhyme, could not but prove a welcome, an all but necessary, means of articulating or sectioning the somewhat spineless flow of sonorous syllables.

English was hospitable to the French suggestion of rhyme, but did not seriously need it in its rhythmic economy. Hence rhyme has always been strictly subordinated to stress as a somewhat decorative feature and has been frequently dispensed with. It is no psychologic accident that rhyme came later into English than in French and is leaving it sooner. Chinese verse has developed along very much the same lines as French verse.

The syllable is an even more integral and sonorous unit than in French, while quantity and stress are too uncertain to form the basis of a metric system. Syllable-groups — so and so many syllables per rhythmic unit — and rhyme are therefore two of the controlling factors in Chinese prosody. The third factor, the alternation of syllables with level tone and syllables with inflected (rising or falling) tone, is peculiar to Chinese.

To summarize, Latin and Greek verse depends on the principle of contrasting weights; English verse, on the principle of contrasting stresses; French verse, on the principles of number and echo; Chinese verse, on the principles of number, echo, and contrasting pitches.

Each of these rhythmic systems proceeds from the unconscious dynamic habit of the language, falling from the lips of the folk. Study carefully the phonetic system of a language, above all its dynamic features, and you can tell what kind of a verse it has developed — or, if history has played pranks with its phychology, what kind of verse it should have developed and some day will.

Whatever be the sounds, accents, and forms of a language, however these lay hands on the shape of its literature, there is a subtle law of compensations that gives the artist space. If he is squeezed a bit here, he can swing a free arm there. And generally he has rope enough to hang himself with, if he must. It is not strange that this should be so. Language is itself the collective art of expression, a summary of thousands upon thousands of individual intuitions.

The individual goes lost in the collective creation, but his personal expression has left some trace in a certain give and flexibility that are inherent in all collective works of the human spirit. The language is ready, or can be quickly made ready, to define the artist's individuality. If no literary artist appears, it is not essentially because the language is too weak an instrument, it is because the culture of the people is not favorable to the growth of such personality as seeks a truly individual verbal expression.

LITERACY EVENTS

In this chapter we use a microethnographic approach to discourse analysis to illuminate issues of social identity in classroom language and literacy events. Social identity has many meanings. Traditionally, social identity has been used to refer to the social group to which an individuabelongs, such as an ethnic group, gender, racial group, economic class, and so on. Within a classroom, a student's social identity might also include membership in a reading group or a friendship group. A student might have a social identity as a "top student, " a "troublemaker, " a "teacher's pet, " and so on. Social identity has recently been used to describe more subtle, situated, and dynamic social relationships. Instead of fixed, predetermined, and stable, social identities (also described as social positions) are viewed as being constructed through the interactions people have with each other (sometimes referred to as social positioning) and as a consequence of the evolving social structures of social institutions.

In this we focus on how microethnographic analysis can contribute to a better understanding of the dynamics of social identity in and through classroom language and literacy events—that is, how microethnographic analysis can help theorize the dynamics of social identity and the relationship of social identity to classrooms and to literacy events and practices. Stated simply, we are interested in how participation in classroom language and literacy events affects "who you are" and how "who you are" affects your participation in classroom language and literacy events.

It is necessary to work back and forth across theoretical concerns, methodological issues, and findings and we have found this to be the case with regard to the discourse analysis of social identity in classroom language and literacy events. Therefore, we have organized this chapter to reflect the recursive processes involved in microethnographic discourse analysis. We take the reader through the recursive process, beginning with a discussion of theoretical and methodological issues (what we call Round 1).

We then shift to a microethnographic analysis of a storytelling event in a kindergarten, followed by a microethnographic analysis of three related events in a 6thgrade social studies/language arts lesson. We then return to a discussion of theoretical and methodological issues (what we call Round 2).

By organizing the chapter in this manner, we illustrate how a recursive process can identify new questions and issues to explore and how it can lead to reinterpretations of data. The organization of the chapter emphasizes the importance of recursive design as a part of the microethnographic discourse analysis of classroom language and literacy events.

SOCIAL IDENTITY

One way to view social identity is as an appellation indicating membership in a particular social group or a social position within a social institution or social group. Thus, social identity would include appellations such as Jew, woman, middle class, student, teacher, banker, parent, quarterback, vice president, or some combination of these. For some theorists, social identities such as these are similar to various roles that a person might assume, metaphorically acting out a role like an actor in a dramatic production, with the real person hidden underneath the roles.

At different times, a person/actor might act out different roles. However, other scholars reject the dualism implied in this view of social identity. They claim instead that social identity defines the person, even if those definitions are multiple and conflicting and vary across situations. There is no "real" person hiding underneath various roles, waiting to express itself.

There is no separation of the material existence of the body, social interaction, the social group, situation, social identity, and the person. How people interact with others, how people are located historically and geographically—these visible features of social life simultaneously define social identity and who and what people are. Thus, one does not merely act out the dramatalurgical role of being a Jew, a woman, and a teacher; in a particular situation one is a Jew, a woman, and a teacher.

So far the theoretical issues we have raised with regard to social identity concern the relationship between an appellation of social identity and cultural ideologies. However, the process of appellation itself is a complex, dynamic, and problematic one. What is meant by an appellation such as Jew, woman, and teacher changes and is negotiated, and the assignment of these social identity appellations and their meanings are often contested. For example, does the appellation of Jew mean membership in a religious, cultural, ethnic, or biological group? Who decides? How is a decision made? Is it only in some formal or legalistic process, well defined and bounded, or is it assigned through how people act and react to each other in a broad range of informal and everyday situations? When and where does the appellation apply?

Similar questions can and have been asked about the social identity of teacher. Is it just a job classification, or is it a social identity both within a social institution (school) and across social institutions? Does one maintain the social identity of teacher in one's family? In government? As a patient in health institutions? In romantic and sexual domains? Does the social identity of teacher depend on the existence of persons who take on the social identity of student? Does it require proximity of social processes defined as "teaching" and "learning"?

As the preceding questions suggest, part of the difficulty with treating social identity as fundamentally an appellation is that doing so obfuscates the social processes involved in the production, evolution, and use of social identity. Rather than focusing on labels per se, attention can be focused on the processes involved in labeling and on the functions that labels provide.

Among the functions labels provide are inclusion and exclusion (a member of the group or not a member of the group), backgrounding (a peripheral member of the group), designation of histories and social relationships, suppression (no existence of a social actor), impersonalizadon (representing someone or a group without the quality of being human), relationship (an identity based on a relationship to another), and abstraction (identity based on a quality associated with the person or group), among others.

The processes through which social identities are named and constituted are language processes; that is, it is through the use of language that people name, construct, contest, and negotiate social identities. Analysis of social identity, therefore, requires attention to language use. Building on Van Leeuwen's work, Reisigl and Wodak (2001) described how the process of predication is an essential part of the presentation of self and others. "Predication" is the very basic process and result of linguistically assigning qualities to persons, animals, objects, events, actions and social phenomena.

Through predication, persons, things, events and practices are specified and characterized with respect to quality, quantity, space, time and so on. Predications are linguistically more or less evaluative (deprecatory or appreciative), explicit or implicit and—like reference and argumentation—specific or vague/evasive.

Among other things, predicational strategies are mainly realised by specific forms of reference (based on explicit denotation as well as on more or less implicit connotation), by attributes (in the form of adjectives, appositions, prepositional phrases, relative clauses, conjunctional clauses, infinitive clauses and participial clauses or groups) by predicates or predicative nouns/adjectives/pronouns, by collocations, by explicit comparisons, *similes, metaphors* and other *rhetorical figures* (including *metonymies, hyperboles, litotes* and *euphemisms*) and by more or less implicit *allusions, evocations* and *presuppositions/implications*.

Labeling a social identity is a social and linguistic move, a move to establish a sense of permanence by establishing a shared (and named) category with presumably shared boundaries. The attempt to create a sense of permanence may apply to either the person being labeled or to the social structure from which the social identity was derived.

For example, when school officials label students as "Black," "white," "Hispanic," and so on, they are ascribing to students social identities intended to be permanent, and at the same time they are implicitly giving a sense of permanence to the social structure based on race and ethnicity. Of course, such moves may be contested.

Students may protest such labeling because it does not apply (e.g., they may have multiple racial-ethnic identities and therefore not fit any of the categories) or because they disagree with a social policy that organizes people in terms of racial-ethnic identities. This is merely to say that although labeling may attempt to give a set of social identities a sense of permanence, it does not necessarily mean that either those social identities, or the social structure from which they were derived, will be permanent.

Over time, the boundaries of an appellation may change (e.g., what counts as being "Black, " "white, " or "Hispanic" may change), the appellation itself may evolve and change, or, the social structure that generated the appellations might change (with the consequence of changing the meaningfulness and the use of the appellations of the social identities).

Beyond social identities with appellations are social identities that are not named. Consider a classroom in which the teacher has asked the students to sit in a group and read a poem silently. Assume that most of the students follow the teacher's directions but that a small number of students do not and that their behaviour is visible to many, if not all, of the students.

There is no extant appellation for this group of noncooperating students or for the others who observe them, yet their existence as two different social groups is evident as the teacher calls out "Those of you who aren't reading need to get going, and the rest of you need to put your eyes on the poem."

Such social identities may lack a sense of permanence but nonetheless be powerful in orienting social behaviour, assigning morality, and asserting a social structure. For example, by dividing the students into a group of cooperating students and a group of noncooperating students, the teacher is asserting a social structure based on a hierarchy of cooperative participation.

The noncooperating students have been positioned as errant, as operating outside of the moral bounds of the reading group, and as at risk of negative consequences because of their membership in that social group. These theoretical issues raise a series of methodological warrants, constraints, and complexities. Our discussion focuses attention on the processes involved in appellation; the relationship among social identity, social structure, cultural ideology, and personhood; and the tension between situated and evolving social identities and moves to promote permanence.

METHODOLOGICAL ISSUES

In this section we focus on three methodological issues: (a) the movement from the "givens" of social identity appellations as expressed in social theories to the processes of face-to-face interaction, and vice versa; (b) identification of the discourse processes involved in the production, evolution, and use of social identities; and (c) capturing, describing, and labeling social identities as they evolve within an event.

Among the most frequently used "givens" of social identity are the categories of race, ethnicity, gender, and class. These four categories are frequently treated as inherent to the human condition, as if they need no explanation as to what they are or how they are defined. In numerous studies, researchers begin with assigning these social identities to the people participating in the study.

Then, findings are related to these given categories of social identity. Consistent with our earlier theoretical discussion, we reject such an uncritical acceptance of these categories of social identity and at the same time reject the claims of neoconservatives who argue that race, ethnicity, gender, and class do not matter and in fact do not exist.

In brief, we hold that racial, ethnic, gender, and class identities are social constructions. These social constructions, however, are not ethereal; neither are they matters of whim that an individual can change, the way one changes one's necktie or brand of soap.

Rather, like social identitles in general, they are material; they are built into how people act and react to each other; into social and governmental policy; into the architecture of the buildings and open spaces we inhabit; into our social institutions of law, family, religion, business, health, education, science, and so on. They are also built into the literacy practices that dominate our social institutions, including schools. We argue that two of the dynamics that distinguish "given" social identities such as race, ethnicity, gender, and class from other identities, such as friend, good reader, author, problem child, and so on, are (a) the ubiquity and hegemony of the categories of race, gender, ethnicity, and class in so many countries across the continents and (b) the vehemence with which the categories of race, gender, ethnicity, and class are maintained and their sense of permanence (including the maintenance of the rationale for the accompanying inequalities, inequities, and suffering).

Yet, we would claim that even given the ubiquity and vehemence of the given categories of race, ethnicity, gender, and class, there has been resistance to these categories, and they have been evolving as a result of people's resistance to how these categories have been defined and of how people have lived their daily lives.

The difficulty for researchers is that "given" categories of social identity exist in the settings and situations being studied and in the traditions and protocols of research. Schools use given categories of race, gender, and class to describe students and teachers with a series of concomitant qualities. Sometimes they get these given categories from folk theories of social life, but others take them from the research and scholarly community.

Regardless, these given categories are part of the social scenes and social interactions being analyzed, and a discourse analysis needs to take account of these categories of social identity and that they are "given." Researchers engaged in microethnographic analysis must ask, "What do people make of these given categories?," in which make of refers to the construction and reconstruction of the given categories.

From a practical point of view, researchers can start with the given categories and bump them up against what people do with them, or they can start with how people interact with each other and how they constitute given categories. In either case, the constraint is to work within the setting and event and with the people involved. Consider these issues within the context of classroom language and literacy events. These events can be distinguished from nonclassroom language and literacy events by the presence of school discourse. Thus, writing a letter as part of a classroom lesson differs from writing a letter or telling a story at home or at work, because in the classroom the activity is surrounded and permeated by school discourse.

In writing a letter, the student is involved simultaneously in an immediately present pedagogic event and in an event involving the interaction of an author and an audience mediated through the production of a written text. Stated more simply, the student is interacting with the teacher and students in the classroom, and the student is interacting with the people who will be receiving the letter (the addressee).

Of course, it may be that there was never any intention to mail the letter, in which case the audience for the letter is an imaginary construction. Savvy students will recognize that in some classrooms they are really writing a letter to the teacher and, although they pretend to write the letter to some addressee they adjust the text they create accordingly.

Even so, there is still the premise of (a) the schooling context and immediate, face-to-face event and (b) the context of author-audience for the written or spoken text being produced or consumed. In our view, it is always the case that the immediate, schooling event always contextualizes the author-audience event, and this is so whether the author-audience event is authentic or an artifice—which is merely to state that an author-audience event (the writing of a letter, the telling of a story, the reading of a novel) is constructed within and through the immediate, face-to-face, pedagogic event.

The complex relationship between the immediate, face-to-face pedagogic event and the author-audience event results in complex explications of social identity work in classroom language and literacy events. We illustrate part of this complexity through an analysis of the storytelling of a student, Shannon, in a kindergarten classroom. In this classroom lesson, students volunteered to tell a story to their peers as a precursor to writing down their stories.

Shannon begins telling a story that is structured the way many previous stories in the class have been structured. She tells about an activity that she (the protagonist of the story) and the teacher did (lines 05–09). Although fictional, it has the characteristics of a narrative report. Then there are major silences (lines 10–19) that indicate a transition and separation between the first story and the second one.

The second story has some of the characteristics of a report, as if Shannon is telling about a sleepover party at her house. But the structure of her storytelling and her interaction with the audience make clear that the reporting is a weak artifice for identifying her friends in the classroom and entertaining her classmates by invoking a taboo topic (people sleeping with each other; lines 36–61).

She is improvising a structure, adapting the reporting structure, perhaps importing structures from other stories she has heard, and in so doing creating a new story structure (at least new to this class and setting). She continues her improvisation as she counts the amount of money her mother gave the students (lines 68–83), encouraged by the positive response of the students.

It may be that Shannon is building on call-and-response storytelling structures she has heard elsewhere, and she may be using structures from various children's counting books she has read. The map reveals a number of language processes she used in creating a series of social identities for herself and others through the use of extant language and literacy practices and through improvisation.

The table actually contains two parallel maps: The first traces the evolution of social identities of Shannon and her classmates within the narrative being told—that is, within the text world or situation model being created as the narrative is created, and the second map traces Shannon's social identity as a storyteller (the immediate face-to-face event).

The two maps parallel the theoretical construct just discussed; namely, that classroom language and literacy events often involve an immediate, face-to-face pedagogic event (which in this case is the interaction of Shannon with her peers and her teacher) and an author-audience event mediated through the creation of a text world (situation model).

In line 05 Shannon creates a two-person group, she and the teacher (linked through the use of various conjunctions). They are friends who do things outside of school, highly valued activities such as the teacher buying her a necklace and going to the park, all of which give Shannon special social status. Defining a group and affiliating with highly valued activities are two strategies for constructing a social identity and social position.

LANGUAGE DISCOURSE

We can "know" the real and represent it through language — offer an analogy of it, a mirrored reflection, so to speak. He established three primary criteria for such discourse. Discourse should be coherent — a whole consisting of interrelated parts; comprehensive — an exhaustive representation of the relevant parts and their relationships to themselves and to the whole; and simple — uncomplicated in its representation of truth by issues of contingency, locality, established opinion, or other matters that might blur the distinction between discourse and reality. In short, the world is and discourse should be compositional.

Plato's chief notion that meaning is produced by correlating language with the real continued to exert its influence long after his suggestion that Being was a totality of Ideal Forms. I only hinted at this rather complicated history of the transformation of "substance", discussing just enough, I hope, to suggest that the concept of "culture" in the late nineteenth and early twentieth centuries could be seen as a transformation of God-substance (as Burke would have put it), one taking over the discursive function of the ground or foundation that had previously been attributed to Scripture.

As such transformations, concepts of culture cannot help but contribute to the creation of the conditions they purport to describe. Cultures exist by virtue of their being believed to exist. They are a peculiar product of compositional discourse. When alternatives are available, it is impossible for an individual to make the distinctions and decisions that consistently would associate her or him with one culture rather than another unless that individual intentionally defers to a preconceived notion of cultural wholeness. Once that deferral takes place, however, something strange happens. First, the world divides up into two types of people, those who "belong" to our culture and those who do not. The way we actually behave and interpret then changes. We interpret the actions of those whom we presume to be "one of us" precisely as we would our own behaviour under the same conditions, as a set of systematic conformities to and deviations from the norm we ourselves project.

This mode of "cultural understanding" prevents us from even considering the possibility that the conditions affecting the other's behaviour may be quite different from those that would affect us. We presume to understand and so free ourselves to judge. Obviously, such a mode of understanding can be very efficient and therefore have considerable survival value for small groups of people living in similar conditions, and who thus actually say and do similar things for similar purposes.

As societies become more complex, however, maintaining the illusion of living under the same conditions — a requirement of cultural understanding — becomes more and more difficult. Laws have to become more abstract and generalized as behaviours become more diverse and the society's need to "transcend" particular differences becomes more acute. The less effective the sameness among individuals' activities and their aims and purposes becomes, the more consciously the society has to impose standards of unity if it is to maintain its old modes of interpretation and persuasion. There have been, of course, many strategies for imposing standards of unity.

Besides law, however, the standardization of language has been attempted the most aggressively. In this chapter I am particularly interested in a line of change that leads to the structural theories of language and the political and rhetorical paralysis associated with modernism and postmodernism. I'm not so much interested in historical correctness here, in the sense of an exposition of cause and effect, as I am in exposing the consistency of an assumption about the requirements of meaningful discourse – an assumption deriving from the Platonic distinction between reality and appearance that reduced power to force, opposed truth to opinion, and so eventually led toward the twentieth century's sense of human powerlessness within a relativistic universe. Church scholasticism following Augustine had put the world out of the epistemological loop.

To Augustine, the world as perceived was insignificant; the Bible, however, was "the canon" of "divinely inspired writings" that "could not have been said in any other way". Consider what this pronouncement implies. As a canon, the Bible is a closed system of writings. That the writings could contradict themselves or one another is, to Augustine, inconceivable.

As he exclaims when examining an apparent contradiction in Paul's first epistle to Timothy, "Does the Apostle contradict himself?" Of course, he cannot. It is not just that Paul speaks truth and, therefore, as with Plato's texts, that any apparent contradictions have to be resolved in favour of coherence; it is that Paul could not have spoken otherwise. Augustine, concerned about the apparent ineloquence of Biblical writings in comparison to pagan, declared that where "I do not understand these [Biblical writings] their eloquence appears to me to be less, but I do not doubt that it is like that eloquence I find in places where I do understand them".

By declaring that the Biblical authors could not have spoken otherwise, he implies that they could not have stylistically varied their words and still said the same thing, could not vary the part without substantially altering the whole. With this declaration, Augustine establishes the Bible as a closed system reflecting the cosmic totality, a unity of form and content, and therefore the standard of Truth and Beauty against which historically concrete beliefs and values are to be measured.

In short, with a gesture he created the grounds of a discursive tradition that would last more than a thousand years. During the Renaissance, however, the medieval assumption that the Bible alone could sufficiently ground discourse had begun to dissolve. As it did, rhetorical theory, which had received little attention after Augustine, again became a central intellectual concern.

The reasons for this renewed interest are, of course, multifold. Thomas M. Conley in Rhetoric in the European Tradition refers to two significant conditions in particular. The first is the internecine conflict both among Western Christians and between Rome and Constantinople. Something more than a mutual reference to Biblical authority was evidently required, and something less destructive than force of arms was urgently desired as a means toward resolving differences. Rhetoric seemed to be a practical, although hardly an ideal, instrument for peace.

The second change in condition was the radical revision of the past stimulated in the Latin world by the discovery and dissemination of significant, previously unknown Latin and Greek rhetorical texts. Especially influential were Cicero's speeches, correspondence, and, crucially, his De oratore. Together these presented an image of thought and speech actively engaged in solving concrete human problems, in resolving human conflicts, and, perhaps most important, debating the nature and aims of rhetoric itself.

One response to this new set of conditions has become known as "humanism," primarily because of the humanists' redirection of interest away from celestial and toward mundane concerns. One of the humanists, Erasmus, is of special interest to the story I am now telling because he represents a way not taken that contrasts sharply with the narrative lines leading to today's culturalist rhetoric. Erasmus was indeed Christian, but he was also a skeptic for whom the chief characteristic of human beings is our finitude, a characteristic that so limits our rationality that faith necessarily overshadows epistemology at every turn.

For Erasmus, the severe limits of reason suggest that true rationality requires devising modes of thought and discourse that foreground uncertainty and make it obvious that decisions spring from ultimately unjustifiable beliefs guided by individual desire. Erasmus's understanding of the human condition resulted in a rhetoric that in practice consumed all invention and magnified it through the ideal of copia. . . an abundance of alternatives in both expression and subject matter that "are so interconnected in reality that one cannot easily separate one from the other".

Copia exerted itself in argumentation through a balanced presentation of possibilities, rather like the Sophists' antilogic. These possibilities were primarily generated from scholarly tradition, classical thought, and Scripture, all of which, the Bible included, were open to multiple interpretations that weighed more heavily in some contextualizations than in others, but that ultimately had to be remanded to the individual for a decision.

Social coherence — peace — then, depended, first, upon the persuasive power of learned individuals capable of taking an enormous number of possibilities into consideration and, second, upon the willingness of those individuals to submit to authority once the possibilities had been played out. In an uncertain world, faith in authoritative figures must ultimately prevail. Erasmus's political and religious conservatism notwithstanding, the important thing to note is that for him the very grounds of discourse are negotiable and debatable, even though ultimately the authority of those grounds, once established, must be treated as if absolute.

Moreover, that authority rests upon its access to and active consideration of the alternatives discovered in a controversial and very obviously plural scholarly tradition. And most important, fluency in that tradition defined membership in the community the humanist addressed, not narrow political, geographical, or linguistical boundaries.

Such a community was certainly elitist; nevertheless, those with the education and training necessary to enter it could have the sense of actively shaping their world, not simply sojourning in a world ready-made. For Ramus the world was ready-made, and by God. Unlike Erasmus, who doubted the ability of humans to understand the world, Ramus thought he knew precisely how both the world and God's mind worked. The real and the divine were sublimely logical, binomially logical, and an integrated whole. Theoretically, one could catalogue the entire universe in terms of its dichotomous logical interrelationships of part to part — an epistemological and ontological totality Ramists would call "encyclopedia."

Thus, by aligning the closed Biblical canon with a closed system of logic to create an image of total intelligibility, Ramus could claim that meanings and beings were knowable in terms of their relationships. Even human beings were to be understood in relational terms. Richardson would extend this claim saying that the truth of how things are — including what the Bible means — is to be found only through involvement in social life, through engagement with the world and with others, not through detachment from social life and encyclopedic natural life.

In other words, "God's Idea" regulated the natural world, and if social life was meant to mirror the mutual dependencies of natural elements, then "God's Word" could be understood as reflecting the former and refracting the latter. The Bible's meaning, therefore, was accessible to anyone to whom God had given the grace to "experience," and not merely to know abstractly, the isomorphism of God's World and Word. To anyone without grace, however, the Bible was as subject to multiple, self-interested interpretations as any other text.

Since to Ramus God's Word was logos, binomially logical, and the world, made by God, was also logical, and since dialectical logic was available to and in fact defined human beings, it was possible to know with near certainty exactly how God wanted human beings to resolve their controversies. Ramists like Richardson would argue, for instance, that human relationships could function logically only in what Ramus had called "relative" relationships (relationships of mutual causality such that, for one half of a dichotomy to exist the other half has to exist) of which there are only two types, natural (as a father and son) and consensual (as a buyer and seller, or husband and wife).

To be legitimate (i.e., divinely authorized because logical), the latter required mutual consent. By this logic, the appointment of a minister to a congregation without the prior consent of both minister and congregation is simply, flatly wrong. There can be no argument about it. The difference between Erasmus and Ramus can be described as one between an assumption that discursive grounds are fully negotiable until authoritatively established and the contrary assumption that they are fixed in advance.

For Erasmus, what matters most is what the individual believes others will believe, thus his focus upon tradition, historical situations, and the invention of copious alternatives to the description and solution of problems. For Ramus, what matters most is a non-negotiable truth completely unaffected by what others believe, by historical circumstances, or by personal desire — a truth accessible because the method for finding it and the language for expressing it have been fixed in advance.

In short, Erasmus is concerned almost exclusively with discursive power — persuasion to a possible conceptual whole from elements that others will consider relevant; Ramus is concerned almost exclusively with rhetorical force — persuasion from a conceptual whole toward conclusions that others will (by virtue of the method entailed in the whole to which they have already agreed) consider necessary.

Historically, Ramus won and Erasmus lost; that is, force won out over power in the battle for theoretical attention. The single notable exception lay in the work of Giambattista Vico, who, in his struggle against the domination of Cartesianism during the early eighteenth century, argued that the concept of truth should not be restricted to "eternal" abstract truth. Prudence demands attention as well to those "concrete or specific truths" which "change momentarily from truths to untruths".

Part of truth, part of the reality of any situation, was the opinions about it held by others. Vico considered the failure to be concerned "with the opinions of others" to be the chief source of political and rhetorical ineptitude, whereas attention to the opinions of one's audience was the "essence" of eloquence. When we recognize human opinion as being part of the reality one is trying to describe, we can no longer, like the abstract scientist, be satisfied with "reducing a large multitude of physical effects of a single cause"; instead, we will "ferret out the greatest possible number of causes which may have produced the single event, and . . . conjecture which of all these causes is the true one".

To Vico, in the world as lived, appearance is as effective as reality, and to ignore reality's social dimension was simply foolish. Unfortunately, although today scholars have recognized that Vico was grappling with issues that would not reemerge until the late nineteenth and twentieth centuries, he had almost no influence during his time and was seen by most as a reactionary against the new science.

The revolutionary spirit of the times demanded a view of discourse and truth that could ignore tradition and the beliefs of others. Unlike Erasmus's and Vico's humanism, Ramism had encouraged a casual disregard of traditional authority and, through its alignment with Protestantism, reliance upon individual experience.

Ramism, too, would lose adherents as that same reliance upon experience, once it became directed toward the natural world, would contradict the Ramist claim that the logical mechanisms of the universe could be known a priori and knowledge of individual truths could be deduced from it. Nevertheless, Erasmus and Ramus continued to influence discourse theory after the Renaissance in its two opposing tendencies predominant in the eighteenth and nineteenth centuries.

One tendency would be to claim that normative discursive patterns are discoverable and accessible, while the other would be to claim that such patterns have yet to be discovered or produced. Both, however, will subscribe to the old Platonic assumption that discourse *should* be "correct" and subordinated to some normative pattern.

FIXING LANGUAGE

The modern world would put its faith in perceivable experience, but that, in turn, shifted the burdens of coherence and comprehensibility onto everyday discourse, while simplicity demanded the bracketing of personal and communal faith. No one had ever believed that everyday discourse was unified and coherent in itself. Whatever unity and coherence it achieved was by virtue of it's reflecting either Biblical discourse or encyclopedic form.

Now it became obvious that if truth consisted of a correspondence between an unknown unified totality and a known one, and if arriving at the truth of the unknown had to be progressive, not the immediate total vision of the mystic, but a labored, incremental development, then the communication process had to be purified. How could anyone build upon what others had learned if the language muddied the information?

Francis Bacon was one of the first to target language as an epistemological hindrance. In The New Organon, he declared that "the human understanding is like a false mirror" because our very perceptions are distorted. They are distorted on account of what he calls the four "Idols": the Idols of the Tribe are those endemic to human nature and finite perception; the Idols of the Cave are those peculiar to individuals, either their personal nature or their education and particular experiences; the Idols of the Market Place are peculiar to particular societies and social practices; and the Idols of the Theatre stem from philosophies and religions that have virtually created worlds of their own.

Each of these is the product of false or imprecise discourse, and each distorts and limits our apprehension of reality, "For men believe that their reason governs words; but it is also true that words react on the understanding".

Bacon believed that "the formation of ideas and axioms by true induction is no doubt the proper remedy to be applied for the keeping off and clearing away of idols". A number of projects followed upon Bacon's suggestion that language be subjected to an inductive critique. In the late seventeenth century, the British Royal Society endorsed working toward a one-thing, one-word language.

A founding member, Bishop Wilkins, proposed an entirely

new system of symbolization, Esperanto, that would eradicate the deceptive ambiguities of rhetorical devices. Still, most Baconians were content to believe that through a disciplined critique guided by a properly scientific examination of the world, language may gradually come to approximate more closely the true nature of things.

Others, however, followed Wilkins in believing that language had to be purified or standardized before proper scientific procedures could proceed fruitfully. One of the more influential, John Locke, held that we can have unmediated knowledge only of our own ideas. We do have direct sensations of phenomena, of course, and some of these directly result in what he called "simple ideas."

But to all our ideas we assign words. While words allow us to convey our ideas to others, because simple ideas combine to form complex ones that may have no necessary relation to reality, our language may be more deceiving than it is enlightening. Language may deceive us especially when (1) we use words to which we can assign no particular idea (as, for example, when someone discusses the taste of pineapple without ever having eaten a pineapple), (2) when our vocabulary is inadequate to our complex ideas, (3) when we use words inconsistently, (4) when we use words in ways different from their common use, and (5) when words refer to imagined substances.

These deficiencies could be remedied, at least partially, by submitting discourse more strenuously to experience and by standardizing language. The development of dictionaries and prescriptive grammars followed naturally from Locke's concerns. Although Locke saw language as a "medium" whose "obscurity and disorder" is likely to "cast a mist before our eyes, and impose upon our understandings", he did not see language as conditioning knowledge.

Discourse merely recorded our own thoughts and communicated them to others, so that a conventionally standardized language would effectively promote the goal of accumulating and spreading knowledge. Some, however, saw language — the right language — as one of the necessary conditions of understanding, Etienne Bonnot de Condillac was one of these. After Descartes had found in geometry what he believed to be a model for developing a universal method for all the sciences, one that would link all knowledge in encyclopedic unity, and after Leibniz had sought the same sort of unity in a universal grammar modeled upon algebraic symbolization, Condillac concluded that "the progress of the sciences depends uniquely on the progress of language, and that well constructed languages alone can give analysis the degree of simplicity and precision of which it is susceptible". Languages, he believed, are "so many analytical methods. . . . We think with them. Rulers of our judgment, they determine our knowledge, opinions, and prejudices".

By asserting, somewhat like Bacon, that language conditioned knowledge and perception, Condillac parted significantly with the Cartesians, who held to the doctrine of the "essential identity of reason." As Pierre Swiggers has said, "This [doctrine] entails a radical distinction between thought and speech: the former is, by nature, uniform, whereas the latter is flexible and varies from one language to another". This same doctrine had led the Port Royal solitaires in their Grammar and Logic to posit the theory of the arbitrariness of linguistic signs.

This theory supports the notion that language is transparent and "grounded in the conscious use of the total set of linguistic signs, which are arbitrary at the level of constitution". Because language use is grounded in conscious intentionality, the Port-Royalists considered it possible "to rephrase, in a systematic way, the control exerted by the speaker over the system of signs he uses".

In other words, a language can artificially be made more rational, by, for instance, altering its syntax to conform to the natural order of reason (subject-predicate-object). But this new rationality only makes the language's use more convenient; it does not determine how one thinks.

To Condillac, however, we can reason only as well as our language will permit us. He speculated that because of inadequate languages that allow or encourage "the habit of using words before determining their meanings," human beings now live dominated by "monstrous systems" in which error supports error, and in which, while we may "believe we think for ourselves, we still continue thinking second hand". The only way to restore order to thought, now, is "to forget everything we have learned, to take up our ideas again at their origin and to reconstitute human understanding". If we were to think under the guidance of a rational language that tied our words to our sensational experience, our linguistic system would correspond to the natural system.

Nature is "a system whose parts are all perfectly well ordered. If there are in me needs and desires, there are outside of me objects appropriate for satisfying them, and I have the faculty of knowing and making use of them". In other words, Condillac believed some sort of rationally guided, universal grammar was necessary to make Locke's sensationalism work. Closing the gap between world and word required guidance. But the initial contact between word and world could not be empirically induced.

That contact was not provided by supernatural intervention, by grace, but by "genius" — that typically Romantic substitute for God or substance-which intuited a core "analogy" around which the rest of a rational language could develop. Before the nineteenth century had begun, then, two trends had emerged in reaction to the loss of the medieval faith in an available, immediately accessible, normative discursive pattern.

One trend assumed that such a pattern was needed but had yet to be discovered. For those moving this direction, language conditioned perception, so that establishing truth required first finding a true or proper language, one fitting either physical nature (analogously to mathematical laws or geometrical relationships), as with Descartes and Leibniz; or one fitting human nature (a rational language attuned by genius to nature) as with Condillac.

The other trend, including Bacon, Wilkins, and Locke, assumed that language's alignment with nature had to be achieved incrementally, guided by a proper method of positive investigation. The main requirement for the second trend was that language should not hinder the recording and communication of knowledge; therefore, an adequate language could be produced conventionally and arbitrarily, so long as the language was coherent and unambiguous.

Different as they were in method, these projects to purify language were intended to further scientific investigation, not to alter society; nevertheless, they quickly began to affect social life, as well, primarily by encouraging an increased demand for and expectation of greater linguistic standardization and conventionality. Of course, it is true that rhetorical theory and practice had emphasized conventionality significantly at least since the Roman era.

Quintilian had demanded, "Let no one however demand from me a rigid code of rules such as most authors of text books have laid down, or ask me to impose on students of rhetoric a system of laws immutable as fate", but his only protest was that "most rules are liable to be altered by the nature of the case, circumstances of time and place, and by hard necessity itself". In short, he understood particulars only as deviations from known norms.

Earlier, the Rhetorica ad Herennium had defined taste in terms of "Correct Latinity" which "keeps the language pure, and free of any fault," and "Clarity" which "renders language plain and intelligible." Clarity was to be achieved by the use of "current terms and proper terms" as defined by everyday speech and the discursive practices typical of various occupations.

Of course, both Quintilian's stricture and the Ad Herennium's dictum were derived from Cicero who had insisted that "in oratory the very cardinal sin is to depart from the language of everyday life, and the usage of the community". For Cicero, one adhered to "correct Latinity" and sought clarity in order to achieve identification with one's audience and thus to effect persuasion.

Identification (as we might say today, solidarity) with an audience was both the means and the end of persuasion. The idea was to make the audience see and feel that what it and the orator want were, at bottom, the same. It was the rhetor's responsibility to become one with the audience. The rhetor "ought to feel the pulses of every class, time of life, and degree, and to taste the thoughts and feelings of those before whom he is pleading or intending to plead any cause". To the Roman rhetoricians, speaking as the audience spoke reflected such an identification.

However, the rhetoric that emerged in England during the eighteenth and nineteenth centuries under the influence of the "conventionality" trend in linguistics sought correctness and clarity for entirely different reasons and through entirely different means.

NEW RHETORIC

These reasons may be best seen through a brief examination of how Bacon revised the traditional rhetorical canon. In traditional rhetoric, the processes of invention were designed to discover what a rhetor's audience believed and how they thought. Aristotle's rhetoric, by far the most influential, had pursued invention through two lists of topics, or "places," where arguments could be found.

One of these lists mapped out general modes of thinking; the other was an incomplete list suggesting that people used different kinds of arguments for different subjects in different settings. The aim here was to know the audience. If the ancients believed that knowledge was power, the knowledge was of the communities to whom they spoke.

In contrast, for Bacon, who coined the phrase "knowledge is power," the knowledge was of empirical "reality," as for Ramus it had been knowledge of the dialectical encyclopedia. Accordingly, like Ramus, Bacon degraded rhetorical invention. The only knowledge that matters, knowledge about how the world works, Bacon assigned to science. Rhetorical invention was "no Invention, but a Remembrance or Suggestion" of what we have learned through scientific methods.

Bacon's famous definition of rhetoric therefore completely altered the very notion of persuasion. He said, "The duty and office of Rhetoric is to apply Reason to Imagination for the better moving of the will". If classical rhetors had adjusted their arguments in order to accommodate the established will of their audiences, this new rhetoric sought to alter the audience's will itself, by subordinating it to "reason" — to scientific, inductively established knowledge. This is why knowledge is power.

In effect, empirical knowledge became the rhetorical substitute for the Holy Scripture that in the Middle Ages had founded communion. Whereas in classical rhetorics, power was achieved through establishing one's solidarity with a community, through the identification of the rhetor's desires with those of a community's members, now power was defined as the capacity to alter what the audience wants — to change the audience's minds by bringing them under the domination of reason, as defined by scientific method.

With the alteration of the notion of persuasion came corresponding alterations in the aims and methods of persuasion. Primarily, rhetoric came to be seen unabashedly as manipulative power-seeking, although ideally subservient to scientific truth. By the late eighteenth century, as George Campbell put it in his highly influential treatise The Philosophy of Rhetoric, the best orator was thought to combine appeals to the intellect and the passions in order to produce "an irresistible power over the thoughts and purposes of his audience." Seeking such manipulative power was, however, quite legitimate:

It is this which hath been so justly celebrated as giving one man an ascendant over others, superior even to what despotism itself can bestow; since by the latter the more ignoble part only, the body and its members are enslaved; whereas from the dominion of the former, nothing is exempted, neither judgment nor affection, not even the inmost recesses, the most latent movements of the soul.

In other words, people want, and should want, what reason says is best, just as once they should have wanted to obey God. Nature becomes the general standard of what is desirable. However, we must remember that the trend influenced by Bacon and Locke saw the communication of the truth of nature facilitated by strict linguistic conventionality. What this meant socially and rhetorically can be quickly illustrated by Hugh Blair Lectures on Rhetoric and Belles Lettres.

For Blair, what correctness of diction was to communicability, correctness of taste was to desirability. It therefore could no more be possible that individuals could legitin.ately disagree about the desirability of the same object than they could legitimately disagree about the meaning of the same word.

A standard was necessary. Of course, "nature is the standard of taste", and if there were "any one person who possessed in full perfection all the powers of human nature, whose internal senses were in every instance exquisite and just, and whose reason was unerring and sure" we could rely upon that person for our standard (just as Jesus's life had provided a moral standard).

There being no one person with this kind of authority, however, the next best standard is human nature in general. That is, "That which men concur the most in admiring, must be held the most beautiful. His taste must be esteemed just and true, which coincides with the general sentiments of men". Blair's standard is certainly not a simple majority rule; rather, "when we refer to the concurring sentiments of men as the ultimate test of what is to be accounted beautiful in the arts, this is to be always understood of men placed in such situations as are favorable to the proper exertions of taste". These, obviously, are the educated men of "polished and flourishing nations".

All that is to be said about correctness of taste goes also for correctness of diction. Thus, linguistic and rhetorical standards are to be found in the established conventionality of the upper classes. Richard Whately articulated this as a general principle in his Elements of Rhetoric: "There is a Presumption," he said, "in favour of every existing institution".

When language is perceived as a kind of measuring stick, a tool for the correct transmission of information, then it is obvious that "a change is not good in itself"; so, "he that demands change should show cause for it:"

STANDARDIZING LANGUAGE

Nineteenth-century theories of rhetoric and language did offer cause for altering, or rather, standardizing, language, which had now come to be regarded as an institution, and in the Victorian age, institutions had come to be regarded as the proper seats of power. Tony Crowley has done a fine, although brief, study of the history of the English movement toward standardization. The term "standard language," he says, was "coined in the 1858 Proposal for the New/Oxford English Dictionary" during the debate over what was to be included in its volumes.

He notes that "the arguments about whether there was such a standard form had raged for well over a century and a half, its locus classicus being Locke's extension of his arguments in favour of social stability to language, particularly in his warnings of the dangers of formal and semantic instability." According to Crowley, nineteenth-century scholars saw "standard language" as a project to be accomplished rather than as a fact to be described.

Unlike their eighteenth-century counterparts, they saw linguistic unity as more a political than an epistemological necessity. As one nineteenth-century linguistic historian put it, "Unity of speech is essential to the unity of a people. Community of language is a stronger bond than identity of religion or government, and contemporaneous nations of one speech, however formally separated by differences of creed or of political organization, are essentially one in culture, one in tendency, one in influence".

The felt need for linguistic norms for politics' sake was echoed in other areas, as well, especially in education and aesthetics. In literary aesthetics, the eventual conviction that there was a norm would lead during the first half of the twentieth century to an extraordinary emphasis upon aesthetic effects such as parody, irony, and personal "style" that rely for their recognition upon the assumption of there being linguistic norms. Typically, those who believe in the necessity of such norms also believe that in their time the language is degraded and in need of rehabilitation. For example, in 1948 Cleanth Brooks would lament "the depletion and corruption of the very language itself" and insist that "the modern poet has the task of rehabilitating a tired and drained language so that it can convey meanings once more with force and with exactitude".

Crowley's study makes it clear, however, that norms such as those Brooks laments exist only as an ideal for the elite. Thus, we should suspect claims that "linguistic fragmentation" is a recent and specifically postmodern phenomenon. Fredric Jameson, for instance, has suggested that postmodern "pastiche" has displaced high modernist parody, and this in turn, has been followed by a linguistic fragmentation of social life itself to the point where the norm itself is eclipsed: reduced to a neutral and reified media speech (far enough from the Utopian aspirations of the inventors of Esperanto or Basic English), which itself then becomes but one more ideolect among many. The loss of the "norm," however, could only be a loss for those few who had convinced themselves that there ever was a norm to lose.

Chapter 9

Impact of Linguistic

ACCENTS OF LITERATURE

English includes some words that can be written with accent marks. These words have mostly been imported from other languages, usually French. But it is increasingly rare for writers of English to actually use the accent marks for common words, even in very formal writing.

The strongest tendency to retain the accent is in words that are atypical of English morphology and therefore still perceived as slightly foreign. For example, *café* and *paté* both have a pronounced final *e*, which would be "silent" by the normal English pronunciation rules.

Some examples: appliqué, attaché, blasé, bric-à-brac, brötchen, café, cliché, crème, crêpe, façade, fiancé(e), flambé, naïve, naïveté, né(e), papier-mâché, passé, piñata, protégé, raison d'être, résumé, risqué, über-, vis-à-vis, voilà. For a more complete list, see List of English words with diacritics.

Some words such as *rôle* and *hôtel* were first seen with accents when they were borrowed into English, but now the accent is almost never used. The words were considered very French borrowings when first used in English, even accused by some of being foreign phrases used where English alternatives would suffice, but today their French origin is largely forgotten.

The accent on "élite" has disappeared from most publications today, though *Time* magazine still uses it. For some words such as "soupçon" however, the only spelling found in English dictionaries (the OED and others) uses the diacritic. Italics, with appropriate accents, are generally applied to foreign terms that are uncommonly used in or have not been assimilated into English: for example, *adiós, coup d'état, crème brûlée, pièce de résistance, raison d'être, über (übermensch), vis-à-vis.*

It was formerly common in English to use a diaeresis to indicate a syllable break: for example, coöperate, daïs, reëiect. One publication that still uses a diaeresis for this function is the *New Yorker* magazine. However, this is increasingly rare in modern English. Nowadays the diaeresis is normally left out (cooperate), or a hyphen is used (co-operate). It is, however, still common in loanwords such as naïve and noël.

Written accents are also used occasionally in poetry and scripts for dramatic performances to indicate that a certain normally unstressed syllable in a word should be stressed for dramatic effect, or to keep with the metre of the poetry. This use is frequently seen in archaic and pseudoarchaic writings with the "-ed" suffix, to indicate that the "e" should be fully pronounced, as with *cursèd.*

In certain older texts (typically British), the use of ligatures is common in words such as archæology, diarrhœa, and encyclopædia. Such words have Latin or Greek origin. Nowadays, the ligatures have been generally replaced in British English by the separated letters "ae" and "oe" ("encyclopaedia", "diarrhoea") and in American English by "e" ("encyclopedia", "diarrhea"); however, the spellings "oeconomy" and "oecology" are now generally replaced by "economy" and "ecology" outside the U.S. as well.

For further information on how one can type diacritics and ligatures, see British and American keyboards, keyboard layouts. In the nineteenth century, though, such norms were still seen as something to be established, and once established, spread.

As Tony Crowley emphasizes, the "forces of centripetalisation . . . were not confined to a united language internal to the British state". Many British scholars believed that English, by right of the accomplishments of its speakers, was on its way toward being, and deserved to become, the universal language.

As one apologist for imperialism proclaimed, "English is emphatically the exponent of commerce, of civilization, of social and religious freedom, of progressive intelligence, and of an active catholic philanthropy; and beyond any tongue ever used by man, it is of right the cosmopolite speech".

One might observe in this argument for linguistic imperialism more going on than Locke's requirements for recording and communicating ideas. By now, another notion had become imported into British linguistic discourse, one justifying the belief that language reflected, indeed created character. This notion encouraged British linguist G. F. Graham, for example, to describe language as follows:

Language is the outward expression of the tendencies, turn of mind, and habits of thought of some one nation, and the best criterion of their intellect and feelings. If this explanation be admitted, it will naturally follow that the connexion between a people and their language is so close, that the one may be judged of it by the other; and that the language is a lasting monument of the nature and character of the people.

The belief that the character and intelligence of a people was determined by their language descended not from Bacon or Locke, but from Condillac, who in his Essay on the Origin of Human Knowledge had declared not only that "every language expresses the character of the people that speak it" and that a nation's great works begin only "when the language begins to have fixed principles and a settled standard", but also, more importantly, that "the language of rude and ignorant people obstructs the progress of the mind," an obstruction that cannot "diminish, but in proportion to the degrees of perfection added to that language".

Such pronouncements lent authority to the ideologues' plan to impose a standardized French throughout the country. In the late eighteenth century, they sought to replace not only foreign languages but also French dialects. According to Hans Aarsleff, The chief support for these efforts came in fact from the non-French speakers who wished to be part of the events they did not understand. Since the republic was one and indivisible under a single law and the equality of patriots, it must also have one language and do away with the distinction between the French-speaking elite and the rest of the population. The aim was liberation, not repression.

However noble the intent of the ideologues may have been, their project to standardize the language within French borders soon combined with the idea that some languages were better, because more "rational," than other languages, and therefore it was equally noble to impose a more rational language upon the speakers of those less so.

An important linguist whose work sometimes was used to support such linguistic imperialism — although he himself did not support it — was Wilhelm von Humboldt. His influential text, The Diversity of Human Language-Structure and Its Influence on the Mental Development of Mankind (1836), claimed, as its title suggests, that the language and mental capability of a people were identical, "For," as he explains, "intellectuality and language allow and further only forms that are mutually congenial to one another".

According to Humboldt's theory, some language types more closely reflect the principles of universal grammar than others because they have had, from their very origin, a better intuitive grasp of the goals of speech. A language's "primordial form" determines from the start its ultimate development, just as the initial configuration of a crystal determines its ultimate structure.

Humboldt concluded that certain linguistic properties such as regular inflection were more conducive to creativity and intellectual rigor. Accordingly (to continue my analogy), just as it is legitimate to value a diamond more than a quartz crystal, it is legitimate to value some languages (as it turns out, unsurprisingly, "Sanskrit" or Indo-European languages) more than others. Humboldt does not want to eliminate the inferior languages anymore than he would want to eliminate "inferior" crystals and gems. As he put it,

I can never avoid a clear and open adoption of the decisive contrast between languages of purely regular form, and those of a form that deviates from this. It is my sincere conviction that what is expressed thereby is just an undeniable fact. The excellence of even these deviant languages, with the particular advantages it confers, the artistry of their technical construction, is neither misapprehended nor despised; we simply deny them the capacity to act, of themselves, in so ordered, so versatile and so harmonious a fashion upon the mind.

Later British efforts to standardize English, as Crowley has noted, "did not exclude differences but hierarchished them: posited as the central form, it [standard English] then ranged around it dialectal, class, gender and race-related differences in an inferior relation to its own powerful status". Humboldt clearly provides a rationale for such a hierarchalization. Deriving his standard from the values held by his own society and then imposing it upon others, thus "proving" that otherness leads to inferiority, Humboldt set the pattern for later attempts to purify languages and cultures of foreign elements.

Humboldt's main argument for such purification, however, came from his habit of describing the differences among languages as being analogous to differences among works of art. Previously, Condillac had described languages as developments of an initial, formative analogy, one that continues to govern the language's structure and give it its unity. A language's beginning, Condillac had said, may be arbitrary, but afterwards linguistic relationships are not: "Signs are arbitrary the first time they are employed, which is the reason perhaps that some imagine they can have no character. But I would fain know whether it be not natural for every nation to combine their ideas according to their own peculiar genius".

Humboldt took this idea further to claim that the totality of a language was, like an artistic genius' initial inspiration, inherent in the sparking analogy that initiates the development of a language: "Language, as is evident from its very nature, is present to the soul in its totality. Every detail in it, that is, behaves in such a way as to correspond to another that has yet to become clear, and to a whole given, or rather capable of creation, by the sum of the phenomena and the laws of the mind. The actual development goes on gradually, however, and the new increment is formed by analogy with what is already present." For Humboldt, then, a language is like organic art. And, like art, when conceived organically, a language suffers when it is not kept pure. As Hans Aarsleff explains:

"For Condillac the genius of each language is controlled by the analogy that determines its individuality and organization. It is by virtue of its analogy that a language can be said to be an organism, and for Condillac as well as Humboldt this analogy and thus also the organism are impaired when a language becomes mixed with elements taken from a language that obeys another analogy."

Humboldt understands language as the working out of an intrinsic relationship between an initial "form" or "analogy" that cannot be artificially created and a totality that has yet to be realized but whose intimated nature as an integral whole determines what does and does not belong to it.

Despite major differences between Humboldt's romanticism and the rationalisms of Locke, Leibniz, and Condillac — including the obvious difference of Humboldt's insistence upon the "genius" of the initial formation — Humboldt presumes as the rationalists did that nature itself is an integrated system and that ideally language mirrors that integrative totality.

Even so, a very important difference exists between Humboldt's theory and those of the universal grammarians on the one side and the Lockian conventionalists on the other. The difference lies in Humboldt's treating language as a process rather than a product. We usually think of language as being the lexicon and the grammatical laws that determine the correctness of speech. Humboldt says, on the contrary, that "the break-up into words and rules is only the dead makeshift of scientific analysis".

Such structures are descriptions of moments of stasis that in fact do not occur: "Language, regarded in its real nature, is an enduring thing, and at every moment a transitory one. . . .

In itself it is no product, but an activity". This language activity, or speech, Humboldt sometimes describes as a "labour," or a "work of the spirit", and sometimes as an "inner striving" of the individual to, on the one hand, express the requirements of a particular situation and, on the other, to be understood, which requires submitting to the way in which a listener "under similar circumstances, would have spoken to [the speaker]".

Such "labour," which "produces the expression of thought, is always directed at once upon something already given; it is not purely creative, but a reshaping activity". Humboldt claims that the "labour operates in a constant and uniform way", according to a certain form — or what he sometimes, following Condillac, calls the central "analogy."

This form, not grammatical form, constitutes the very essence of language, and language, therefore, cannot be regarded as a totality of signs and a set of rules for their combination. We can regard "only the totality of this speaking as the language". Only particular utterances are "present."

V. N. Volosnov, in his germinal text Marxism and the Philosophy of Language, has described Humboldt as "the most important representative" and founder of one of the two most important trends in language theory prior to his own work in the 1930s.

That trend, individualistic subjectivism, adhered to four basic principles:

1. Language is activity, an unceasing process of creation (energeia) realized in individual speech acts;
2. The laws of language creativity are the laws of individual psychology;
3. Creativity of language is meaningful creativity, analogous to creative art;
4. Language as a ready-made product (ergon), as a stable system (lexicon, grammar, phonetics), is, so to speak, the inert crust, the hardened lava of language creativity, of which linguistics makes an abstract construct in the interests of the practical teaching of language as a ready-made instrument.

The opposing major trend, established by Ferdinand de Saussure, Volosinov called abstract objectivism, and he gives these as its basic principles:

1. Language is a stable, immutable system of normatively identical' linguistic forms which the individual consciousness finds ready-made and which is incontestable for that consciousness.
2. The laws of language are the specifically linguistic laws of connection between linguistic signs within a given, closed linguistic system. These laws are objective with respect to any subjective consciousness.
3. Specifically linguistic connections have nothing in common with ideological values (artistic, cognitive, or other). Language phenomena are not grounded in ideological motives. No connection of a kind natural and comprehensible to the consciousness or of an artistic kind obtains between the word and its meaning.
4. *Individual* acts of speaking are, from the viewpoint of language, merely fortuitous refractions and variations or plain and simple distortions of normatively identical forms; but precisely these acts of individual discourse explain the historical changeability of linguistic forms, a changeability that in itself, from the standpoint of the language system, is irrational and senseless. There is no connection, no sharing of motives, between the system of language and its history. They are alien to one another.

I borrow Volosinov's antithetical contrast here because it highlights nicely the difference between the Romantic and Modernist conceptions of the grounds of meaning, the nature of discursive force, and the individual's relationship to a language. Whereas the Romantics believed that discursive force originated from the individual's grasp of a core analogy that generates an organic linguistic whole, the Modernists, like the eighteenth-century Rationalists, saw the whole itself as the ground. The chief differences between the Modernists and their Rationalist predecessors, of course, were that while the Rationalists thought the whole in question was Nature, the Modernists thought it was language; and while the Rationalists thought language could be fixed and altered to correspond to the logic governing the universe, the Modernists thought that language was not subject to the individual's control.

Just as Darwin argued that the success or failure of the individual act or life had no effect upon the evolution of its species, except insofar as that act or life is the consequence of an accidental mutation affecting the individual's inheritable capacities correlated with accidental alterations in the species' environment, Saussure argued that the system of language that mediates speech, that determines or limits what an individual thinks, and that "in great part . . . makes the nation" that speaks it, is completely "unassailable by the human will" and changes only by chance.

Saussure's founding methodological premises are well known. He defines language (la langue) and speech (la parole) in terms of a difference between "the product passively registered by the individual" and "an individual act of the will and the intelligence". This distinction allows him to establish language as an isolated, homogeneous object for a science distinct from those appropriate to studying speech.

Language as the object of linguistics is a closed system of arbitrary signs, and signs are "real objects", unities of signifiers and signifieds whose identities are determined by their differences from one another within the closed system. His very definition of language therefore compels him to distinguish between synchronic linguistics (the study of a language at a particular moment in time) and diachronic linguistics (the study of historical changes in states of the system).

Apparently, Saussure intended for these constitutional definitions to establish only a particular point of view, one that would not delegitimate the study of individual speech or motivated discourse but would assign to such studies entirely different methodologies. However, his claims that signs are real and not merely analytical abstractions and, more importantly, that the history of a language is conceptually and causally independent of the state of a language, led inevitably to "structuralism" and the belief in the abyss between desire and knowledge, motive and effect, that structuralistic thinking supposedly reveals.

This "abyss," however, is less a revelation than a presupposition. That this is so can best be observed by revisiting Saussure's explanation of the difference between "static linguistics" and "evolutionary linguistics." In this section of his Course, as in several other places, Saussure draws an analogy between a language and a game of chess. The recurrence of this analogy leads me to believe that Saussure consciously modeled his theory on the game. Whether he did so or not, the analogy provides considerable insight to the limitations of the theory.

Saussure offers three points of comparison between chess and language in order to illuminate his distinction between synchrony and diachrony. First, he says, "a state of a chessboard corresponds exactly to a state of the language. The value of the chess pieces depends on their position upon the chess board, just as in the language each term has its value through its contrast with all the other terms". This correspondence tells us a number of things.

For one, it reminds us that the capacity of a sign to substitute for an idea is conditioned by the sign's comparative relationship to other signs in the system. Saussure, when explaining the difference between value and meaning, said that "the content of a word is determined in the final analysis not by what it contains [i.e., by "the concept or meaning for which it is a token"] but by what exists outside it. As an element in a system, the word has not only a meaning but also — above all — a value."

And that value is "assessed against comparable values, by contrast with other words". In the analogy with chess, then, the "meaning" of a knight is "can move up two spaces and over one," while its value is the product of that capacity and its position on the board in relation to the other pieces, each with its own meaning and value. This correspondence also suggests that the board itself, its configuration and size, is not determined by the play even if the board's order determines the potential value of every piece on it.

What in language corresponds to the board? "It is true," Saussure notes, "that the values also depend ultimately upon one invariable set of conventions, the rules of the game, which exist before the beginning of the game and remain in force after each move". These rules, he says, correspond to "the unchanging principles of semiology." So the rules, no doubt, establish the board. Still, we have no idea what in language might correspond to it.

But the only thing the board could correspond to in Saussure's system is reality, which, for his system to work, would have to be a fixed scheme, like the scheme of squares on the board. As Saussure says, though, "If words had the job of representing concepts fixed in advance, one would be able to find exact equivalents for them as between one language and another.

But this is not the case". Instead of "predetermined categories" or "ideas given in advance" are "values emanating from a linguistic system." Furthermore, "If we say these values correspond to certain concepts, it must be understood that the concepts in question are purely differential. What characterizes each most exactly is being whatever the others are not".

In other words, Saussure presupposes a reality that is formally fixed but blank; in itself it is meaningless, like the squares of a chess board, except when a linguistic game is being played upon it. What the squares "mean" is nothing; their value is determined by the pieces upon them, just as are the values of the pieces themselves.

The board, then, is Saussure's metaphor as the chora, the ground of discourse. It may be helpful to compare Saussure's notion of the ground as a fixed structure, a notion typical of philosophies of being, with a more historicized notion of ground typical of philosophies of becoming. Julia Kristeva, for instance, has argued that chora's "organization is subject to an objective ordering [ordonnancement], which is dictated by natural or sociohistorical constraints such as the biological difference between the sexes or family structure". In contrast, Saussure's theory clearly implies that changes in linguistic order have no effect upon social order as such, even if various "moves" may effectively re-value elements within the social order. Individuals remain in the grip of a system with no rational means of altering it. We may draw similar conclusions from Saussure's second and third points of comparison between chess and language. The second is that "the system is only ever a temporary one. It varies from one position to the next."

The third is that "in order to pass from one stable position to another or, in our terminology, from one synchronic state to another, moving one piece is all that is needed". The consequence of these characteristics is that changes in the linguistic order are necessarily irrational, senseless. Any one move "has a repercussion upon the whole system," but "it is impossible for the player to foresee exactly where its consequences will end".

Prediction is impossible because there is an absolute break between diachrony and synchrony. "In a game of chess," as in linguistics, any given state of the board is totally independent of any previous state of the board. It does not matter at all whether the state in question has been reached by one sequence of moves or another sequence. Anyone who has followed the whole game has not the least advantage over a passerby who happens to look at the game at that particular moment.

In order to describe the position on the board, it is quite useless to refer to what happened ten seconds ago. All this applies equally to a language. Although alterations in linguistic systems usually take place through "blind forces of change," even deliberate changes are necessarily irrational. As Saussure says, "If the game of chess were to be like the operations of a language in every respect, we would have to imagine a player who was either unaware of what he was doing or unintelligent". Just as to Darwin the evolution of life is not going anywhere in particular; to Saussure the evolution of language is not going anywhere. Both the physical environment and the social order are beyond the individual's control; just as the survival value of an individual's genetic characteristics and the value of a sign's meaning are products of previous changes in the system, changes that will have taken place through "blind force" and that no one could have predicted. The net result is a view of discourse that implies that anyone who is surviving or making sense now has every reason to try to maintain the system exactly as it is and has no reason at all to try to change it.

CONSEQUENCES

Discourse about discourse has tended toward what I will call "linguistification" — toward more and more emphasis upon language as a medium of force between "mind" and "reality," one of greater or lesser transparency, but always toward more formality, abstraction, and disconnection from historical process and individuals' situations and their desires. Linguistic discourse has been hardly value-free, "objective," or descriptive; instead, the ideal of formal coherence has almost always been its goal. Once this goal has been articulated, the desire for linguistic standardization or purification has been the usual unfortunate consequence. Only in a few historic instances has the "substantiality" of the others' discourse been recognized at all.

Even in these, however, recognition of the other has depended upon first subordinating the other's discourse to some authoritative standard: Erasmus's copia, although acknowledging a multiplicity of finite perspectives, relied not only upon a community of Latinity, but ultimately upon Papal authority to achieve final consensus; Vico, although fighting the substitution of Cartesianism for common sense, saw Cartesian logic not as being itself imbued with the temporality that prudence accounts for, but as being actually universal, although in need of being supplemented by common sense; and Humboldt, as pathbreaking as his view was of discourse as a struggle or labour of the individual desire and the particular instant against the petrified or crystallized remains of prior linguistic activity, he still saw true discourse as a struggle toward a new form of coherence and unity that required a cleansing of alien elements to achieve its destined perfection.

The remaining theories of discourse, from Augustine through Saussure, tend to suppress completely the effects of individual speech acts, particular discursive situations, and others' opinions about speech. Therefore, linguistification tends to suppress, if not bury completely from view, the effects of power at work in discourse.

Instead of a flow of discursive process, it presents a sequence of linguistic states; and instead of the effective word, it presents the arbitrary sign. As "language," discourse is set apart from reality, thus obscuring the way things are. Language is said to have a different ontological status from reality and to operate according to different sets of laws; accordingly, language is understood differently from the way we understand "reality as such."

Moreover, linguistification implies that because languages are unified wholes, we have numerous, incommensurable languages. And it is not just that Swahili differs from French, but that poetic languages differ from scientific languages, and that both differ from "ordinary" languages. Such languages are said to be "translatable" into the others only insofar as they "refer" to the same thing in a world that is presumed to be unaffected by mere discourse.

By the same logic, or rather by the same need to grasp "meaning" as sets of relations within integrated totalities, language itself is said to be split into incommensurable "levels," so that what can be said to be true at the level of phonetics cannot be said to be true at the level of syntax, and so on. Of course, such beliefs about language led to spectacular attempts to impose the syntax of the sentence upon wholes greater than the sentence (structuralism), attempts to reconcile the event of speech, which can be "deviant" and new, with the grammar of the language, and attempts to locate and distinguish the levels of discourse that function according to different sets of rules than those of the sentence.

All this breaking up of discourse, this cognitive shattering of the world, underwrites "alienation," the central "problem" of discourse. Ironically, alienation is a problem only to the processes of linguistification, a fact that is obscured by understanding discourse in terms of language. Because they defined the phenomena of discourse as "language" problems, whole generations of intellectuals ignored the rhetorical tradition with its emphasis upon concrete discursive situations, social constraints, choice, responsibility, and persuasive force.

As late modernist and postmodernist writers began to tackle the problems that had been caused by linguistification, they did so within linguistic terminology, usually completely in ignorance of the rhetorical alternatives available to them. This forgetting of the tradition is especially evident in European scholarship. Chaim Perelman, for instance, could, upon visiting The Pennsylvania State University in the late 1960s, be genuinely surprised to find out that what he thought he had discovered had been the subject of debate for centuries. He could then go on in The New Rhetoric to reclaim this "lost" tradition.

Other Europeans, however, seem to have never acknowledged rhetoric or seem to have had a very limited view of its issues. Mikail Bakhtin, J. L. Austin, Michel Foucault, Jacques Derrida, Stephen Toulmin, and many others who have battled against alienating dichotomies of modernism and who have sought to reclaim an understanding of discourse as situated events, apparently have done so completely without the benefit of knowing the work of their predecessors who had fought to prevent the splits from occurring in the first place.

Of course, this neglect of the tradition is understandable since what was left to the discipline of rhetoric after Plato split it from philosophy, and after Ramus and then Bacon eliminated invention from its canon, was distributed after the Enlightenment into logic, literary criticism, anthropology, psychology, linguistics, etc. But removing a particular subject from the rhetorical field could not remove rhetoricity from the subject. Eventually, the twentieth century had to account for the discursive processes of all these disciplines. Sooner or later, they have all had to confront the fact that the saying is never innocent of what is being said, that appearance is a mode of reality. Regrettably, attempts to account for the effects of saying were made so not by resubordinating the disciplines to the study of what the Sophists had called logos but by importing linguistics into the various disciplines, on the assumption that linguistics explained scientifically how discourse worked.

Richard Rorty book The Linguistic Turn explains marvelously how this occurred in philosophy. Similar "turns" took place in the other "human sciences." Rorty has suggested that the "three hundred years' worth of attempts to bridge the gap which the Cartesian, representationalist picture of knowledge and inquiry led us to imagine existed" is coming to an end. Would that it were so simple! Rorty's hopeful comment reveals just how deeply the picture he deplores still dominates even the best of us, for it suggests that that picture is just an illusion, an appearance, with no real effects, and so it can be simply dismissed and forgotten.

But, as I have said several times in this book, even if belief in such a picture cannot produce the effects the belief would lead us to expect, it produces effects nevertheless. However unnecessarily or inappropriately, people *do* interpret and persuade through linguistic and cultural conceptual schemes.

Given this, our interpretive and rhetorical strategies must take these beliefs and effects into account. We may say there are situations where it would be better if there were no linguistic effects in discourse. We may say linguistification and culturalization have produced situations we find undesirable, situations we would prefer to alter.

If so, we may want to develop a study of discourse that has as its purpose de-linguistification and de-culturalization, one that produces alternative ways of interpreting and persuading to those who do rely upon ideas of "culture" or "language," when these are understood as "structured [media] of representation, capable of standing in determinate relations to a distinct entity called 'the world'.

Chapter 10

Global Literature and Language

GLOBAL ENGLISH

Also significant beginning around 1600 AD was the English colonization of North America and the subsequent creation of American English. Some pronunciations and usages "froze" when they reached the American shore. In certain respects, some varieties of American English are closer to the English of Shakespeare than modern Standard English ('English English' or as it is often incorrectly termed 'British English') is. Some "Americanisms" are actually originally English English expressions that were preserved in the colonies while lost at home (e.g., *fall* as a synonym for autumn, *trash* for rubbish, and *loan* as a verb instead of lend).

The American dialect also served as the route of introduction for many native American words into the English language. Most often, these were place names like *Mississippi, Roanoke,* and *Iowa*. Indian-sounding names like *Idaho* were sometimes created that had no native-American roots. But, names for other things besides places were also common. *Raccoon, tomato, canoe, barbecue, savanna,* and *hickory* have native American roots, although in many cases the original Indian words were mangled almost beyond recognition.

Spanish has also been great influence on American English. *Mustang, canyon, ranch, stampede,* and *vigilante* are all examples of Spanish words that made their way into English through the settlement of the American West. A lesser number of words have entered American English from French and West African languages. Likewise dialects of English have developed in many of the former colonies of the British Empire. There are distinct forms of the English language spoken in Australia, New Zealand, South Africa, India and many other parts of the world.

English has now inarguably achieved global status. Whenever we turn on the news to find out what's happening in East Asia, or the Balkans, or Africa, or South America, or practically anywhere, local people are being interviewed and telling us about it in English. To illustrate the point when Pope John Paul II arrived in the Middle East recently to retrace Christ's footsteps and addressed Christians, Muslims and Jews, the pontiff spoke not Latin, not Arabic, not Italian, not Hebrew, not his native Polish. He spoke in English.

Indeed, if one looks at some of the facts about the amazing reach of the English language many would be surprised. English is used in over 90 countries as an official or semi-official language. English is the working language of the Asian trade group ASEAN. It is the de facto working language of 98 per cent of international research physicists and research chemists.

It is the official language of the European Central Bank, even though the bank is in Frankfurt and neither Britain nor any other predominantly English-speaking country is a member of the European Monetary Union. It is the language in which Indian parents and black parents in South Africa overwhelmingly wish their children to be educated. It is believed that over one billion people worldwide are currently learning English.

One of the more remarkable aspects of the spread of English around the world has been the extent to which Europeans are adopting it as their internal lingua franca. English is spreading from northern Europe to the south and is now firmly entrenched as a second language in countries such as Sweden, Norway, Netherlands and Denmark.

Although not an official language in any of these countries if one visits any of them it would seem that almost everyone there can communicate with ease in English. Indeed, if one switches on a television in Holland one would find as many channels in English (albeit subtitled), as there are in Dutch. As part of the European Year of Languages, a special survey of European attitudes towards and their use of languages has just published.

The report confirms that at the beginning of 2001 English is the most widely known foreign or second language, with 43% of Europeans claiming they speak it in addition to their mother tongue. Sweden now heads the league table of English speakers, with over 89% of the population saying they can speak the language well or very well.

However, in contrast, only 36% of Spanish and Portuguese nationals speak English. What's more, English is the language rated as most useful to know, with over 77% of Europeans who do not speak English as their first language, rating it as useful. French rated 38%, German 23% and Spanish 6% English has without a doubt become the global language.

VARIETIES OF ENGLISH

- Basic English is simplified for easy international use. It is used by some aircraft manufacturers and other international businesses to write manuals and communicate. Some English schools in Asia teach it as an initial practical subset of English.
- Special English is a simplified version of English used by the Voice of America. It uses a vocabulary of 1500 words.
- English reform is an attempt to improve collectively upon the English language.
- Seaspeak and the related Airspeak and Policespeak, all based on restricted vocabularies, were designed by Edward Johnson in the 1980s to aid international cooperation and communication in specific areas. There is also a tunnelspeak for use in the Channel Tunnel.
- English as a lingua franca for Europe and Euro-English are concepts of standardising English for use as a second language in continental Europe.
- Manually Coded English — a variety of systems have

been developed to represent the English language with hand signals, designed primarily for use in deaf education. These should not be confused with true sign languages such as British Sign Language and American Sign Language used in Anglophone countries, which are independent and not based on English.

- E-Prime excludes forms of the verb "to be."

Euro-English (also Euroenglish or Euro-Englich)terms are English translations of European concepts that are not native to English-speaking countries. Due to the United Kingdom's (and even the Republic of Ireland's) involvement in the European Union, the usage focuses on non-British concepts. Examples are the concept of spatial planning or something being "degressive", and the word "Euro-".

It also refers to dialects of English spoken by Europeans for whom English is not their first language, especially since English is frequently used by two Europeans to communicate even when neither of them know English as the first language. (For example, a French person who doesn't know German and a German who doesn't know French, but both of whom know English, would use English to communicate with one another, even though it is not the native language of either - such as at the first meeting of Jacques Chirac and Angela Merkel at the Elysée palace after Merkel's confirmation as chancellor).

English is a member of the Indo-European family of languages. This broad family includes most of the European languages spoken today. The Indo-European family includes several major branches: Latin and the modern Romance languages (French etc.); the Germanic languages (English, German, Swedish etc.); the Indo-Iranian languages (Hindi, Urdu, Sanskrit etc.); the Slavic languages (Russian, Polish, Czech etc.); the Baltic languages of Latvian and Lithuanian; the Celtic languages (Welsh, Irish Gaelic etc.); Greek. The influence of the original Indo-European language can be seen today, even though no written record of it exists. The word for *father*, for example, is *vater* in German, *pater* in Latin, and *pitr* in Sanskrit. These words are all cognates, similar words in different languages that share the same root. Of these branches of the Indo-European family, two are, as far as the study of the development of English is concerned, of paramount importance, the Germanic and the Romance (called that because the Romance languages derive from Latin, the language of ancient Rome).

English is a member of the Germanic group of languages. It is believed that this group began as a common language in the Elbe river region about 3,000 years ago. By the second century BC, this Common Germanic language had split into three distinct sub-groups.

- East Germanic was spoken by peoples who migrated back to southeastern Europe. No East Germanic language is spoken today, and the only written East Germanic language that survives is Gothic.
- North Germanic evolved into the modern Scandinavian languages of Swedish, Danish, Norwegian, and Icelandic (but not Finnish, which is related to Hungarian and Estonian and is not an Indo-European language).
- West Germanic is the ancestor of modern German, Dutch, Flemish, Frisian, and English.

ANCIENT ENGLISH

West Germanic invaders from Jutland and southern Denmark: the Angles (whose name is the source of the words England and English), Saxons, and Jutes, began to settle in the British Isles in the fifth and sixth centuries AD. They spoke a mutually intelligible language, similar to modern Frisian - the language of the northeastern region of the Netherlands - that is called Old English. Four major dialects of Old English emerged, Northumbrian in the north of England, Mercian in the Midlands, West Saxon in the south and west, and Kentish in the Southeast.

These invaders pushed the original, Celtic-speaking inhabitants out of what is now England into Scotland, Wales, Cornwall, and Ireland, leaving behind a few Celtic words. These Celtic languages survive today in the Gaelic languages of Scotland and Ireland and in Welsh. Cornish, unfortunately, is, in linguistic terms, now a dead language. (The last native Cornish speaker died in 1777) Also influencing English at this time were the Vikings.

Norse invasions and settlement, beginning around 850, brought many North Germanic words into the language, particularly in the north of England. Some examples are *dream*, which had meant 'joy' until the Vikings imparted its current meaning on it from the Scandinavian cognate *draumr*, and *skirt*, which continues to live alongside its native English cognate *shirt*. The majority of words in modern English come from foreign, not Old English roots. In fact, only about one sixth of the known Old English words have descendants surviving today. But this is deceptive; Old English is much more important than these statistics would indicate. About half of the most commonly used words in modern English have Old English roots. Words like *be, water,* and *strong,* for example, derive from Old English roots.

Old English, whose best known surviving example is the poem Beowulf, lasted until about 1100. Shortly after the most important event in the development and history of the English language, the Norman Conquest.

MIDDLE ENGLISH

William the Conqueror, the Duke of Normandy, invaded and conquered England and the Anglo-Saxons in 1066 AD. The new overlords spoke a dialect of Old French known as Anglo-Norman. The Normans were also of Germanic stock ("Norman" comes from "Norseman") and Anglo-Norman was a French dialect that had considerable Germanic influences in addition to the basic Latin roots.

Prior to the Norman Conquest, Latin had been only a minor influence on the English language, mainly through vestiges of the Roman occupation and from the conversion of Britain to Christianity in the seventh century (ecclesiastical terms such as *priest, vicar,* and *mass* came into the language this way), but now there was a wholesale infusion of Romance (Anglo-Norman) words. The influence of the Normans can be illustrated by looking at two words, beef and cow. *Beef,* commonly eaten by the aristocracy, derives from the Anglo-Norman, while the Anglo-Saxon commoners, who tended the cattle, retained the Germanic *cow.* Many legal terms, such as *indict, jury,* and *verdict* have Anglo-Norman roots because the Normans ran the courts. This split, where words commonly used by the aristocracy have Romantic roots and words frequently used by the Anglo-Saxon commoners have Germanic roots, can be seen in many instances.

Sometimes French words replaced Old English words; *crime* replaced *firen* and *uncle* replaced *eam.* Other times, French and Old English components combined to form a new word, as the French *gentle* and the Germanic *man* formed *gentleman.* Other times, two different words with roughly the same meaning survive into modern English. Thus we have the Germanic *doom* and the French *judgment,* or *wish* and *desire.*

It is useful to compare various versions of a familiar text to see the differences between Old, Middle, and Modern English. Finally, in Early Modern English (King James Version, 1611) the same text is completely intelligible.

- Our father which art in heauen, hallowed be thy name.
- Thy kingdom come. Thy will be done in earth as it is in heauen.
- Giue us this day our daily bread.
- And forgiue us our debts as we forgiue our debters.
- And lead us not into temptation, but deliuer us from euill. Amen.

For a lengthier comparison of the three stages in the development of English. In 1204 AD, King John lost the province of Normandy to the King of France. This began a process where the Norman nobles of England became increasingly estranged from their French cousins.

England became the chief concern of the nobility, rather than their estates in France, and consequently the nobility adopted a modified English as their native tongue. About 150 years later, the Black Death (1349-50) killed about one third of the English population. And as a result of this the labouring and merchant classes grew in economic and social importance, and along with them English increased in importance compared to Anglo-Norman. This mixture of the two languages came to be known as Middle English. The most famous example of Middle English is Chaucer's Canterbury Tales. Unlike Old English, Middle English can be read, albeit with difficulty, by modern English-speaking people.

By 1362, the linguistic division between the nobility and the commoners was largely over. In that year, the Statute of Pleading was adopted, which made English the language of the courts and it began to be used in Parliament. The Middle English period came to a close around 1500 AD with the rise of Modern English.

EARLY MODERN ENGLISH

The next wave of innovation in English came with the Renaissance. The revival of classical scholarship brought many classical Latin and Greek words into the Language. These borrowings were deliberate and many bemoaned the adoption of these "inkhorn" terms, but many survive to this day. Shakespeare's character Holofernes in *Loves Labour Lost* is a satire of an overenthusiastic schoolmaster who is too fond of Latinisms.

Many students having difficulty understanding Shakespeare would be surprised to learn that he wrote in modern English. But, as can be seen in the earlier example of the Lord's Prayer, Elizabethan English has much more in common with our language today than it does with the language of Chaucer. Many familiar words and phrases were coined or first recorded by Shakespeare, some 2,000 words and countless idioms are his.

Newcomers to Shakespeare are often shocked at the number of cliches contained in his plays, until they realise that he coined them and they became cliches afterwards. "One fell swoop," "vanish into thin air," and "flesh and blood" are all Shakespeare's. Words he bequeathed to the language include "critical," "leapfrog," "majestic," "dwindle," and "pedant." Two other major factors influenced the language and served to separate Middle and Modern English. The first was the Great Vowel Shift. This was a change in pronunciation that began around 1400. While modern English speakers can read Chaucer with some difficulty, Chaucer's pronunciation would have been completely unintelligible to the modern ear.

Shakespeare, on the other hand, would be accented, but understandable. Vowel sounds began to be made further to the front of the mouth and the letter "e" at the end of words became silent. Chaucer's *Lyf* (pronounced "leef") became the modern *life*. In Middle English *name* was pronounced "nam-a," *five* was pronounced "feef," and *down* was pronounced "doon." In linguistic terms, the shift was rather sudden, the major changes occurring within a century. The shift is still not over, however, vowel sounds are still shortening although the change has become considerably more gradual.

The last major factor in the development of Modern English was the advent of the printing press. William Caxton brought the printing press to England in 1476. Books became cheaper and as a result, literacy became more common. Publishing for the masses became a profitable enterprise, and works in English, as opposed to Latin, became more common. Finally, the printing press brought standardization to English. The dialect of London, where most publishing houses were located, became the standard. Spelling and grammar became fixed, and the first English dictionary was published in 1604.

LATE-MODERN ENGLISH

The principal distinction between early- and late-modern English is vocabulary. Pronunciation, grammar, and spelling are largely the same, but Late-Modern English has many more words. These words are the result of two historical factors. The first is the Industrial Revolution and the rise of the technological society. This necessitated new words for things and ideas that had not previously existed. The second was the British Empire. At its height, Britain ruled one quarter of the earth's surface, and English adopted many foreign words and made them its own. The industrial and scientific revolutions created a need for neologisms to describe the new creations and discoveries. For this, English relied heavily on Latin and Greek. Words like *oxygen, protein, nuclear,* and *vaccine* did not exist in the classical languages, but they were created from Latin and Greek roots. Such neologisms were not exclusively created from classical roots though, English roots were used for such terms as horsepower, airplane, and typewriter.

This burst of neologisms continues today, perhaps most visible in the field of electronics and computers. *Byte, cyber-, bios, hard-drive,* and *microchip* are good examples. Also, the rise of the British Empire and the growth of global trade served not only to introduce English to the world, but to introduce words into English. Hindi, and the other languages of the Indian subcontinent, provided many words, such as *pundit, shampoo, pajamas,* and *juggernaut.* Virtually every language on Earth has contributed to the development of English, from Finnish (*sauna*) and Japanese (*tycoon*) to the vast contributions of French and Latin. The British Empire was a maritime empire, and the influence of nautical terms on the English language has been great. Phrases like *three sheets to the wind* have their origins onboard ships.

Finally, the military influence on the language during the latter half of twentieth century was significant. Before the Great War, military service for English-speaking persons was rare; both Britain and the United States maintained small, volunteer militaries. Military slang existed, but with the exception of nautical terms, rarely influenced standard English.

During the mid-20th century, however, a large number of British and American men served in the military. And consequently military slang entered the language like never before. Blockbuster, nose dive, camouflage, radar, roadblock, spearhead, and landing strip are all military terms that made their way into standard English.

SUPRA-SEGMENTAL FEATURES

TONE GROUPS

English is an intonation language. This means that the pitch of the voice is used syntactically, for example, to convey surprise and irony, or to change a statement into a question. In English, intonation patterns are on groups of words, which are called tone groups, tone units, intonation groups or sense groups. Tone groups are said on a single breath and, as a consequence, are of limited length, more often being on average five words long or lasting roughly two seconds. The structure of tone groups can have a crucial impact on the meaning of what is said.

CHARACTERISTICS OF INTONATION

English is a *stress-timed language,* i.e., certain syllables in each multi-syllabic word get a relative prominence/loudness during pronunciation while the others do not. The former kind of syllables are said to be *accentuated/stressed* and the latter are *unaccentuated/unstressed*. All good dictionaries of English mark the accentuated syllable(s) by either placing an apostrophe-like sign either before or after (as in many other dictionaries) the syllable where the stress accent falls. In general, for a two-syllable word in English, it can be broadly said that if it is a noun or an adjective, the first syllable is accentuated; but if it is a verb, the second syllable is accentuated.

Hence in a sentence, each tone group can be subdivided into syllables, which can either be stressed (strong) or unstressed (weak). The stressed syllable is called the nuclear syllable.

For Example

That | was | the | best | thing | you | could | have | done! Here, all syllables are unstressed, except the syllables/words "best" and "done", which are stressed. "Best" is stressed harder and, therefore, is the nuclear syllable. The nuclear syllable carries the main point the speaker wishes to make.

For example:

John hadn't stolen that money. (... Someone else had.)

John *hadn't* stolen that money. (... You said he had. or ... Not at that time, but later he did.)

John hadn't *stolen* that money. (... He acquired the money by some other means.)

John hadn't stolen *that* money. (... He had stolen some other money.)

John hadn't stolen that *money*. (... He stole something else.)

Also:

I didn't tell her that. (... Someone else told her.)

I *didn't* tell her that. (... You said I did. or ... But now I will!)

I didn't *tell* her that. (... I didn't say it; she could have inferred it, etc.)

I didn't tell *her* that. (... I told someone else.)

I didn't tell her *that*. (... I told her something else.)

The nuclear syllable is spoken louder than all the others and has a characteristic change of pitch. The changes of pitch most commonly encountered in English are the rising pitch and the falling pitch, although the fall-rising pitch and/or the rise-falling pitch are sometimes used.

For example:

When do you want to be paid?

Now? (Rising pitch. In this case, it denotes a question: "can I be paid now?" or "do you desire to be paid now?")

WORDS IN ENGLISH

English has an extraordinarily rich vocabulary and willingness to absorb new words. As the *General Explanations* at the beginning state: The Vocabulary of a widely diffused and highly cultivated living language is not a fixed quantity circumscribed by definite limits... there is absolutely no defining line in any direction: the circle of the English language has a well-defined centre but no discernible circumference.

The vocabulary of English is undoubtedly vast, but assigning a specific number to its size is more a matter of definition than of calculation. Unlike other languages, there is no Academy to define officially accepted words. Neologisms are coined regularly in medicine, science and technology and other fields, and new slang is constantly developed. Some of these new words enter wide usage; others remain restricted to small circles. Foreign words used in immigrant communities often make their way into wider English usage. Archaic, dialectal, and regional words might or might not be widely considered as "English". The difficulty of defining the number of words is compounded by the emergence of new versions of English, such as Indo-Pakistani English. The editors of *Merriam Webster's Third New International Dictionary, Unabridged* (475,000 definitions) in their preface, estimate the number to be much higher.

ORIGINS

One of the consequences of the French influence is that the vocabulary of English is, to a certain extent, divided between those words which are Germanic (mostly Old English) and those which are "Latinate" (Latin-derived, either directly from Norman French or other Romance languages).

Numerous sets of statistics have been proposed to demonstrate the various origins of English vocabulary. None, as yet, are considered definitive by a majority of linguists.

Other estimates have also been made:

- French, 40%
- Greek, 13%
- Anglo-Saxon (Old English), 10%
- Danish, 2%
- Dutch, 1%
- And, as about 50% of English is derived from Latin — directly or otherwise — another 10 to 15% can be attributed to direct borrowings from that language.

DUTCH ORIGINS

Words describing the navy, types of ships, and other objects or activities on the water are often from Dutch origin. Yacht (Jacht) and cruiser (kruiser) are examples.

FRENCH ORIGINS

There are many words of French origin in English, such as competition, art, table, publicity, police, role, routine, machine, force, and many others that have been and are being anglicised; they are now pronounced according to English rules of phonology, rather than French. Approximately 40% of English vocabulary is of French language origin, most derived from, or transmitted via, the Anglo-Norman spoken by the upper classes in England for several hundred years after the Norman Conquest.

VOICING AND ASPIRATION

Voicing and aspiration of stop consonants in English depend on dialect and context, but a few general rules can be given.

- Voiceless plosives and affricates (/p/,/t/,/k/, and/tʃ/) are aspirated when they are word-initial or begin a stressed syllable — compare *pin* [p°jn] and *spin* [spjn].
  - In some dialects, aspiration extends to unstressed syllables as well.
  - In other dialects, such as Indo-Pakistani English, all voiceless stops remain unaspirated.
- Word-initial voiced plosives may be devoiced in some dialects.
- Word-terminal voiceless plosives may be unreleased or accompanied by a glottal stop in some dialects (e.g. many varieties of American English) — examples: *tap* [t°æp], *sack* [sæk].
- Word-terminal voiced plosives may be devoiced in some dialects (e.g. some varieties of American English) — examples: *sad* [sæd], *bag* [bæa]. In other dialects they are fully voiced in final position, but only partially voiced in initial position.

AMERICAN AND BRITISH ENGLISH

American English in its *written* form is standardized across the U.S. (and in schools abroad specializing in American English). Though not devoid of regional variations, particularly in pronunciation and vernacular vocabulary, American speech is somewhat uniform throughout the country, largely because of the influence of mass communication and geographical and social mobility in the United States. After the American Civil War, the settlement of the western territories by migrants from the east led to dialect mixing and levelling, so that regional dialects are most strongly differentiated in the eastern part of the country that were settled earlier.

The *General American* accent and dialect (sometimes called 'Standard Midwestern'), often used by newscasters, are traditionally regarded as the unofficial standard for American English. British English has a reasonable degree of uniformity in its formal written form. On the other hand, the forms of *spoken* English – dialects, accents and vocabulary – used across the British Isles vary considerably more than in any other English-speaking areas of the world, and more so than in the United States, because of a much longer history of dialect development in the English speaking areas of Great Britain and Ireland.

Dialects and accents vary, not only between England, Northern Ireland, Scotland and Wales (which constitute the United Kingdom), and the Republic of Ireland, but also within these individual countries. There are also differences in the English spoken by different socio-economic groups in any particular region. *Received Pronunciation (RP)* has traditionally been regarded as 'proper English' – 'the educated spoken English of south-east England'. The BBC and other broadcasters now intentionally use a mix of presenters with a variety of British accents and dialects, and the concept of 'proper English' is now far less prevalent.

British and American English are the reference norms for English as spoken, written, and taught in the rest of the world; for instance, the English-speaking members of the Commonwealth of Nations often (if not usually) closely follow British orthography, and many new Americanisms quickly become familiar outside of the United States.

Although the dialects of English used in the former British Empire are often, to various extents, fairly close to standard British English, most of the countries concerned have developed their own unique dialects, particularly with respect to pronunciation, idioms, and vocabulary; chief among them are, at least for number of first-language speakers, Australian

English and Canadian English. The English language was first introduced to the Americas by British colonization, beginning in the late 16th century. Similarly, the language spread to numerous other parts of the world as a result of British colonization elsewhere and the spread of the former British Empire, which, by 1921, held sway over a population of about 470–570 million people: approximately a quarter of the world's population.

Over the past 400 years, the form of the language used in the Americas – especially in the United States – and that used in the United Kingdom and the rest of the British Isles have diverged in many ways, leading to the dialects now commonly referred to as American English and British English. Differences between the two include pronunciation, grammar, lexis, spelling, punctuation, idioms, formatting of dates and numbers, and so on, with a small number of words having completely different meanings between the two dialects or even being unknown or not used in one of the dialects.

One particular contribution towards formalizing these differences came from Noah Webster, who wrote the first American dictionary (published 1828) with the intention of showing that the United States spoke a different dialect from Britain. This divergence between American English and British English once caused George Bernard Shaw to say that the United States and United Kingdom are "two countries divided by a common language"; a similar comment is ascribed to Winston Churchill.

Likewise, Oscar Wilde wrote, "We have really everything in common with America nowadays, except, of course, the language". Henry Sweet predicted in 1877 that within a century, American English, Australian English and British English would be mutually unintelligible. It may be the case that increased world-wide communication through radio, television, the Internet, and globalization has reduced the tendency to regional variation. This can result either in some variations becoming extinct (as, for instance, *truck* has been gradually replacing *lorry* in much of the world) or in the acceptance of wide variations as "perfectly good English" everywhere. Often at the core of the dialect though, the idiosyncrasies remain. Nevertheless, it remains the case that although spoken American and British English are generally mutually intelligible, there are enough differences to cause occasional misunderstandings or at times embarrassment – for example, some words that are quite innocent in one dialect may be considered vulgar in the other.

PRONUNCIATION

In BrE, collective nouns can take either singular (formal agreement) or plural (notional agreement) verb forms, according to whether the emphasis is, respectively, on the body as a whole or on the individual members; compare a committee was appointed ... with the committee were unable to agree. Some of these nouns, for example staff, actually combine with plural verbs most of the time.

The difference occurs for all collective nouns, both general terms such as *team* and *company* and proper nouns (for example, where a place name is used to refer to a sports team). For instance,

BrE: The Clash are a well-known band; AmE: The Clash is a well known band. BrE: Indianapolis are the champions; AmE: Indianapolis is the champion. Proper nouns which are plural in form take a plural verb in both AmE and BrE; for example, The Beatles are a well-known band; The Colts are the champions.

VERB MORPHOLOGY

The past tense and past participle of the verbs *learn, spoil, spell* (only in the word-related sense), *burn, dream, smell, spill, leap,* and others, can be either irregular (*learnt, spoilt,* etc.) or regular (learned, spoiled, etc.). BrE allows both irregular and regular forms, but the irregular forms tend to be used more often by the British (especially by speakers using Received Pronunciation), and in some cases (*learnt, smelt, leapt*) there is still a strong tendency to use them; in other cases (for example, dreamed), in current British usage, the regular form is more common. The forms with *-ed* are preferred by many careful writers of English since they are regular verbs. In AmE, the irregular forms are never or hardly ever used (except for *leapt* and *dreamt*). Nonetheless, as with other usages considered nowadays to be typically British, the *t* endings are often found in older American texts.

However, usage may vary when the past participles are actually adjectives, as in burnt toast. Finally, the past tense and past participle of *dwell* and *kneel* are more commonly *dwelt* and *knelt* on both sides of the Atlantic, although *dwelled* and *kneeled* are widely used in the U.S.

- *Lit* as the past tense of *light* is more common than *lighted* in the UK; the regular form enjoys more use in the U.S., although it is somewhat less common than *lit*. By contrast, *fit* as the past tense of *fit* is much more used in AmE than BrE, which generally favours *fitted*.
- The past tense of *spit* "expectorate" is *spat* in BrE, *spit* or *spat* in AmE.
- The past participle *gotten* is rarely used in modern BrE (although it is used in some dialects), which generally uses *got*, except in old expressions such as *ill-gotten gains*. In AmE, *gotten* emphasizes the action of acquiring and *got* tends to indicate simple possession (for example, *Have you gotten it?* versus *Have you got it?*). Interestingly, AmE, but not BrE, has *forgot* as a less common alternative to *forgotten* for the past participle of *forget*.
- AmE further allows other irregular verbs, such as *dive* (*dove*) or *sneak* (*snuck*), and often mixes the preterite and past participle forms (*spring–sprang* (U.S. also *sprung*)*–sprung*), sometimes forcing verbs such as *shrink* (*shrank–shrunk*) to have a further form, thus *shrunk–shrunken*. These uses are often considered nonstandard; the AP Stylebook in AmE treats some irregular verbs as colloquialisms, insisting on the regular forms for the past tense of *dive, plead* and *sneak*. *Dove* and *snuck* are usually considered nonstandard in Britain, although *dove* exists in some

British dialects and *snuck* is occasionally found in British speech.

- By extension of the irregular verb pattern, verbs with irregular preterites in some variants of colloquial AmE also have a separate past participle, for example, "to buy": past tense *bought* spawns *boughten.* Such formations are highly irregular from speaker to speaker, or even within idiolects. This phenomenon is found chiefly in the northern U.S. and other areas where immigrants of German descent are predominant, and may have developed as a result of German influence. Even in areas where the feature predominates, however, it has not gained widespread acceptance as "standard" usage.

ROLE OF TENSES

- BrE uses the present perfect tense to talk about an event in the recent past and with the words *already, just* and *yet.* In American usage, these meanings can be expressed with the present perfect to express a fact or the simple past (to imply an expectation. This American style has become widespread only in the past 20 to 30 years; the "British" style is still in common use as well.
  - "I've just got(ten) home."/"I just got home."
  - "I've already eaten."/"I already ate."
- Similarly, the pluperfect is occasionally replaced by the preterite in the U.S.; this is generally regarded as sloppy usage by those Americans who consider themselves careful users of the language. U.S. usage sometimes substitutes the conditional for the pluperfect ("If I would have cooked the pie we could have had it for lunch").
- In BrE, *have got* or *have* can be used for possession and *have got to* and *have to* can be used for the modal of necessity. The forms which include *got* are usually used in informal contexts and the forms without *got* in more formal contexts. In American speech the form

without *got* is used more than in the UK. AmE also informally uses *got* as a verb for these meanings, *for example,* "I got two cars," "I got to go"; but these are nonstandard and will be considered sloppy usage by most American speakers.

- The subjunctive mood is more common in AmE in expressions such as: "They suggested that he apply for the job". BrE would have "They suggested that he should apply for the job" (or even "They suggested that he applied for the job", although this last sentence can be ambiguous). However, the British usage ("should apply") is also heard in the United States, but is often regarded as erroneous in writing.

AUXILIARIES

Shall (as opposed to *will*) is more commonly used by the British than by Americans. *Shan't* is no longer used in AmE (almost invariably replaced by *won't* or *not going to*), and very much less so amongst Britons. American grammar also tends to ignore some traditional distinctions between *should* and *would*; however, expressions like *I should be happy* are rather formal even in BrE.

TRANSITIVITY

The following verbs show differences in transitivity between BrE and AmE.

- *Agree*: Transitive or intransitive in BrE, usually intransitive in AmE (*agree a contract/agree to* or *on a contract*). However, in formal AmE legal writing one often sees constructions like *as may be agreed between the parties* (rather than *as may be agreed* to *between the parties*).
- *Catch up* ("to reach and overtake"): Transitive or intransitive in BrE, strictly intransitive in AmE (*to catch sb up/to catch up with sb*).
- *Cater* ("to provide food and service"): Intransitive in BrE, transitive in AmE (*to cater for a banquet/to cater a banquet*).

- *Claim*: Sometimes intransitive in BrE (used with *for*), strictly transitive in AmE.
- *Meet*: AmE uses intransitively *meet* followed by *with* to mean "to have a meeting with", as for business purposes (*Yesterday we met with the CEO*), and reserves transitive *meet* for the meanings "to be introduced to" (*I want you to meet the CEO; she's such a fine lady*), "to come together with (someone, somewhere)" (*Meet the CEO at the train station*), and "to have a casual encounter with". BrE uses transitive *meet* also to mean "to have a meeting with"; the construction *meet with*, which actually dates back to Middle English, appears to be coming back into use in Britain, despite some commentators who preferred to avoid confusion with *meet with* meaning "receive, undergo" (*the proposal was met with disapproval*). The construction *meet up with* (as in *to meet up with someone*), which originated in the U.S., has long been standard in both dialects.
- *Provide*: Strictly monotransitive in BrE, monotransitive or ditransitive in AmE (*provide sb with sth/provide sb sth*).
- *Protest*: In sense "oppose", intransitive in BrE, transitive in AmE (*The workers protested against the decision/The workers protested the decision*). The intransitive *protest against* in AmE means "to hold or participate in a demonstration against". The older sense "proclaim" is always transitive (*protest one's innocence*).
- *Write*: In BrE, the indirect object of this verb usually requires the preposition *to*, for example, *I'll write* to *my MP* or *I'll write* to *her* (although it is not required in some situations, for example when an indirect object pronoun comes before a direct object noun, for example, *I'll write* her *a letter*). In AmE, *write* can be used monotransitively (*I'll write my congressman; I'll write him*).

SYNTACTIC ELEMENTS

- Where a statement of intention involves two separate activities, it is acceptable for speakers of AmE to use *to go* plus bare infinitive. Speakers of BrE would instead use *to go and* plus bare infinitive: thus where a speaker of AmE might say "I'll go take a bath", BrE speakers would say "I'll go *and* have a bath". (Both can also use the form *to go to* instead to suggest that the action may fail, as in "He went to take/have a bath, but the bath was full of children.") Similarly, *to come* plus bare infinitive is acceptable to speakers of AmE, where speakers of BrE would instead use *to come and* plus bare infinitive: thus where a speaker of AmE might say "come see what I bought," BrE speakers would say, "come and see what I've bought" (notice the present perfect tense: a common British preference).
- Use of prepositions before days denoted by a single word. Where British people would say "She resigned on Thursday", Americans often say "She resigned Thursday", but both forms are common in American.

what in later work he called "pre-specified", that is specified before any information about the outcome is known. The value of the universal probability bound corresponds to the inverse of the upper limit of "the total number of possible specified events throughout cosmic history," as calculated by Dembski. Anything below this bound has CSI.

The terms "specified complexity" and "complex specified information" are used interchangeably. In more recent papers Dembski has redefined the universal probability bound, with reference to another number, corresponding to the total number of bit operations that could possibly have been performed in the entire history of universe. Dembski asserts that CSI exists in numerous features of living things, such as DNA and other functional biological molecules, and argues that it cannot be generated by the only known natural mechanisms of physical law and chance, or by their combination.

He argues that this is so because laws can only shift around or lose information, but do not produce it, and chance can produce complex unspecified information, or unspecified complex information, but not CSI; he provides a mathematical analysis that he claims demonstrates that law and chance working together cannot generate CSI, either. Moreover, he claims that CSI is holistic, with the whole being greater than the sum of the parts, and that this decisively eliminates Darwinian evolution as a possible means of its creation. Dembski maintains that by process of elimination, CSI is best explained as being due to intelligence, and is therefore a reliable indicator of design.

For almost two decades, some of the most visible and influential research in written composition has followed Kellogg W. Hunt in examining student writing from the standpoint of syntax. Most of this research relies at least to some extent on one or more of the quantitative indices posited by Hunt as gross measures of syntactic sophistication—mean number of words per clause, mean number of words per sentence, mean number of words per T-unit, mean number of T-units per sentence, and mean number of clauses per T-unit.

Although ill-defined conceptually, the phenomenon these indices purportedly measure is variously referred to as syntactic complexity, syntactic maturity, or syntactic fluency.

Researchers using Hunt's syntactic indices generally pursue one of two lines of inquiry. Hunt's own research—together with the researches is primarily concerned with identifying normative levels of syntactic complexity for different age groups. Other researchers pursue a second line of inquiry, seeking to measure the degree to which the syntactic skills of different experimental groups are enhanced through sentence-combining exercises.

Most of these studies seem to be motivated by the assumption that a more sophisticated command of syntax in writing is positively associated with writing quality. Although Hunt himself does not argue explicitly for a direct relationship between syntactic complexity and writing quality, the nature of his samples and the higher levels of syntactic complexity found for his older, and presumably better, writers at least imply a positive relationship between syntactic complexity—as measured by his indices—and writing quality.

For each successively older, and presumably more skilled, group of writers, these researchers report longer T-units, longer clauses, and more clauses per T-unit. In fact, each of these normative studies suggests that as writers grow older their writing becomes better as it becomes syntactically more sophisticated or complex.

The findings of these normative studies have influenced the direction of pedagogical research. In fact, Hunt's earlier studies prompted instructional researchers such as Mellon and O'Hare to look for ways of teaching students to write sentences that were syntactically more complex or sophisticated than would be typical for their age group. We believe it no exaggeration to say that the sentence-combining research cited above is predicated on the assumption of a positive and linear relationship between writing quality and syntactic complexity. If increasing syntactic complexity were not assumed to increase writing quality, then there would have been no reason to investigate the use of sentence-combining instruction in writing classes. Indeed, it is no accident that most experiments designed to enhance syntactic complexity through sentence-combining exercises also looked for, and found, parallel gains in writing quality. All of this, of course, suggests that the underlying assumption of a positive linear relationship between writing quality and syntactic complexity is valid. However, in the few studies that regress data for Hunt's indices against ratings of writing quality, Hunt's indices predict very little of the variance (usually less than 7 per cent) in the quality ratings. Moreover, in these same studies the indices proposed by Francis Christensen fared no better.

LIMITATIONS OF PREVIOUS RESEARCH

While previous research in the area either assumes or suggests a positive linear relationship between syntactic complexity and writing quality, as defined by Hunt's indices, to our knowledge no one study has directly addressed the question of whether this relationship is in fact linear. And even when researchers conducting experimental studies in sentence-combining methods have indirectly explored the relationship between syntactic complexity and writing quality, they have not been able to do so unambiguously. Two related problems in experimental studies of sentence-combining instruction have precluded a clear and unconfounded test of the linearity assumption. The first problem stems from the limited range of syntactic complexity displayed in essays rated for quality in experimental studies. In virtually all sentence-combining studies, the range of syntactic complexity is relatively narrow.

For example, in the Miami University sentence-combining experiment, essays by the control and experimental groups displayed a posttest mean difference in clause length of less than one word and a posttest mean difference in T-unit length of only 1.1 words. Nevertheless, the Miami investigators report that the experimental group—the group exposed to sentence-combining practice—wrote essays at the end of the experiment that were significantly better than those written by the control group. Similarly narrow ranges in syntactic complexity are found in many normative studies, which tend to associate chronological age and syntactic complexity. For example, the investigation by O'Donnell, Griffin, and Norris of syntactic growth revealed a mean difference in clause length of only 1.2 words between grades three and seven; and Hunt found mean differences of only two words per clause between grades four and twelve. In both experimental and normative studies that have employed Hunt's indices, similar restricted ranges of syntactic complexity often appear. It is possible, however, that a limited range of syntactic complexity in essays used to elicit quality ratings might significantly attenuate any effects of syntactic complexity on judgments of writing quality. Thus, until something approaching the full range of possible values for syntactic complexity is used in a rating situation, the relationship between complexity and quality must remain ambiguous. A clear test of the relationship between syntactic complexity and writing quality would require ratings of essays along an extended range of complexity values.

The second problem, which is in some ways the obverse of the first one, appears exclusively in the experimental studies. These studies usually investigate the relationship between syntactic complexity and writing quality to one degree or another. Most of these studies employ an essay-rating procedure that requires raters to judge the quality of particular essays in relation to other essays read during the rating session. Standards are thus inferred and rating criteria established in terms of differences that exist among essays within the pool of essays rated. Consequently, evaluations of essays are, in fact, relative judgments of writing quality.

Because discourse mode, purpose, and topic are often controlled in such studies, and because raters are often instructed to ignore handwriting and mechanical problems such as spelling, small differences among the essays in terms of syntactic complexity may exaggerate differences in quality. Such rating procedures may bias results by cuing distinctions along dimensions—such as syntactic complexity—which under other circumstances may not have a pronounced effect on judgments of quality. Undue attention to syntactic features may produce results that suggest a positive relationship between writing quality and syntactic complexity but that may in reality be an artifact of the rating procedure. Before differences in quality can be attributed to levels of syntactic complexity, the potential bias that may result from rating essays in relation to one another must be assessed.

This can be done by contrasting ratings given to the same essay under two conditions: one where the essay is read alone and another where the essay is read as one essay in a series of essays. To demonstrate an unambiguous relationship between writing quality and syntactic complexity, it is necessary for essays differing in syntactic complexity, but read by themselves without any contrasting essays, to vary systematically in quality ratings.

PURPOSE OF STUDY

In this study we attempt to clarify the relationship between syntactic complexity and writing quality by addressing directly (1) the issue of extremes in syntactic complexity and (2) the issue of dependence among ratings of texts. We examine quality ratings for texts that differ in syntactic complexity and assess whether there is a significant linear relationship between perceived writing quality and syntactic complexity. In this respect, the present study resembles certain aspects of sentence-combining studies. However, the present study differs from those studies in two ways. First, we extend the range of syntactic complexity values in stimulus passages. In previous research, differences in levels of complexity among the texts rated have been small; in contrast, the texts in our study represent a wide range of complexity values. Second, we contrast conditions under which raters form judgments of writing quality. In one condition, raters are exposed to a series of passages that vary widely in syntactic complexity. In the second condition, raters evaluate only a single passage. The latter condition eliminates the influence of previously rated passages on judgments of writing quality.

INVESTIGATION I

The purpose of our first investigation was to examine the relationship between syntactic complexity and writing quality by having teachers rate a series of texts that varied widely in syntactic complexity. This investigation required teachers to read and evaluate five short passages that were written on the same topic but that differed in syntactic complexity. The entering expectation was for a positive linear relationship between syntactic complexity and writing quality. Sixty-two high school teachers served as evaluators in this investigation. All participated in the investigation as part of a graduate course in communication. Passages on two different topics were used so that an internal replication would be possible and to preclude a confounding between any effect and discourse topic. Thirty-five teachers read and evaluated short passages on the topic of making aluminum; the remaining twenty-seven read papers on the use of alcohol and marijuana.

In this investigation, the ratings of the passages on the "alcohol and marijuana" topic were used as part of the replication study. Because the procedures for creating the experimental stimuli and for collecting data were identical for each group of five passages, those procedures will be described only once. The investigators composed five short texts for each topic. The five passages in each set represented five different levels of syntactic complexity, ranging from very simple to very complex. However, the passages were, as much as possible, similar in all other respects. Discourse mode, discourse purpose, and content were held constant across all five passages in each set. The first set of five passages was based on the "aluminum" task used in Hunt's 1970 study of syntactic complexity.

The original "aluminum" passage, which served within the first set of passages as the passage with the lowest level of syntactic complexity, reads as follows: Aluminum is a metal. It is abundant. It has many uses. It comes from bauxite. Bauxite is an ore. Bauxite looks like clay. Bauxite contains aluminum. It contains several other substances. Workmen extract these other substances from the bauxite. They grind the bauxite. They put it in tanks. Pressure is in the tanks. The other substances form a mass. They remove the mass.

They use filters. A liquid remains. They put it through several other processes. It finally yields a chemical. The chemical is powdery. It is white. The chemical is alumina. It is a mixture. It contains aluminum. It contains oxygen. Workmen separate the aluminum from the oxygen. They use electricity. They finally produce a metal. The metal is light. It has a luster. The luster is bright. The luster is silvery. The metal comes in many forms. This passage consists entirely of single-clause sentences, each of which is a single T-unit.

It is a passage notable for its syntactic simplicity rather than its complexity. For the other end of the spectrum of five passages on the first topic, we constructed a passage delivering the same content, but in a much more syntactically complex way. Two sentences from the passage at the other end of the spectrum will illustrate the differences in syntactic complexity: Aluminum, an abundant and useful metal, comes from bauxite, a claylike ore. Although bauxite contains several other substances, workmen remove them by grinding the ore and placing it in pressurized tanks where the other substances form a mass which is removed by filters. This latter version differs in important ways from the simpler passage. Some sentences from the original version, for example, appear as appositives in the first sentence of the more syntactically complex version. Other sentences from the original version are reduced to subordinate or relative clauses in the second version, while still others become participial constructions, adjectives, and prepositional phrases.

Such reductions to dependent-clause status or to less than-clause status have the effect of (1) increasing the average length of resultant clauses and T-units and (2) increasing the ratio of dependent clauses to independent clauses (i.e., the mean number of clauses per T-unit). Complementing the increase in syntactic complexity is a corresponding decrease in the total number of words needed to deliver essentially the same content. Similar differences exist between the least and most syntactically complex passages devised for the second topic. Those five passages were all based on a sentence-combining exercise entitled "Alcohol and Marijuana" from William

Strong's Sentence Combining: A Composing Book. Because this passage is considerably longer than the least complex "aluminum" passage, only the first part of the original is reproduced below: There is much talk. The talking occurs today. The talking is about evils. The evils are from marijuana. But few people talk about alcohol. Alcohol represents a hazard. The hazard is to health. The hazard is greater than marijuana. Consider an example. Consider our consumption. The consumption is of alcohol. The nations [sic] drinks 650 million gallons. The gallons are distilled spirits. The drinking is done each year. Americans guzzle 100 million barrels. The barrels contain beer. The guzzling is done each year. We also drink wine. The volume is 200 million gallons.

These first 19 sentences from the simplest version of "Alcohol and Marijuana" indicate that the passage is comparable with respect to syntactic complexity to the least complex version of the "aluminum" passage. The following two sentences are from the most syntactically complex of the five versions of "Alcohol and Marijuana." Although much is said today about the evils of marijuana, few people talk about alcohol, which may represent as great a health hazard and social threat as marijuana. Consider, for example, Americans, who each year drink 650 million gallons of distilled spirits, consume 200 million gallons of wine, and guzzle 100 million barrels of beer.

Using the procedures set down in the Miami University sentence- combining study for segmenting extended texts into clauses and T-units and for counting words, we calculated the mean T-unit length, mean clause length, and mean number of clauses per T-unit for each of the five passages in the two sets used in the present investigation. Although questions may be raised about the artificial nature of these stimuli, we decided to compose the passages rather than use student essays in order to gain better control over not only the levels of syntactic complexity but also the content. Such controls were mandatory for a direct and unambiguous test of the relationship between writing quality and syntactic complexity. It is impossible to find actual student essays that deliver exactly the same content and exhibit the range of syntactic complexity necessary to test the linear hypothesis. By using these stimuli, we avoided several problems that we identified in the earlier literature on syntactic complexity and writing quality. Having constructed these brief texts, we presented each of the sixty-two teachers with a packet of materials that included the five passages on one of the two topics. Each of the passages was followed by a rating form that asked the teacher to rate the passage on five evaluative scales: high quality/low quality; effective/ineffective; good/bad; interesting/uninteresting; clear/unclear. The polarities of the scales were randomly set, and the five passages were randomly sequenced within each packet.

INVESTIGATION

For our second investigation of the effects of syntactic complexity on writing quality, we had teachers read and evaluate a single text. The entering hypothesis was for a positive relationship between writing quality and syntactic complexity, although a relationship of smaller magnitude than that found in our first investigation. We expected a smaller effect because the teachers participating in the second investigation would rate a single passage without comparing it to any others. Syntactic complexity would thus be less salient as a differentiating variable.

The second investigation provided (1) an additional test of the linearity hypothesis and (2) a test of whether the findings of previous research have been biased by raters having made judgments of essays in the context of rating a number of essays. Two hundred and fifteen high school teachers participated in this phase of the investigation. One hundred and eleven teachers evaluated one of the five "aluminum" essays, while the remaining 104 evaluated one of the five texts on the use of alcohol and marijuana. As in the first investigation, the use of passages on two different topics allowed us to conduct two independent studies at the same time. Because the two studies were conducted simultaneously, only one description of the procedures is presented here. The texts used in the two studies in the second investigation were the same ones used in our first investigation. The patterns of means for both topic sets indicate that the predominant effect is again for the least syntactically complex passage in either set 5 in both cases) to be rated significantly lower in quality than any of the other texts in a given set. Beyond this effect for syntactic complexity, no significant differences among ratings emerged when ratings were assigned independently of one another. It is important to contrast our two investigations in terms of the limitations in previous research on syntactic complexity and writing quality described in the introduction. Recall that our first concern was with the restricted range in syntactic complexity found in previous studies, studies that seem to assume a positive linear relationship between syntactic complexity and writing quality. In both of our investigations, we used as stimulus passages brief texts that spanned a greater range in syntactic complexity than the writing examined in most previous research, especially pedagogical research on sentence-combining instruction. It was fortuitous that we did. In every case, the least syntactically complex passage had a significant impact on the results.

Differences consistently emerged between the quality ratings assigned the least complex passage and the other, more syntactically complex passages on the same topic. Usually, the differences in the ratings assigned the passages within the mid-range of syntactic complexity were not significant. It is important to note that these midrange passages were comparable in syntactic complexity to the essays studied in, for example, Faigley's generative rhetoric experiment and the Miami University sentence-combining experiment. Had we chosen to use only passages within the mid-range of complexity, no significant effect on writing quality would have emerged. In that case, our findings would have paralleled more closely those of studies that have regressed data for one or more of Hunt's indices against quality scores. In short, in order to obtain large and significant effects for syntactic complexity, it is necessary to use stimulus essays that span a wide range of levels of syntactic complexity.

It is essential that relatively extreme values, especially at the lower end of the spectrum of syntactic complexity, be used if an effect is to be obtained. Previous research, whether normative or experimental, has consistently implied a positive and linear relationship between syntactic complexity and writing quality. The results of the present study on this issue are mixed. In three of the four analyses we performed, the most complex passage received a lower mean quality rating than the next-to-the-most complex passage. In only one of the four analyses presented here was the difference in quality between the most complex and the next most complex passage statistically significant. In the other three analyses we performed, the differences in quality among the three most syntactically complex passages were not statistically significant.

In short, the only time a significant difference in quality emerged among the three most complex passages was when the next most complex passage was judged to be of significantly higher quality than the most complex passage. Thus, at the upper end of the syntactic complexity range, a positive and linear relationship between complexity and writing quality does not appear to exist. However, all four analyses performed in the present study indicate that the least syntactically complex passage is inferior in quality to all other brief texts with which it was compared. Thus our analyses suggest that a positive and linear relationship between writing quality and syntactic complexity obtains only when ratings of texts at the lower end of the syntactic complexity range are contrasted with texts in the middle or higher ranges of syntactic complexity. Plots of the mean values suggest a tendency towards a positive linear relationship only when ratings of extremely noncomplex passages are included. And beyond the extremely noncomplex passages, there is little evidence of a systematic relationship.

We were also concerned in the present study with the potential effects that multiple essays have on the quality ratings assigned to individual essays in a set. Our first investigation used a rating procedure similar to that used in much composition research, whether experimental or evaluative. In that investigation, teachers read five passages, all on the same topic but differing with respect to level of syntactic complexity. In our second investigation, teachers read only one brief text. The research we have reported here suggests that studies using procedures that call for raters to evaluate a series of essays may be biased by those procedures. Such procedures can exaggerate the magnitude of effects due to characteristics of the essays rated.

The investigations we have reported here also suggest why, in spite of their expectations to the contrary, composition researchers have not been able to demonstrate that syntactic complexity is strongly related to writing quality. Our research suggests that syntactic complexity may, after all, be an important phenomenon to investigate in experimental and normative research in composition. But it also suggests that unless there is a wide range of levels of complexity in the writing samples examined, researchers are likely to be disappointed in their attempts to show a relationship between syntactic complexity and writing quality. It looks like your project is off to a good start.

The team got some customers involved in the requirements elicitation stage and you actually wrote a software requirements specification. The spec was kind of big, but the customers signed off on it so it must be okay. Now you are designing one of the features and you've found some problems with the requirements. You can interpret requirement 15 a couple of different ways. Requirement 9 states precisely the opposite of requirement 21; which should you believe? Requirement 24 is so vague that you haven't got a clue what it means. You just had an hour-long discussion with two other developers about requirement 30 because all three of you thought it meant something different.

Index

F

G

I

K

L

M

N

O

P